Is Harpo Free?

RECENT TITLES

Seth Barry Watter, *The Human Figure on Film*

Daniel Varndell, *Torturous Etiquettes*

Jonah Corne and Monika Vrečar, *Yiddish Cinema*

Jason Jacobs, *Reluctant Sleuths, True Detectives*

Lucy J. Miller, *Distancing Representations in Transgender Film*

Tomoyuki Sasaki, *Cinema of Discontent*

Mary Ann McDonald Carolan, *Orienting Italy*

Matthew Rukgaber, *Nietzsche in Hollywood*

David Venditto, *Whiteness at the End of the World*

Fareed Ben-Youssef, *No Jurisdiction*

Tony Tracy, *White Cottage, White House*

Tom Conley, *Action, Action, Action*

Lindsay Coleman and Roberto Schaefer, editors, *The Cinematographer's Voice*

Nolwenn Mingant, *Hollywood Films in North Africa and the Middle East*

†Charles Warren, edited by William Rothman and Joshua Schulze, *Writ on Water*

Jason Sperb, *The Hard Sell of Paradise*

William Rothman, *The Holiday in His Eye*

Brendan Hennessey, *Luchino Visconti and the Alchemy of Adaptation*

Alexander Sergeant, *Encountering the Impossible*

Erica Stein, *Seeing Symphonically*

A complete listing of books in this series can be found online at www.sunypress.edu

Is Harpo Free?

And Other Questions of the Metaphysical Screen

Matthew Cipa

Cover: Harpo Marx, courtesy Photofest New York

Published by State University of New York Press, Albany

© 2024 State University of New York

All rights reserved

Printed in the United States of America

No part of this book may be used or reproduced in any manner whatsoever without written permission. No part of this book may be stored in a retrieval system or transmitted in any form or by any means including electronic, electrostatic, magnetic tape, mechanical, photocopying, recording, or otherwise without the prior permission in writing of the publisher.

For information, contact State University of New York Press, Albany, NY
www.sunypress.edu

Library of Congress Cataloging-in-Publication Data

Name: Cipa, Matthew, 1990– author.
Title: Is Harpo free? : and other questions of the metaphysical screen / Matthew Cipa.
Description: Albany : State University of New York Press, [2024]. | Series: SUNY series, horizons of cinema | Includes bibliographical references and index.
Identifiers: LCCN 2023039403 | ISBN 9781438497358 (hardcover : alk. paper) | ISBN 9781438497365 (ebook) | ISBN 9781438497341 (pbk. : alk. paper)
Subjects: LCSH: Philosophy in motion pictures. | Philosophy on television. | LCGFT: Essays. | Television commentaries. | Film criticism.
Classification: LCC PN1995.9.P42 C48 2024 | DDC 791.4301—dc23/eng/20231229
LC record available at https://lccn.loc.gov/2023039403

10 9 8 7 6 5 4 3 2 1

*In memory of my father, Bob (1950–2009),
who first introduced me to the movies,
and Gracie (2010–2022),
who watched and heard, curled up alongside me,
so many of the works considered herein.*

*Also for Noralie (1957–2023),
a constant supporter.*

I do not perceive any thing with my sense-organs alone, but with a great part of my whole human being. Thus, I may say, loosely, that I "hear a thrush singing." But in strict truth all that I ever merely "hear"—all that I ever hear simply by virtue of having ears—is sound. When I "hear a thrush singing," I am hearing, not with my ears alone, but with all sorts of other things like mental habits, memory, imagination, feeling and (to the extent at least that the act of attention involves it) will. Of a man who merely heard in the first sense, it could meaningfully be said that "having ears" (i.e., not being deaf) "he heard not."

—Owen Barfield (1988, 20–21)

Contents

List of Illustrations		xi
Acknowledgments		xiii
Prelude: Is Harpo Free? Four Ways		xv
1	What Is the Metaphysical Screen? Artistic Form, Content, and Philosophy	1
2	Can Lola Choose? Causality, Contingency, and Narrative Form	31
3	Is Shane Virtuous? Goodness and *Telos* in the World of the American Western	71
4	How Does Julie Grieve? Qualia and the Texture of Subjective Experience	105
5	Who Are Elizabeth and Philip Jennings? Narrative and Personal Identity	145
6	What Can Film and Television Do? Narrative, Mimesis, and Wonder	183
Afterword: What Does Jerry Do? The Riddle of Selection and the Metaphysics of Performance		209

References 227

Index 237

Illustrations

Figures

P.1	Does Harpo have freedom in *A Night at the Opera*?	xvii
P.2	Harpo chooses to act in *A Night at the Opera*.	xix
P.3	Harpo responds to his surroundings in *At the Circus*.	xxi
1.1	Irena and Krzysztof stand side by side in *Dekalog 1*.	9
1.2	Resisting the oppression of existence in *The Turin Horse*.	16
1.3	The toll of war in *The Thin Red Line*.	23
2.1	Fate unifies in *Grand Canyon*.	46
2.2	Continuity across time in *Looper*.	55
2.3	The past and present displayed at once in *Dark*.	57
2.4	The counterfeit bill in *L'Argent*.	60
3.1	A telos shot from *High Noon*.	84
3.2	A telos shot from *The Shootist*.	87
3.3	A telos shot from *The Assassination of Jesse James by the Coward Robert Ford*.	88
3.4	A telos shot from *Meek's Cutoff*.	92
4.1	Danny's dance of deliberation in *Cover Girl*.	124
4.2	The look of sound in *Sound of Sunshine, Sound of Rain*.	127

4.3	Julie grieves and remembers in *Three Colours: Blue*.	133
4.4	The experience of memory via taste in *Ratatouille*.	144
5.1	Unintentional elusiveness in *Mr. Arkadin*.	151
5.2	A moment's pause in *The Insider*.	153
5.3	Stained dresses in *3 Women*.	161
5.4	The difference in demeanor between Tom and Joey in *A History of Violence*.	168
5.5	Philip and Elizabeth disguised in *The Americans*.	173
6.1	Elwood says farewell (top), and Elwood is reunited (bottom) in *Harvey*.	192
6.2	A billboard creates a brave sea captain in *The Secret Life of Walter Mitty*.	193
6.3	Morvern touches the earth in *Morvern Callar*.	203
6.4	Facial and architectural angles in *The Limits of Control*.	205
A.1	A selection by Hubert Hawkins in *The Court Jester*.	213
A.2	Oscar Jaffe forcibly selects the right scream in *20th Century*.	217
A.3	Selections of staging, setting, and performance in *The Band Wagon*.	221

Table

2.1	An overview of *The Phantom of Liberty*'s parametric narrative form.	63

Acknowledgments

The very fact of this book's existence is a testament to the patience, encouragement, friendship, and personal and professional investment of a number of people to whom I am grateful in ways that are extraordinarily difficult to express.

As this book grew out of my PhD dissertation, I offer my deepest thanks to Ted Nannicelli and Jane Stadler, my supervisors, who grew into colleagues and friends. Your genuine interest and unfailing support and guidance made the completion of that dissertation possible, and your expertise, intelligence, and intellectual charity resonates in this book in innumerable ways.

Throughout my PhD candidature, I was further supported by the critical insights of Tom O'Regan, Andrea Bubenik, Gillian Whitlock, Marguerite La Caze, and Melissa Harper. The examiners of my PhD dissertation—Robert Sinnerbrink and Lucy Bolton—offered a range of extremely perceptive comments that provided invaluable guidance when I began the process of developing it into the present book. A very early version of a part of chapter 1 was presented at the 2018 SSAAANZ conference, where I received helpful and encouraging comments from Richard Rushton, Hamish Ford, Paul Atkinson, and Daniel Binns.

I here make special mention of Tom O'Regan, whose legacy both to me personally and institutionally at the University of Queensland (and doubtless beyond the sandstone of Brisbane, too) is profound. As an examiner of my honors thesis, he not only took the time to provide extensive comments and remarks but happily and with great energy sat and talked with me about Stanley Kubrick, existential philosophy, and the wildness of Hans-Georg Gadamer in a completely unplanned meeting. It is an occasion I will always hold very dear.

The completion of this book would not have been possible without the institutional support of the University of Queensland, especially the School of Communication and Arts, the School of Languages and Cultures, and the Institute for the Advanced Studies of the Humanities. Nor would this book have been possible without the support of the publisher, SUNY Press. I make specific mention of my understanding and gracious editor James Peltz (whose middle name surely is Patience), the design team and copyeditors, and all those who toiled behind the scenes working on this volume.

To the Horizons of Cinema series editor, Murray Pomerance, I offer my deepest appreciation for not just your keen editorial eye but, more important, the friendship and mentorship you have selflessly provided over many years (not to mention your encouragement and support of my work). Your good humor, attentive ear, encyclopedic knowledge of film, and unhesitant willingness to catch up for a chat have been a perennial source of personal fulfillment across a long and significant period of time.

I am grateful to those whose friendship began in academia, but whose importance has extended beyond that world: Elliott Logan, David Richard, Jason Jacobs, Tim Mehigan, Jess Wilkinson, Alberto N. García, Lisa Bode, Murray Smith, Bonnie Evans, Meg Thomas, and Keya Makar.

I am immeasurably appreciative of the support and ability of my friends outside of academia to keep things in perspective and especially to help me to stay on the straight and narrow: Mitchell, Max, Matthew, Austin, Alex, Connor, Matthew, Eamon, Joseph, Samuel, Jordan, and Brett.

Finally, I am grateful, as ever and always, for the unfailing love and support of my whole family, especially my mother, Leigh; my brother, Anthony, and sister-in-law, Caz; my sister, Catherine, and brother-in-law, Chris; my nieces, Therese and Rose; my nephew, Joseph; and my grandmother, Margaret.

Prelude

Is Harpo Free? Four Ways

IN WHAT WAYS MIGHT ONE LOOK to answer the question, Is Harpo free? I will offer four tentative responses, and these will illustrate the complexity of the question more than they will provide a concrete and confident answer. At the same time, they will frame the interests of this book. A prior question first, though: Who is Harpo?

When I write of Harpo, I do not mean Arthur Marx (born Adolph on November 23, 1888), and I do not mean Pinky of *Duck Soup* (1933), Tomasso of *A Night at the Opera* (1935), Stuffy of *A Day at the Races* (1937), Punchy of *At the Circus* (1939), Rusty of *Go West* (1940), or Wacky of *The Big Store* (1941). Nominally individuated though they may be, separated across eight years though they are, these personae are all ostensibly different manifestations of one and the same being. The transcendent being who acts as the thread that connects the aforementioned instantiations is whom I refer to as Harpo.

Who, or what, is the metaphysical Harpo? He is the Harpo that sets the conditions, shapes the boundaries, and conducts the possibilities for Pinky, Tomasso, Stuffy, and company in their own little adventures. The metaphysical Harpo could be understood as a matter of authorship or a matter of stardom or celebrity—Harpo's persona, the ways in which he is identifiable to us (the silent, frenzied, red-haired harpist). The features that make Pinky and the rest recognizable denote the importance of these instantiations (or embodiments, manifestations, appearances). We observe them, combine them, and pursue them back to where they lead: the transcendent, metaphysical Harpo. This same dynamic of observation and pursuit underpins the approach of this book—understanding the ways in which films and television programs give an artistic life to metaphysical concepts such as free will, causality, personal identity, and so on, to pursue an understanding of the concepts themselves. To pursue, indeed, a richer understanding of the artistic possibilities of film and television.

The transcendent dimension of Harpo and the approach of observation and pursuit allow us to ask, Is Harpo free? There is no singular answer to the question, but there are multiple ways in which we might respond to it—to observe, pursue, and better understand what is at stake in asking it. The first considers whether Harpo has freedom—can he deliberate, can he choose, does he have a will? The second considers his availability—is Harpo free to meet us? Is he free to meet others with whom he is interacting? How does he interact? The third possesses a whisper of concern—is Harpo . . . out there? Has he escaped? Is this madman, this force of chaos, free? And finally, is Harpo available to us freely—what is the cost, or what must we give over to experience him? These are but four different ways of considering what is gained in response to asking the question, Is Harpo free?

Freedom

In a famous moment from *A Night at the Opera*, underhanded business manager Otis T. Driftwood (Groucho Marx) finds himself aboard an ocean liner—the expanse of which contrasts in absolute terms with the confinement of his quarters. He is there to continue his attempts at wooing (for financial and romantic reasons) the impossibly wealthy widow, Mrs. Claypool (Margaret Dumont). His competitor, New York Opera company director Herman Gottlieb (Sig Ruman) is responsible for the insult that is Driftwood's meager stateroom.

Driftwood's absurdly large suitcase fills much of the room. It is fortunate that he has brought such capacious luggage, as contained therein are aspiring opera singer Ricardo Baroni (Allan Jones), his close friend and business manager Fiorello (Chico Marx), and a profoundly asleep Tomasso. Once the three have emerged clown-car-esque from Driftwood's trunk (Tomasso with laborious help from the others), the already tightly framed and confined space of the stateroom is full to the point of bulging (fig. P.1). As we will soon see, though, it possesses a curiously elastic sense of space.

Tomasso is asleep, with little room to move. Does he have freedom? He is so confined mentally and cognitively, physically and spatially: How can he enact his will, if indeed he has one? His responses to the events of the scene suggests that he acts, but he perhaps has little capacity for deliberation (at least in this moment).

On behalf of the stowed-away trio, Fiorello makes a demand: they don't leave Driftwood in peace unless they eat. With no room to negotiate, Driftwood leaves his quarters and yells for the steward to place an order—although he is now spatially freer than earlier, he is nevertheless constrained (and burdened) by those, both conscious and unconscious, who wait in his room. He begins by ordering one juice of each the liner has on offer and then "two fried eggs, two poached eggs, two scrambled eggs, and two medium-boiled eggs."

Figure P.1. Does Harpo have freedom in *A Night at the Opera*? *Source:* Wood, Sam, dir. *A Night at the Opera*. 1935. Burbank, CA: Warner Bros. Pictures, 2021. Blu-ray Disc, 1080p HD.

Cut to the stateroom, where Fiorello calls out, "and two hard-boiled eggs." We hear offscreen from beyond the stateroom door Driftwood's confirmation—"and two hard-boiled eggs"—just as Tomasso, still apparently in a deep sleep, squeezes the horn attached to the top of his cane to produce a deep honk. Cut back to the two shot of Driftwood and the steward, where Driftwood clarifies in response to Tomasso's request, "Make that three hard-boiled eggs."

Driftwood continues the order, his irritation growing as he is repeatedly interrupted by Fiorello's desire for two hard-boiled eggs, closely followed by Tomasso's cane speaking for him ("Make that three hard-boiled eggs"). This part of the scene approaches culmination, as Tomasso offers a staccato honk (Driftwood's interpretation: "and a duck egg") before, prefiguring Ornette Coleman in his freest and most experimental moments, Tomasso lets out a series of rhythmically disjointed honks. Driftwood: "It's either foggy out or make that twelve more hard-boiled eggs."

Driftwood returns to the stateroom—shot again now in the tightest possible framing—as the second part of the scene commences. A parade of liner workers and fellow travelers appearing ex nihilo come to take care of the room and its occupants: two women to make up the beds (a task made inconvenient by Tommaso's resting on them, before he amorously attaches himself to one of the women; he is still fast asleep, mind you); the engineer to turn off the heat; a manicurist; the engineer's assistant (a larger physical presence than the engineer himself); a woman searching for her aunt, who asks to use the phone; and a cleaner looking to mop the floor. Finally, the food arrives, which has Tomasso launching himself lovingly (though still apparently in a stupor) across the multiple trays—many of which, presumably, are laden with hard-boiled eggs (fig. P.2).

Tomasso consistently finds himself in the wrong place— draped over the woman, or with his boot on the manicurist's tray, or lengthened across multiple trays of food—requiring him to be pushed, rolled, pivoted, and shifted throughout the stateroom. Is his somnambulism an act, though? Harpo, with his laser-beam attention toward females who catch his eye (even, as in this scene, through his eyelids) and his ravenous love of food, is like an English pointer detecting hidden game on a hunt. For him, these are consistent features identifiable across his many different filmed embodiments. Here, Harpo's will is apparently explicitly constrained—mentally by

Figure P.2. Harpo chooses to act in *A Night at the Opera*. *Source:* Wood, Sam, dir. *A Night at the Opera*. 1935. Burbank, CA: Warner Bros. Pictures, 2021. Blu-ray Disc, 1080p HD.

sleep, spatially by the stateroom—but he nevertheless reacts to that which he desires with nary a thought or a moment's deliberation. He is responsive with an immediacy that precludes deliberation—at least in this scene. As a mute (a willing mute, according to legend—a choice, then, that suggests a will), he does not speak, so he must give voice through other means—he must act and express through his cane horn, through his body. The scene suggests competing answers to the central question, or if not answers in competition, certainly multiple responses that suggest the question's complexity. Harpo's will is strong enough to break through the dense constraints of sleep and restricted space, while at the same time he is a being that has a severely restricted will that can respond and not deliberate. The question remains, though: Does Harpo have freedom—the capacity to choose and deliberate?

A scene from *At the Circus* has Punchy and Tony (Chico Marx) preparing to search strongman Goliath's (Nat Pendleton) room. They are looking for $10,000, which they believe Goliath has had some involvement in stealing. Before entering the room, Tony reminds the mute Punchy to "keep-a quiet." Confirming his understanding, Punchy, a maniacal look written across his face, pushes his finger to his lips briefly and then spreads his mouth into a broad grin. If we are familiar with the metaphysical Harpo, we anticipate with our own sense of glee the chaos that we presume to ensue.

Goliath rhythmically snores and whistles on a lower bunk—confident and at ease, Tony says to Punchy "Hey, he's asleep-a like a baby." A sweet smile on his face, Punchy closes his hands against each other and rests his head on them, before immediately taking a large (and full) glass baby's bottle from his trench coat pocket, wielding it ready to pummel the resting strongman. Tony quickly puts an end to all that—dissuading Punchy from violence—as, Goliath beginning to waken, he rushes to his bedside singing "Rock-a-bye baby, on the treetop . . ."

Punchy begins to play the harmonica in tune with Tony's singing, before the search for the money recommences. Punchy's pockets are apparently laden with objects that preempt Tony's comments. "I think it would be better if we work in the dark" is met with Punchy putting on dark sunglasses. "If anything happens, we should meet right here" (the center of the room and shot) is met with Punchy's drawing with chalk an X on the floor. A bump causing Goliath to wake again is met with more of Tony's singing before being accompanied by Punchy not on a harmonica but a recorder. Still wearing the glasses, Punchy walks and plays before walking and playing into a wall, and this time Goliath really does wake up. Tony, thinking quickly, turns off the light and leaps into the top bunk. Punchy leaps into the coat hanging next to the door, swaying in rhythm with the room's movement (the scene takes place on a train) (fig. P.3).

Harpo's responsiveness again suggests a lack of deliberation—he responds to the comments of his brother; he responds to the events of the scene and Goliath's stirring. But it is a restriction of will, rather than an absolute absence of one. Hanging from the wall, he flicks the light switch off as Goliath, half-asleep, flicks it confusedly on (only for Punchy to flick it off again). He decides, with the strongman safely asleep once again, to look for the money throughout the room. His hand resting on the steps leading down from the bunk bed is painfully stepped on—Punchy yells out in (silent) anguish, the crunch

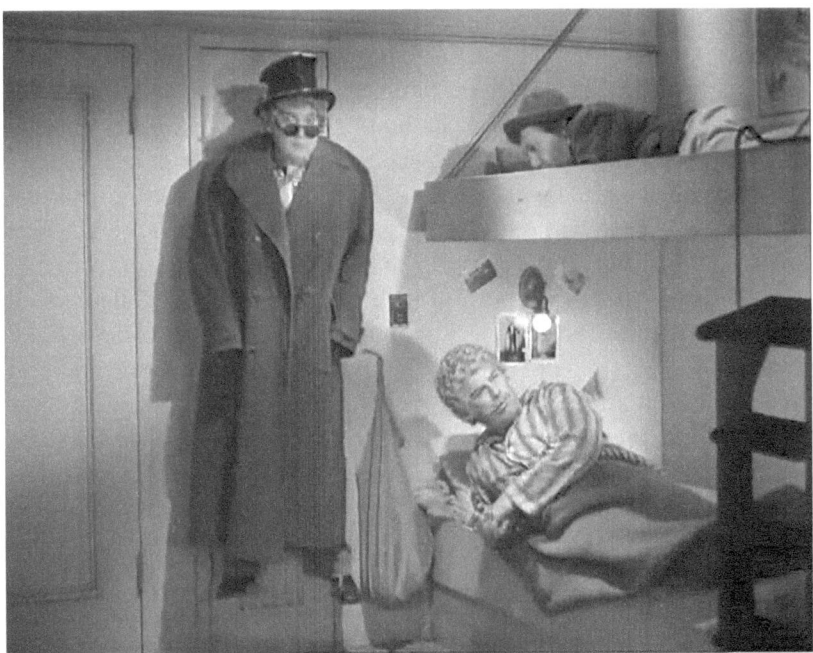

Figure P.3. Harpo responds to his surroundings in *At the Circus*. *Source:* Buzzell, Edward, dir. *At the Circus*. 1939. Burbank, CA: Warner Bros. Pictures, 2020. DVD, 480p SD.

of boot on fingers clearly heard. He makes his way to the medicine cabinet to regather himself. Pouring some apparently medical tonic on the affected hand, he then flaps and slaps the hand up and down on the wall recklessly as though brandishing a flesh-and-blood human paintbrush.

Punchy's deliberation and his will to act are fairly consistently restricted. He is responsive and locked in to the things that are happening around him, the environment in which he finds himself, and those who are acting in their own right. Tony is not just looking for the money but trying to keep Punchy on track. Punchy's magical trench coat pockets contain (with an element of the preternatural) the exact props for responding to what Tony will say. It might be fate or destiny, or it might be that Harpo can see the future (or, to demystify things completely, it might be that he has what is needed in order for the written gags to work). Harpo does seem to have free will in that he clearly acts, but like a train he can go forward or back, but not anywhere he likes. His will is confined both by what is needed in the circumstances in which he finds himself, and by the predictable unpredictability, the absurdity, the bombastic and overflowing joy with which he conjures chaos that is dictated by the metaphysical Harpo.

Considering Harpo's capacity to deliberate and choose is the most obviously metaphysical response to the question of whether Harpo is free. But it is a question in response to figures on screen—in this case films—and so does not attain a rigorously philosophical clarity in its answer. Two embodiments of Harpo—Tomasso and Punchy—instead cinematically illustrate some of the pieces that relate to the puzzle of free will: deliberation, the imposition of one's environment, the role of desire, one's cognitive abilities, action and reaction. As films they do not seek to settle the philosophical problem. Instead, as films they give artistic life to elements of the question itself, as observed and pursued through the figure of Harpo.

Availability and Chaos

In *Duck Soup*, Rufus T. Firefly (Groucho Marx) has been appointed leader of the nation of Freedonia. A conniving ambassador from neighboring country Sylvania has appointed two spies—Chicolini (Chico Marx) and Pinky—to dig up some dirt on Firefly. Chicolini sets up a popcorn stand on the street outside Firefly's office—he tenderly prepares a pickle to eat, but Pinky, who has sidled into shot behind the stand (and taken several large handfuls of popcorn to place in his bottomless trench coat pockets for later), walks around and cuts the pickle in half with a pair of scissors just as Chicolini is to take his first bite.

Chicolini, his frustration bubbling and growing, asks Pinky what he's found out about Freedonia's leader, but Pinky can only stand there dumbly. Chicolini's gestures become more exaggerated, the volume of his voice grows, and his speech increases in rapidity and urgency. Harpo-as-Pinky interrupts his partner twice—once to take Chicolini's hand as a rest for Pinky's leg, and once to place some food in Chicolini's mouth midsentence such that he begins to chew. A fight breaks out, interrupting the lemonade stand vendor nearby. Harpo is free to fight, despite having a task he needs to accomplish—his is a schedule that seems to exist beyond the conventional.

A moment in *Animal Crackers* (1920) sees Signor Emanuel Ravelli (Chico Marx) involved in a game of bridge. His playing partner is the Professor (Harpo Marx). Ravelli is commentating on the endless supply of aces of spades that the Professor is producing, much to the bewilderment and frustration of their opponents. Before the game begins, the four go through the process of picking partners—it will be the Professor and Ravelli against Mrs. Whitehead (Margaret Irving) and Mrs. Rittenhouse (Margaret Dumont). Mrs. Whitehead notifies the Professor that he has choice of seat (she clearly presumes him to have free will), at which point the Professor gets up and sits on her lap. She hurriedly ushers him back to his original spot. Ravelli: "He thought it was contact bridge."

The Professor begins dealing before he is implored to shuffle the cards, at which point he cuts them into two piles, flicking the corners of the cards in each pile individually, before combining the two piles once again, shuffling absolutely nothing. As the Professor begins to deal, he looks to streamline the process by licking the thumb of one of his hands—the only problem being that he is dealing singlehandedly from the other hand.

The Professor clearly knows what he is doing—the wild bridge game is a kind of controlled chaos, and it is being orchestrated by Harpo as the Professor. His fake shuffling, his dealing to ensure that he and Ravelli get the best cards—essentially his well-trained routine to cheat his opponents—suggests a will and a capacity for deliberation, but it also suggests time to rehearse and refine the act, the performance. Clearly this isn't his first game of bridge—clearly, he has the freedom of time to practice and, behind the scenes, the freedom of choice to dedicate his time to perfecting his art of chaotic deception.

Can Harpo and the instantiations of him choose how to spend his and their time? The very question brings to mind the earlier one regarding his freedom of will, but there is a kind of existential freedom that suggests a limitless availability that is crystallized in the two situations briefly mentioned here. The idea of chaos suggests an "anything can happen" quality to Harpo—a feature that runs somewhat counter to the observations earlier that he seems at points locked into and constrained by his environment and those around him, his trench coats and reactions loaded up, presaging the events that unfold or the things that are said to him.

Anything can happen because Harpo can be anywhere. He can fit into any situation. He can fit into any situation because he is free from the responsibility to fit in as a matter of convention or expectation in the first place. That is, Harpo's transcendence makes him identifiable, makes him limitlessly available, and—because he is free from the constraints of situation—renders him a joyous force of chaos. He upsets things by being himself: ontologically distinct and dropping in where necessary rather than adapting to the demands of convention that a game of bridge, a conversation, or anything else might dictate.

The interplay of availability and chaos—the second and third responses to the question, Is Harpo free?—calls to mind again the approach of observation, pursuit, and understanding. We understand the presence of Harpo's chaos and the breadth of his freedom by accumulating our experiences with the different instantiations of his being and following them back to the metaphysical Harpo himself. This is the approach brought to choice, goodness, qualia, personal identity, wonder, and other concepts central to what I term the metaphysical screen and pursue throughout this book. I begin with the films and television programs themselves and the way they animate certain ideas through narrative, form, and style and then consider how the artistic life given to such ideas makes them present to our aesthetic experience. The concepts begin in the works of art and can extend out to the spectator, ripe and ready for contemplation. But what the spectator brings to these films also intersects with the artistic and narrative means of conceptual representation: it is a two-way street. This parallels the way Tomasso, Punchy, Pinky, the Professor, and the rest extend out and reach Harpo himself, while at the same time being shaped and bound by the metaphysical Harpo.

Affordability

What is gained by asking the question, Is Harpo free? And if there is anything gained, does that mean there is something that we must give over to Harpo and to the films in which he appears? That is, is there a particular kind of cost involved, or is Harpo free? The different ways in which we can conceive of and think through Harpo's freedom seem to suggest different sorts of cost—at least to those with whom he interacts. I mentioned earlier Harpo's decision to remain mute. In *A Day at the Races*, Stuffy is trying to convey to Tony (Chico Marx) that Dr. Hugo Z. Hackenbush (Groucho Marx) is in trouble. Rather than deploy his cane horn, he opts instead for a mime act accompanied by whistles. Stuffy places one finger horizontally across his face between his upper lip and nose and then impersonates Groucho's trademark walk while whistling the syllables of "Doctor Hackenbush." The elaborate game of charades has Tony struggling, until Stuffy starts miming a person hacking away at a nearby bush—now the duo are on a roll.

There is a cost to Harpo's choices—deliberative, responsive, reactionary, preternatural choices. They inform the behavior of those around him and play a part in the unfolding of the occasionally thin narratives in which the embodiment of Harpo finds himself. There is sometimes an environmental cost too, as one might expect when dealing with a whirlwind figure that exhales chaos. But what is the cost for us, the spectators, in asking the question, Is Harpo free? It is a question that parallels and mirrors the interests of this book—what is the cost of thinking about Harpo as metaphysical and thinking of the ways in which the screen (the film and television screen) is metaphysical? What might be gained in return?

The cost: it requires a particular attitude, an effort, and a willingness on the part of the spectator to be anchored in the film or television program they are experiencing, and not to simply leave it there but to contemplate after the fact the fruits of willingly experiencing it in a particular way. To consider the ways in which Harpo is the metaphysical orchestrator of Stuffy, Pinky, and the rest is to maintain a sensitive, aesthetically appreciative balance between what is happening in the work itself—formally, stylistically, narratively— and what is prompted without necessarily being given explicitly by the work. It requires the spectator both to take in the films and to (if one is interested) "select" the aspect of Harpo. The double-edged sword of selection (more on this in the afterword), of course, is that to focus one's attention on one element means necessarily to exclude others. So it is with the metaphysical screen—to focus attention on a film's artistic examination of causality or goodness or personal identity is to take in the stylistic, formal, and narrative ways in which that film or television program examines that concept. It may, of course, examine others. Approaching the metaphysical screen in the way I do in this book also requires a willingness to parse connections between different works—to be motivated by the variable ways films and television programs can artistically examine the same concept, in much the same way that multiple Marx Brothers films afford us a better understanding, appreciation, and love of Harpo.

What is conditionally gained? We gain not just a deeper understanding of the art forms of film and television by way of our aesthetic experiences and close appreciation of the works we experience. We gain, too, a broader sense of the topic or concept under view (be it free will or goodness or anything else). Perhaps of greatest value and meaning is that we gain an expanded sense of wonder for art and the worlds to which it is tied—a wonder tied to the works that refigure the worlds we experience. Do we gain an answer to the question, Is Harpo free? Perhaps not definitively. Do we gain a deeper appreciation of and love for Harpo? How could it not be so?

1

What Is the Metaphysical Screen?

Artistic Form, Content, and Philosophy

Early in Terrence Malick's film *The Thin Red Line* (1998), Private Witt (Jim Caviezel) is speaking to First Sergeant Edward Welsh (Sean Penn). Witt has been AWOL, and was only recently discovered and imprisoned aboard a troop carrier ship. The two men are speaking of existential and metaphysical things—of death and possibly life thereafter and of what constitutes a man. With grizzled demeanor and clipped speech, Welsh insists that a man is nothing in this world, and that "there ain't no world but this one." Witt, with a faraway certainty, disagrees: "I've seen another world," he claims.

What is the significance of the sorts of worlds we see onscreen in films and television programs, and how are they constructed both on their own terms and in relation to reality? What answers can spectators glean in response to these questions by paying close attention to the metaphysical screen—understood as the ways in which the story-worlds of film and television are constructed artistically through form and content, rendering metaphysical ideas such as free will, personal identity, and goodness in different ways? I suggest that the spectator's aesthetic experience of certain films and television programs can be sensitive to the artistic exploration and transformation of the world

1

of ordinary experience, and as a result, experiences of the metaphysical screen provide opportunities to rethink, refine, and contemplate anew our assumptions regarding selfhood and the nature of the world. Across the accumulated experiences of a range of films and television programs, spectators can become attuned to the ways in which certain concepts are explored in different and even contradictory ways: we are not given easy answers or solutions to philosophical problems; rather, cinematic and televisual art can examine such concepts and provide us with new ways of thinking about them in light of our experience with their artistic presentation.

There is a cluster of ideas that organize this chapter and the chapters that follow: the interplay of form and content, aesthetic experience, aesthetic cognitivism, mimesis, and film and television worlds. I will work through each of these in turn and discuss how they help in understanding our spectatorial experience of the metaphysical screen in terms of the questions outlined earlier regarding the ways in which film and television worlds artistically refigure the world of ordinary experience, and what might be gained from our experience of such worlds. First, though, a more detailed understanding of metaphysics and how it relates to the present concerns is necessary so as to outline the aspects of film and television I will explore later.

Metaphysics in Film and Television

Defining metaphysics in a way that is sensitive to the shifts in focus and meaning across its history is a difficult task. For Stephen Mumford, the topics of metaphysics cannot be observed in the way we observe ordinary, physical objects, but they can be abstracted from such objects (2012, 107). In this sense, Mumford's account shares a characteristic feature of Peter van Inwagen's understanding of metaphysics, in that it "attempts to get behind appearances and . . . tell the ultimate truth about things" (2014, 4). Van Inwagen, however, goes further still and suggests that metaphysics attempts to answer three sets of questions about the world. The first regards the world itself: What are its features, what is it like, and what does it (the world) contain? (4). The second regards reasons for the world's existence: Why does the world exist in the manner it does, and why does it exist at all? (4). The third regards humankind's relation to the world:

What is the nature of this relation, and how do we understand the place of humankind's existence in the world? (4). The account of the metaphysical screen I develop throughout this book—anchored as it is in concepts such as causality and free will, goodness, qualia, and personal identity—tends toward the first and third sets of questions.

My interest in the artistic exploration of metaphysical concepts in film and television has several motivations. First, while the metaphysics *of* film (and less so, television) has generated a great deal of literature—addressing questions of the nature (ontology) of film and moving images, for example—sorely lacking is a systematic consideration of metaphysical concepts *through* films and television programs and why this consideration might be significant to our understanding of such concepts, as well as to better establishing the importance of art and experience to our understanding of philosophical ideas. Second, work that has been conducted at the intersection of film and ethics has fruitfully examined the ways that films can illuminate ethical concerns in a distinctive way as well as the way in which philosophical ethics can enhance and deepen our understanding of the spectatorial experience of films and of the films themselves (e.g., Sinnerbrink 2015; Stadler 2008b; Choi and Frey 2013). With this in mind, the account of the metaphysical screen I offer here acts as the kernel of what can develop into something akin to that of cinema and ethics scholarship.

However, there is a distinctive challenge to any attempt to examine metaphysics through or in films and television programs. As articulated earlier, the ultimate concerns of metaphysics are abstract. Looking to film for ethical insight, for example, does not necessarily pose the same potential issues as looking to film for metaphysical insight, given the ways in which screen narratives can problematize or illustrate ethical quandaries. However, as Mumford notes, while metaphysics is "concerned with the world, [it] is not so much concerned with that part of it that can be observed" (2012, 100). Metaphysical concepts cannot necessarily be observed as such; however, we can observe their effects, or at least contemplate their effects and reason back to the abstract concepts themselves. The aesthetic experience of works of the metaphysical screen affords spectators the opportunity to rethink, or contemplate, metaphysical concepts in light of their artistic exploration in certain films and television programs, thereby potentially informing our understanding of how these concepts function in the ordinary world. Therefore, it is precisely because of the abstract nature of metaphysics that the metaphysical screen is philosophically significant, in that it narratively and stylistically explores metaphysical concepts such as those mentioned earlier.

These concerns have been given expression in an earlier work addressing a different art form: T. S. Eliot's consideration of metaphysical poetry, notably the works of seventeenth-century English poets John Donne, Andrew Marvell, and Richard Crashaw. Eliot argues that metaphysical poetry is "that which occurs when an idea, or what is only ordinarily apprehensible as an intellectual statement, is translated in sensible form; so that the world of sense is actually enlarged" (1993, 53–54) and "[so] that it elevates sense for a moment to regions ordinarily attainable only by abstract thought" (55). Two relevant points present themselves. First, given that metaphysical concepts are being artistically transformed into narrative art, to expect such concepts to be presented as they are in a philosophical argument or proposition would be misguided. Because the so-called realm of ideas is given, on the metaphysical screen, an artistic life, any philosophical significance drawn out through a spectator's aesthetic experience relies on treating those works as artworks rather than philosophical propositions. Second, and implied in Eliot's comments, is a certain understanding regarding the inseparability of form and content.

Arthur C. Danto suggests that with art, "if you can answer two questions—these questions really were articulated by Hegel—what's it about—what's the content—and how does it embody the content, you've probably gone as far as anybody knows how to go" (2014, 26). Murray Smith extends Danto's insights into the domain of film: in adopting Danto's understanding of Hegel's definition of art—"the sensuous embodiment of the idea"—Smith notes that this "is a way of recognizing the ideational content of art, while insisting upon the difference between art and philosophy" (2016, 193). As Smith suggests, the difference between Hegel and Danto in the consideration of art and its relation to philosophy is that whereas Hegel emphasizes their differences, Danto looks to highlight what is shared. Smith, therefore, rightly looks to correct the balance and acknowledge "both the ideas and their 'sensuous embodiment' in works of film art" (193) as a means of addressing the relation, specifically, between film and philosophy. (I will return to this question later.)

The understanding of form and content that I adopt here is one advanced by Katherine Thomson-Jones. She suggests that the "thesis of inseparability states that (1) it is impossible to have the same content in two different forms; and (2) it is impossible to have the same form in two different contents" (2005, 375). She identifies three central accounts of form and content: "the container account, the functional account, and the semantic account" (377). The container account understands form as container and content as that which is contained; the functional account identifies "form independently from content as the function of the artwork"; the semantic account designates content as the meaning of a work, and form as the means by which that meaning is expressed or presented: "the way meaning is made manifest" (377). As Thomson-Jones notes, "In its application to our understanding of representational art, the thesis of inseparability invokes the semantic account of form and content" (377). This is the version I develop here.

Thomson-Jones (2005) claims that "a work's treatment of its subject constitutes a certain perspective on, attitude toward, or interpretation of that subject" (381). In the case of the metaphysical screen, it is not just that metaphysical concepts are artistically explored but that part of the exploration involves the expression of particular perspectives on, attitudes toward, or interpretations of metaphysical concepts. Therefore, to take the following chapter as an example, one way in which films and television programs artistically explore the metaphysical concepts of free will and causality is through different narrative forms—such as forking-path narratives, time-travel narratives, and what I term spatially convergent narratives (among others). In works that adopt such narratives, I identify free will and causality as the unifying metaphysical concept. However, in the artistic transformation of the concepts of free will and causality into different narrative forms, they thus present different perspectives on, attitudes toward, or interpretations of those concepts.

The significance of our aesthetic experience with such works now becomes clearer. Thomson-Jones suggests that "insofar as aesthetic experience involves attention to form, appreciation of an artwork *qua* art may involve appreciation of its perspective, attitude, or interpretation of an aspect of human experience" (2005, 381). In an aesthetic experience with a work of the metaphysical screen that adopts a certain perspective on, attitude toward, or interpretation of free will and causality, spectators will be attentive to the formal properties of these works and thus have the opportunity through such experience to contemplate how free will and causality function in the ordinary world, in light of their aesthetic experience with the work. As Noël Carroll notes, "Attending with understanding to the formal, and/or otherwise aesthetic and/or expressive properties of an artwork are examples of aesthetic experience" (2012,173). Therefore, an aesthetic experience in the context of this book will be one where the spectator is attentive to the ways in which the formal, expressive, and aesthetic features of an artwork are artistically exploring particular metaphysical concepts. For André Bazin, "As good a way as any towards understanding what a film is trying to say to us is to know how it is saying it" (2010, 98). An aesthetic experience is one where the spectator is attentive to the inseparability of form and content.

At the most basic level, the sort of attention that is necessary for experiencing a film or television program aesthetically is reflected in the fact that, while there is much that is shared between contemporary television and film, one needs to be sensitive to the differences between these art forms too. The recent trend in television scholarship to adopt an aesthetic approach that favors detailed consideration of the formal characteristics of television certainly informs treating it alongside film, though one notable difference is in the narrative form of film and television. Ted Nannicelli identifies a key distinguishing feature between film and television as that of "temporal prolongation" that "carries with it connotations of a temporally unfolding, yet organically unified structure" (2016, 65). Alongside temporal prolongation there is also the feature of interruption. Television series, even in the contemporary age of Netflix and other streaming services that do not need to work around advertising breaks within episodes, still maintain a formal structure of episodes and seasons. Both features—temporal prolongation and interruption—are characteristic of television and generate a different sort of experience than that of films, which are, in general, temporally shorter though uninterrupted in terms of narrative form.

There is an authorial point worth briefly touching on here: other medium-specific features (such as screen size and sound technology) will likely dictate the sorts of aesthetic decisions filmmakers and showrunners will make in creating their works. (Television programs will potentially limit extreme long shots and will design sound around the technological capacities of televisions, for example.) The convergence of media and the breakdown of expected normative viewing conditions further complicate the ways in which films and television programs remain separate mediums. Without discounting these important technological developments and their influence on the aesthetic features of films and television programs, my approach with regard to the works considered in this book emphasizes the medium-specific features as they are embodied in the work, rather than the ways that the constraints of each medium will influence the artistic decisions made by creators.

How, then, can the particulars of television's narrative form be put to productive use, and how does this shape television's use of form and content to artistically explore metaphysical concepts? Krzysztof Kieślowski's television program *Dekalog* (1989–1990) offers an instructive example. Although the narrative does not develop in a linear sense from episode to episode, and two of the episodes were made into films (the episodes have been referred to as "TV films" or something similar), the program was made for Polish television and involves a narrative form that uses both interruption and prolongation (though its complex and unique take on the latter is not as straightforward as that of more standard television programs). Its structure could even be seen as a precursor to the limited series and compendium series that have proliferated in contemporary television.

As we might expect given the title of the program, many analyses of it seek to establish the magnitude of the connection to the Ten Commandments (Kickasola 2004, 162–163). Writing about the program, Fr. Marek Lis suggests that "*Dekalog* is not a series (meaning a collection of dramatic episodes featuring a closed group of characters) but a cycle, which ... does not form a continuous fictional story but consists of films devoted to different themes" (2016, 21). As mentioned, while temporal prolongation is not present in the typical sense—in the manner of a linear development of story across episodes and subsequently seasons—it is still important to consider *Dekalog* as a whole work. This is in part demanded by the narrative form of the work, which, regardless of how strident we find the connection between commandments and episodes, is relational. Each episode informs the other, perhaps not as spectators of television might expect—such as through the introduction and resolution of plots within an episode, with a larger arc unifying a season, or through the use of the prolonged narrative form of television to gradually and deeply develop a set of characters. Instead, *Dekalog* uses the interruption and prolongation of television's narrative form to develop more subtle connections across episodes. There is still a story present—one that accumulates through smaller stories that are unrelated in the conventional sense, but, in fact, are related when considered in terms of the program's metaphysical preoccupations. Like the form of the Ten Commandments that motivated *Dekalog*, each individual episode can be taken as an isolated and freestanding part, but to appreciate the significance of the work is to take each part in consideration of every other part—to examine the work as a whole. In this sense, attention to the prolongation and interruption present in the program's narrative form is necessary for understanding how *Dekalog* explores metaphysical concepts.

The overarching metaphysical concern of the program regards the nature of one's being in the world, which is drawn out in each episode through a moral confrontation experienced by the central character(s) of that episode. However, these are not separate worlds, so to speak—they are different pockets of the same world. The largely stable setting of an apartment block in which many of the characters live means that they make brief appearances in some of the episodes. The setting combined with the ordinary and unremarkable intersection of characters from different episodes helps to establish the coherence and unity of the world as it is developed throughout the entire program. Furthermore, the presence of the same actor (Artur Basciś) who plays different background characters in most of the episodes of *Dekalog* further establishes a connection across episodes, inviting spectators to maintain an appreciative balance between individual episodes and the program as a whole, unified work.

In her analysis of *Dekalog 1*, Vivian Sobchack is concerned not only with this episode but with how Kieślowski's work is emblematic of "the ambiguous nature of the empirically concrete happenstance to which we ... are always subject" (2004, 85). She continues, suggesting that "as we ... are materially embodied in the space-time of the world with other objective beings and things, we are engaged in incalculable encounters whose scope and consequences exceed not only our vision but also our agency" (85). In considering *Dekalog 1*, therefore, Sobchack looks to draw out how our concrete embodied existence is not just concrete and embodied but ultimately social and ethical. For Sobchack, Kieślowski illustrates through his work that we cannot possibly imagine or speculate on the extent or "scope" of our actions, and this facet of our existence necessarily influences how we understand the ethical dimension of our lives. Sobchack examines the moral dimension of *Dekalog* through the encounters between characters and the effects and consequences of such encounters. However—and in line with the comments offered earlier—in examining the metaphysical dimension of the work, I am interested in extrapolating from such encounters to the concepts that underpin, shape, or inform them.

In the case of *Dekalog*, Sobchack's emphasis is on the limits (or lack of limits) of consequences of action (beyond agency and action), whereas mine is on the metaphysical ground for the characters' being in the world—the metaphysical conditions and qualities of the world, prior to action and agency, that inform, restrict, and make possible the very predicament in which characters find themselves. Therefore, considering *Dekalog* as an example of metaphysical art is not to be ignorant of its central emphasis on the existential dynamics of what it is to be human, or of what it means for a person to exist and be immersed in a world. Furthermore, it is not to suggest a cold, abstract, or overly propositional quality to the program—indeed, Kieślowski's entire body of work, and *Dekalog* in particular, is deeply concerned with the quotidian nuances of human existence. Rather, it is to follow its existential concerns in one of the directions to which they lead—the metaphysical ground of existence, and the nature of one's being in the world.

Across its episodes, *Dekalog* uses the embodied existence and encounters of characters as a way of illustrating and narrativizing concepts such as chance and luck, fatality and determinism and free will. As Paul C. Santilli notes,

> A film director may ... suggest that there are metaphysical and spiritual depths to the scenes being displayed, offering viewers an occasion to reflect on God, freedom, and the human soul. In this respect, film can be taken as a philosophical act expressing ideas about the ground of phenomena, without pretending to offer a conceptual knowledge of that ground. When we watch a good film, we may experience ... the evocation of what may be life's "deepest essences." (2006, 148)

Therefore, we shouldn't expect *Dekalog* to offer a treatise, proposition, or argument regarding metaphysics or a range of metaphysical concepts. Rather, through the artistic exploration of metaphysical concepts within televisual form and content, the program offers the opportunity for a different experience of such concepts.

In *Dekalog 1*, we follow Krzysztof (Henryk Baranowski) and his son Paweł (Wojciech Klata). Krzysztof is enamored with technology and science, and his apartment is regularly aglow from the light of his (for the time period) powerful personal computer. Using the computer, Krzysztof and his son calculate the thickness of the ice of the nearby lake to determine whether it is safe to go ice skating. With the computer's confirmation, and after Krzysztof himself tests the ice, Paweł, upon finding a brand-new pair of ice skates intended as a Christmas gift, is allowed by his father to go skating. Krzysztof does not see his son the next day, and after a frantic and panicked attempt at tracking down his location, watches as what appears to be his son's corpse is pulled from beneath the broken shards of ice that were covering the lake.

This episode is generally attached to the first imperative of the Ten Commandments: "Thou shalt not defy me by making other gods thy own" (or "Thou shalt not have strange gods before me"). It is thus largely understood as a caution against idolatry, which is manifest in the program as the materialist objectives and capacities of technology and science. There is a clear juxtaposition of ideas between Krzysztof—a materialist and atheist—and his sister Irena (Maja Komorowska), who is deeply religious, as well as of their personalities as characters. In an early scene, Paweł asks his father about death, and he answers that it is merely the body's functions ceasing to continue. The boy asks what's left afterward, and his father replies that what a person did remains, as well as the memory of that person, citing various features of physiology and personality that might be particular to an individual. Paweł has a similarly complex conversation with his aunt; however, she prefers to speak of living—that living is a gift and that living is the joy in helping others. The boy asks her what God is, and she replies by hugging him, and saying that God is love—a great big hug.

These quiet and simple moments of experience offer ways into the metaphysical themes of the episode and the program as a whole. The details of the environments inform the responses—the cool lighting and bare-bones setting of Krzysztof's apartment reflect his own being in the world, that of a clinical scientist enamored with technology. The brightness and warm tones of Irena and her softer, familial décor reflect her own being in the world. Furthermore, the difference in setting and aspects of mise-en-scène (including elements of performance such as gesture and dialogue) relate to the thematic concerns of the episode—it makes sense that one aspect of love is expressed through an aunt's hug of her nephew, while a discussion of life that terminates with the body occurs in the cold and dim. The episode, though, complicates the presence of such ideas, as, upon the extraction of Paweł from the lake, both Irena and Krzysztof stand side by side—arriving at the same place, in the same predicament and set of circumstances, with each character potentially reflecting on their own conversations with Paweł (fig. 1.1). Although the adults are certain in their responses to the world up to this point—to the meaning, ground, and conditions of their existence—it is Paweł who perhaps had the most prescience and insight as to the complexity of a person's existence in the world.

Figure 1.1. Irena and Krzysztof stand side by side in *Dekalog 1*. *Source:* Kieślowski, Krzysztof, dir. *Dekalog 1*. 1988. New York: Criterion, 2016. Blu-ray Disc, 1080p HD.

In an earlier scene, in another discussion with his father, the young boy opines that "I was so glad in the morning when I managed to get that calculation right, and then the pigeon came for the breadcrumbs; but I went shopping and saw a dead dog. I knelt over him, and I said to myself, what good is it? Who needs the information how long it will take Miss Piggy to catch up with Kermit? It doesn't make any sense." While Paweł seems to suggest that science and technology can't answer the questions he poses—that perhaps there isn't an equation to quantify the pleasures of achievement or the humble joys of nature—the warm glow of love promised by his aunt strikes the boy as equally inadequate to account for the cruel and apparently uncaring death of a dog. The nature of one's being in the world that is manifested in the lives of Paweł's two closest companions—be it existence sustained through divine love or the calculability and predictability of measured, scientific empiricism—is challenged by the quotidian experiences of Paweł himself. These ordinary moments of experience pose challenging metaphysical questions that rattle the young boy's certainty regarding the nature of things, and it takes a far greater tragedy than a dead dog to do the same to Krzysztof and Irena. It is through the experiences of the characters in *Dekalog 1*, and through a range of experiences developed across the series, that the program's artistic exploration of metaphysical concepts, such as the nature of one's being in the world, occurs.

Mimesis and the Worlds of Film and Television

Given the conceptual nature of metaphysics, it will bear (in different ways, and depending on a particular work) certain similarities to the ordinary world. The metaphysical screen offers a way to reflect on the mimetic relation between work and world—between the different ways in which a metaphysical concept can be explored onscreen and how we might understand that concept (free will, for example) to work in our own lives. That is, there is cause to consider how we understand films and television programs to possess a connection to the world of ordinary experience while also operating as worlds themselves.

Developing a proper understanding of mimesis is one way in which we can (1) better make a distinction between different works and their unique artistic merits or qualities, and (2) more thoroughly understand the relation between the worlds of films and television programs and the reality we inhabit. Paul Ricœur's theory of threefold mimesis offers an informative approach to answering these questions. For Ricœur, mimesis is a creative invention, rather than a strict replication. Such a theory serves Ricœur's broader interests regarding the narrative nature and understanding of selfhood and the world—that we come to understand our existence primarily through the construction of stories.

Threefold mimesis consists of prefiguration, configuration, and refiguration. Ricœur suggests that the composition of plot (emplotment) is a configuration—a narrativization—of the world of ordinary experience (prefiguration) (1984, 54). The role of configuration is to mediate from one side of the story to the other—from prefiguration to refiguration (65). Refiguration, according to Ricœur, "marks the intersection of the world of the text [film/television program] and the world of the hearer or reader [spectators]" (71). According to the concept of threefold mimesis, there is an inherent connection between the configuration of the world and the world itself—on the metaphysical screen, this connection develops out of the (artistic) configuration of a certain perspective on, attitude toward, or interpretation of a metaphysical concept.

It is critical to have a correct understanding of mimesis in order to properly understand this dynamic. As Richard Kearney suggests, "*Mimesis* is not about idealist escapism or servile realism." (2002, 131). Instead, "It remakes the world, so to speak, in the light of its potential truths" (131). When we speak of film and television's mimetic properties, or their mimetic representation of the world, it is a misuse of the term—at least on a historically sensitive understanding of mimesis—to do so in reference to whether or not film and television (and representational arts more broadly) replicate reality, or the world, *tout court*. Instead, understanding the mimetic relation of film and television to reality is not so prescriptive. For example, an Italian neorealist film may be more firmly set within our understanding of the ordinary world, whereas a superhero film might take delight in the flaunting of that understanding. However, it is important to note that while the former seems more grounded in the ordinary world than the latter, in both examples the world is still being artistically transformed—mimetically remade—just to varying degrees and in different ways.

To particularize this in the context of the metaphysical screen, the framework of threefold mimesis helps to explain that in the artistic exploration of metaphysical concepts, it is not a necessary condition that some true statement of, for example, free will and causality is remade in a work, but rather that a particular perspective on, attitude toward, or interpretation of free will and causality is present. This is because the mimetic relation of a work of metaphysical film and television to the world of ordinary experience is not one of replication but one of invention—of development and/or speculation. As Kearney states, "*Mimesis* is 'invention' in the original sense of that term: *invenire* means both to discover *and* to create, that is, to disclose what is already there in the light of what is not yet.... It is the power, in short, to re-create actual worlds as possible worlds" (2002, 132). Therefore, I suggest that threefold mimesis helps to show that the artistic exploration of metaphysical concepts introduces a difference between work and world through the configuration of such concepts via the formal capacities of film and television, and it is through this difference that spectators are offered an opportunity to reconsider and contemplate, in light of their aesthetic experience, how said concepts function in the ordinary world.

In an aesthetic experience of the different worlds of the metaphysical screen, there will be an attention to the ways in which they align or differ from our experience of the ordinary world. For Daniel Yacavone, there is a "basic intuition ... that narrative 'world-making' consists essentially of making imaginary modifications to parts or aspects of genuinely existing reality in ways that are more or less partial and subtle or extensive and obvious. In this view empirical reality ... always remains the standard for the comprehension of every fictional and imaginary world" (2015, 5). From the perspective of authorship, V. F. Perkins notes that the filmmaker's "aim is to organize the world to the point where it becomes most meaningful but to resist ordering it out of all resemblance to the real world which it attempts to evoke" (1993, 70). Taken together, these observations highlight how, in the first instance, the construction of worlds in film and television in terms of artistic creation and spectatorial comprehension will involve the world of ordinary experience as a kind of at least implied reference point and, in the second case, the ways in which these worlds are constructed require an internal consistency, the attention to which allows for a deeper appreciation for the stories that are told within them.

This second point invites consideration of the formal composition of worlds. Ian Garwood notes in his approach to analysis—that of textural analysis—that being sensitive "to the sensuous capacity of cinema . . . might deepen, rather than distract from, or supersede, the viewers' interest in a film as a distinctive fictional world" (2013, 14). One's emphasis on the sensuous and textural elements of a film or television program is not at the expense of narrative and character but considers how such qualities bolster and inform these other aspects. Garwood's comments also allude to the importance of paying attention to the formal construction of works—how all of the different parts come together to make a whole work (world) and are interwoven and related.

Lucy Fife Donaldson also considers the place of texture in terms of a film, noting how it invokes both a "sense of materiality" and "the sense of an overall fabrication, a densely textured world indicating a complex and fully formed fiction, occupied by three-dimensional characters" (2014, 141). The textural composition of film and television involves not just its construction but spectatorial attention to that construction: a sensitivity to how different textural and formal elements are woven together to form an entire narrative world. The disclosure of such a world is not merely a matter of disclosing a story that occurs within it but disclosing the kind of world that makes possible a kind of story (see Bateman 2019).

Belá Tarr's *The Turin Horse* (2011) centers on isolated father-and-daughter farmers whose horse is becoming increasingly uncooperative as it moves toward the end of its life. The film uses a variety of formal elements to reinforce the bleak, punishing quality of the world in which the narrative takes place. The film features black-and-white footage; a haunting and dissonant musical score; an intensity of weather and setting (characterized by the omnipresence of mist and haze, dead and dying foliage, and a seemingly eternal and relentless gale-force wind); the disheveled and run-down home and clothing of the farming family; the gruff and impassive performers and their interaction with the once dependable but now deeply attitudinal horse; the persistent use of low-angle cinematography to render an otherwise ordinary world alien, strange, and unsettled; and the use of long takes (the film is composed of twenty of these) so as to manipulate time to reinforce the punishing slog of existence. The opening scene of the film captures many of these elements: as the old farmer leads his cantankerous horse, every movement is met with struggle, with a kind of rebuttal from the natural forces mentioned earlier, from the limitations of his own body, and from the metaphysical conditions of his life (fig. 1.2).

The different formal elements of the film are woven together for the sake of internal consistency and thus inform the story being told. The world is presented as unforgiving, plodding, difficult, and relentless through form and style in such a way that is internally consistent and that also informs the shape of the story being told within it. Perkins suggests that "To be in a world is to know the partiality of knowledge and the boundedness of vision—to be aware that there is always a bigger picture. To observe a world humanly is to do so from a viewpoint, with angles of vision and points of focus whose selectivity is inflected by the seeing mind" (2020, 275). We witness the world of *The Turin Horse* and any other film or television program of the metaphysical screen in terms of the narratives being

Figure 1.2. Resisting the oppression of existence in *The Turin Horse*. *Source:* Tarr, Béla, and Ágnes Hranitzky, dirs. *The Turin Horse*. 2011. New York: Cinema Guild, 2012. Blu-ray Disc, 1080p HD.

told in it—there is a selectivity involved in that we are focusing on *this* story and *these* characters rather than any others that may populate the world, or only on others insofar as they intersect with the chosen focus of the work. Moreover, an aesthetic experience with works of the metaphysical screen will be attuned to the internal consistency of the world of a work and its formal and textural composition. Attending to the dynamic between world and narrative—between the nature of the world and how this informs what unfolds within it—replicates somewhat how we can treat the relation of a work's world to the world of ordinary experience, too.

Although not discussed in the same terms, the idea of the actual quality of film and television's mimetic relation to reality is one that has been explored throughout film theoretical history. In developing the neoformalist method of film criticism, informed by the Russian formalists, Kristin Thompson suggests that "the basic function of the artwork is to renew perception through a process called *defamiliarization*" (1981, 32). The assumption is that "our everyday perception becomes habitual and dulled" (32) and that therefore artworks can transform the objects and ideas depicted and explored and renew the spectator's appreciation and understanding of them. Elsewhere, Thompson argues that "art defamiliarizes our habitual perceptions of the everyday world, of ideology...of other artworks, and so on by taking material from these sources and transforming them. The transformation takes place through their placement in a new context and their participation in unaccustomed formal patterns" (1988, 11). Following the Russian formalists, Thompson highlights the central place of perception; however, my own point of emphasis is the configuration (that is, the artistic transformation) of aspects of reality—namely metaphysical concepts. What Thompson and I share in approach is an attunement to the philosophical significance of a particular artwork (via, in Thompson's terms, its capacity for defamiliarization) stemming from how the work transforms and remakes the world through the formal capacities of the art forms of film and television. Defamiliarization can occur in an artistically laudable but perhaps less philosophically significant way—for example, how the slowly tracking camera in *The Thin Red Line* parts the long grass of the battlefield; or it can be taken across the entire work in a way that is more experientially and intellectually challenging—*The Thin Red Line*'s questioning of the unseen glory of the world, even in the midst of evil, war, and suffering, or *The Turin Horse*'s examination of existential suffering.

Film and television's exploration of reality is delicate and complex. Stanley Cavell suggests that "the poetry of film ... [is] what it is that happens to figures and objects and places as they are variously molded and displaced by a motion-picture camera and then projected and screened" (2005, 97). The idea of transformation and transfiguration is expressed here, though in different terms. Moreover, implied in Cavell's comments is the notion that the aspects of film and television that establish them as art forms are their formal capacities to configure the world.

For Yacavone, "a cinematic work is not like a mirror of an already illuminated reality ... but, more appositely, a searchlight in the dark, revealing much that we did not even suspect was present before its beam contacted it" (2015, 250). He also suggests that "thus if cinematic art may convey what is true, it does so through an intervention in, and transformation of, what we ordinarily perceive, think, and believe" (249). Shawn Loht makes a similar claim: following Martin Heidegger, Loht suggests that "it is a defining trait of artworks to reveal truth. This happens in a way that they poetically foster insight into the nature of the world" (2017, 6). What is important to note here is that for both Yacavone and Loht, truth does not refer to the correspondence between a proposition and a certain state of affairs (between mind and reality), but rather *aletheia*, or unconcealment. Both scholars, therefore, develop the type of claims offered by Thompson into a stronger one that proposes film's capacity not so much to reveal something about our dulled and apathetic perception of the world but to reveal, or unconceal, something of the world itself. Given the understanding of mimesis with which I work, I do not adopt Loht and Yacavone's claim wholesale; however, I do retain the "interventionist" capacities of film and television to disrupt our ordinary understanding or experience of features of reality.

This scholarly territory is significant when dealing with the metaphysical screen. As I have shown, given what is at stake in metaphysics, nothing could be more philosophically ordinary, and therefore potentially ignored or taken for granted, than metaphysical concepts. The metaphysical screen, therefore, is significant in potentially disrupting our awareness, presumed understanding, or beliefs regarding metaphysical concepts and how they operate in the world of ordinary experience, and such disruption occurs through film and television's artistic exploration of such concepts. For Perkins, "The delicate relationship between what is shown and the way of showing, justifies and exalts the movie's mongrel confusion of reportage with narrative and visual art. A single image is made to act both as a recording, to show us what happens, and as an expressive device to heighten the effect and significance of what we see" (1993, 78). The tension between "reportage" and film (and television's) "expressive" properties or functions elegantly describes the mimetic relation film and television have with reality. It is the configurative capacities of both of these art forms that establish their connection to reality—which, for the metaphysical screen, is by means of the inseparability of form and content (a particular perspective on, attitude toward, or interpretation of metaphysical concepts). However, the metaphysical concepts configured on screen, through the formal capacities that establish the very connection in the first place, enable spectators to contemplate or reflect on them in a new light, and potentially shape how spectators understand the nature of these concepts in the world of ordinary experience. The configuration of such concepts introduces a gap between work and world within which the philosophical significance of such works exists.

Philosophical approaches to film and television studies, or scholarship loosely known as "film-philosophy," can add something to this understanding. This is a diverse field, with approaches including the application of a preexisting theoretical or philosophical framework through which to analyze films (adopting a Deleuzian approach to a work, for example), and what has characteristically been the typical approach to understanding the relationship between philosophical thinking and cinema. While one typical approach within the broad field of film-philosophy addresses the question "Can films philosophize?" I suggest that it misses the main thrust of the relationship between film and philosophy. The multisensory and experiential quality of film and television and their formal exploration of reality highlight how an aesthetic experience draws out the philosophical significance of a work precisely because its expressive form is different from that of philosophy. Therefore, to contemplate a film or television program's philosophical significance as one would a propositional argument is to make a category error. What does connect the philosophical significance of a work with the world of philosophy—if we are to understand philosophy in a historically sensitive way—is the invocation of wonder about the world. As Robert Sinnerbrink notes, "According to tradition, philosophy begins in wonder. We might add that it usually ends in one of two ways, either in self-assured mastery or in thoughtful perplexity" (2011, 38). Adopting this understanding of philosophy is important because it does not impose certain expectations or constraints on film—it does not consider film in terms of a historically or ideologically stringent view of philosophy—but is open to films and television programs as artworks that can invoke wonder about the world. It is this capacity through which the dialogical quality of the relationship between film and philosophy can be understood. Loht argues that "films operating in the guise of philosophy do their work by occasioning insight in the viewer. And this occasioning would seem to occur because of film's capacity for showing, i.e., visually depicting images and situations that stand to be intellectually challenging or provocative" (2015,180). One aspect of Loht's claim requires development: it is not solely through *showing* (visually) that insight is occasioned in the viewer. Spectators, in experiencing film and television, use multiple senses, and therefore it is not just through the visual aspect of these art forms that they occasion insight but through the totality of image, sound, and invocation of tactile responses too. The metaphysical screen has the capacity to provoke contemplation regarding the nature of reality. Therefore, the formal embodiment of metaphysical content in the sorts of films and television programs I examine illuminates their conceptual (i.e., metaphysical) concerns, and invites spectators to consider these ideas in light of their aesthetic experience with such artworks.

Such a perspective, which establishes the philosophical significance of a work in terms of its artistic features, has some connection to the thesis of aesthetic cognitivism. John Gibson notes that "the question of cognitivism is two-place: it not only calls on us to show that there is something we can learn from art; to be cognitivists about art we *further* have to show that what we claim to have learnt from an artwork is a point, insight, or truth, *that is to be found in the artwork itself*" (2008, 575). Gibson continues, noting that cognitivism "asks us to show that if we acquire knowledge from art, it is because artworks themselves are active and competent players in the pursuit of knowledge" (575). Gibson's comments sit within certain claims I have made to this point—that the content, which I have labeled as philosophical for present purposes though in Gibson's terms is cognitivist, is significant precisely because such content is expressed formally (artistically). Furthermore, Gibson is correct in noting the contingent nature of any knowledge (in his terms) to be gained through experiencing art. The claim of art's capacity to reveal knowledge to varying degrees follows on from the comments by scholars such as Thompson, Yacavone, and Loht that I addressed earlier.

However, there is a version of aesthetic cognitivism that emphasizes art's capacity to produce *understanding* rather than knowledge, which I wish to adopt here. Christoph Baumberger highlights several ways in which understanding and knowledge differ: "Understanding is not a species of belief" (2013, 8). It is holistic and gradual, it is not factive, and it is "related to a plurality of epistemic goals" (9). Baumberger concludes that "artworks can provide new perspectives on objects that enhance our understanding of them. By emphasizing and attenuating, exaggerating and downplaying, adding and omitting, deforming and alienating, pictures make us aware of hitherto unnoticed features of objects thereby yielding a new way of conceiving them" (10). Baumberger's claims—directed largely toward visual art—share a significant degree of similarity with the claims about film and television I have defended thus far. It is through the artistic articulation of an attitude toward, perspective on, or interpretation of a metaphysical concept as the content of a work, expressed as it is through the formal capacities of film and television, that creates the mimetic connection to the world and invites spectatorial reflection on it. This involves the understanding that Baumberger writes about, understanding that can influence our conception of metaphysical concepts in a plurality of ways, but which share the feature of reflecting on such concepts in light of an aesthetic experience with the metaphysical screen—to see the metaphysical world in terms of the metaphysical art.

The Thin Red Line is a rich example that illustrates many of the claims being worked through in this section. Robert Pippin suggests, with regard to war films in general, that "an underlying, often implicit question is: what do men need to believe, what do they need to understand, to endure such an ordeal?" (2013, 248). In this way we can see war films wrestling to varying degrees with the question of how war pervades and shapes a given individual's sense of their own being in the world. The voiceovers in *The Thin Red Line* address this explicitly, though such an idea is also located in the narrative form of the film itself. The quiet moments that dwell on and magnify the natural world, and the meandering conversations between soldiers, are interrupted by the brutal flashes of war. Pippin makes a similar point, suggesting that these quiet moments of the film work through an "almost devout concentration on the visual beauty, magisterial indifference, and sublimity of the natural world, and the unusual meditative interior monologue voice-overs by individual characters" (249). Such formal techniques have a curious effect on the film. As Simon Critchley notes in his analysis, "One has the sense of things simply being looked at, just being what they are—trees, water, birds, dogs, crocodiles or whatever. Things simply are, and are not moulded to a human purpose. We watch things shining calmly, being as they are, in all the intricate evasions of 'as.' The camera can be pointed at those things to try and capture some grain or affluence of their reality" (2005, 147). These ordinary things are transformed through the cinematography of the film, but also in their placement in a narrative of war. The grandeur, beauty, and wonder of the natural world is interspersed with the personal and human cost of war. Such artistic transformation, therefore, occurs through both the stylistic and narrative form of the film. Sinnerbrink takes a similar idea a step further, suggesting that *The Thin Red Line* is "an enactment of ... cinematic poesis, revealing different ways in which we can relate to our own mortality, to the finitude of Being, the radiance of Nature, as well as depicting, from multiple character-perspectives, the experience of loss, of violence, of humanity, and of just letting things be" (2006, 36). Sinnerbrink's claim connects to an idea mentioned earlier: that film and television's relation to philosophy is one built on wonder, and that such wonder is invoked because aspects of the world are artistically explored and remade through style and narrative in the film.

The Thin Red Line is notable in part for how it uses cinematography and voiceover to artistically wrestle with what it is to be in a world, and how people draw meaning from their circumstances and experiences. Tracking shots through lush, tall grass, for example, emphasize the immersive quality of the world. At times these natural features overwhelm soldiers, who are crouched or cowering, searching for cover among trenches or trees or grass. Close-ups on the soldiers' faces intensify the emotional register and depths of the individual's attempt to make sense of the world, to cohere and unify their experience of war that has shattered their previous assumptions about the nature of their existence (fig. 1.3). Voiceovers work in a

Figure 1.3. The toll of war in *The Thin Red Line*. *Source:* Malick, Terrence, dir. *The Thin Red Line*. 1998. New York: Criterion, 2010. Blu-ray Disc, 1080p HD.

similar way, but instead take us inside the characters (though we are not always sure which characters), revealing the ways in which certain soldiers attempt to make sense of their predicament and draw out the meaning of their experiences. Furthermore, the voiceovers sustain the human presence of the soldiers—and the deeply human story of the film—even when there is no human present on screen. The meandering and questioning voiceovers in tandem with the close-ups of the natural world establish the connection between humans and the world and the richness and texture of a world in which a person is immersed. The arrangement of such punctuated moments of beauty and calm, interspersed as they are among moments of horror and war, explore how circumstances and experiences can influence, shape, and transform an individual.

Questions regarding what it is to be in a world and what it is to attempt to make sense of such being are posed through the artistic capacities of the film. And although I have pointed briefly toward a few ways this is achieved stylistically, it is in experiencing the film as a total, unified work—as the articulation of a narrative through a particular world—that such ideas are most provocative. As Sinnerbrink suggests, "This showing is enacted not simply at the level of narrative content or visual style; it involves the very capacity of cinema to reawaken different kinds of attunement or mood through sound and image, revealing otherwise concealed aspects—visual, aural, affective, and temporal—of our finite being-in-the-world" (2006, 36). Should spectators wish, they can put such an aesthetic experience to work, so to speak, and reflect on and examine how *The Thin Red Line* can influence their own understanding of the ideas explored in the film. Sinnerbrink notes that the "encounter between film and philosophy opens up a space of mutual interaction or dialogue between images and concepts that might enable us to explore different ways of thinking or indeed different ways of doing philosophy" (2014, 51). He suggests that "Cavell's film-philosophy articulates the aesthetic experience of film such that it opens up new horizons of understanding that might alter the way we think about the relationship between philosophy and film" (58). Therefore, it is in spectators' being attentive to the formal qualities of a film or television program that the work's philosophical significance might be discovered. Such aesthetic experience can be seen to be of value to philosophy insofar as philosophy is motivated by wonder. Spectators need only orient themselves to the transformation of reality on screen, remaining sensitive to the formal exploration of such ideas, so as to potentially have an aesthetic experience with an artwork that could shape how they understand the world.

Sinnerbrink also notes that "aesthetic experience precedes and informs philosophical reflection" (2011, 43). A key element of this experience is an attitude adopted within it, whereby spectators are sensitive and attuned to the formal qualities of the given work, and that the inextricability of such form and metaphysical content can potentially influence how spectators understand such content in the ordinary world. However, the primacy of the aesthetic experience is central—the approach is not to impose philosophical positions or arguments onto a film or television program but rather to be guided by the philosophically oriented contemplation and reflection that can emerge from the spectator's aesthetic experience with the artwork.

Elsewhere, Sinnerbrink notes that "it is the philosophical interpreter who articulates the link between discrete cinematic sequences and particular philosophical ideas" (2014, 62). The philosophical significance drawn out from an aesthetic experience of a particular work is given expression through interpretation and criticism; it is not to replicate the experience but rather to point to what one has experienced—namely, in the case of the metaphysical screen, the artistic exploration (configuration) of metaphysical concepts through the formal capacities of the art forms of film and television. Perkins is also attuned to this point. He suggests that the meanings of a film "are not hidden in or behind the movie, and that my interpretation is not an attempt to clarify what the picture has obscured. I have written about things that I believe to be in the film for all to see, and to see the sense of" (1990, 4). Interpreting a film (or, indeed, a television program) requires an attention to the inextricability of the work's form and content—it is not the process of mapping particular philosophies or claims onto the work. It is a process of discovering what is present in the work itself and articulating those features—a process of paying attention to the construction of the world, its internal features that inform the particular stories that take place within it, and the mimetic connection it has to the world of ordinary experience.

Spectating the Metaphysical Screen

To this point in the chapter, I have been largely concerned with the relation of a work with reality—with what is at stake in the move from prefiguration to configuration. However, Sinnerbrink's and Perkins's comments begin to introduce more substantially the role of the spectator in the process of moving from configuration to refiguration. What can spectators do with the metaphysical screen? How can certain experiences motivate the sort of contemplation with which I am concerned? Kearney suggests that "*mimesis* introduces a 'gap' (however minimal) between living and recounting.... The recounted life prises open perspectives inaccessible to ordinary perception.... So that when we return from story-world to the real world, our sensibility is enriched and amplified in important respects" (2002, 132). In line with what I have been arguing to this point, the "gap" is not a deficient feature of a work but rather an artistically important one. The gap is what allows for the possibility of philosophical significance to be drawn from an aesthetic experience of a work, and it is because of configuration that a gap exists in the first place. The argument I have made thus far implies an active spectator—a spectator willing to reflect on the ordinary world in light of an aesthetic experience or, in Thomson-Jones's terms—to "see the world in terms of art" (2005, 381). There are several factors that influence this aspect of experience of a work. One of those is perceived resemblance to the world itself, as mentioned earlier. Another is the awareness of relevant aspects of the creation of the work—being aware of Terrence Malick's former occupation as a philosopher and scholar, and as a translator of Heidegger, for example, might attune spectators to the means by which the director artistically explores the metaphysical concept of being in a particular way. These two examples address how particulars of the configurative aspect of a work influence that work's reception by spectators. However, there are also aspects of spectatorship that should not be ignored. To return to the example of free will and causality: given the serious tone and explicit dissection of causality and free will in a film such as Rian Johnson's *Looper* (2012), one need not be in a particularly philosophical mood to appreciate and be attentive to the film's philosophical significance. However, given the levity and use of the romantic-comedy genre in a film such as Peter Howitt's *Sliding Doors* (1998), the audience may need to be in a more philosophically charitable mood to develop any philosophical potential drawn out of an aesthetic experience with that work and its treatment of, for example, fate and determinism.

I mention these two examples to clarify several points. First, whatever ways in which a work can motivate the spectator's reflection on the world in terms of that work are developed through and because of an aesthetic experience of that work. Second, I argue that other features—such as aspects of authorship as indicated earlier in the case of *The Thin Red Line*, or generic features typical of a romantic comedy such as *Sliding Doors*—do not dictate but rather influence the extent of a work's reflective significance. The third regards the importance of subjective differences—in terms of how one spectator is different from another, and the ways in which one and the same spectator can differ in two temporally disparate experiences of the same work. Spectators in both senses may differ in terms of their narrative histories, beliefs, assumptions, emotions, mood, and so forth. These factors—which are not to do with the work's configuration of the world—will also influence the aspects of the work that capture the spectator's attention and the ways in which the work is taken up by the spectator in contemplation and reflection.

The active quality of spectatorship is a perspective that is advanced by a range of scholars. In speaking of truth as unconcealment, Loht suggests that such a "truth cannot emerge, it cannot be appreciated without a human viewer who is there, participating in the artwork's disclosure" (2017, 6). For Yacavone, "[film worlds] do not so much simulate or mime our perceptual and emotional capacities as open up new avenues of and for their exercise" (2015, 231). Perkins argues that "in the cinema, as in the world at large, there is a constant interplay between background knowledge and immediate perception" (2020, 35). Once again, as seen earlier in terms of a work's relation to the world, there is a productive difference between subjective, perceptual experience of the world and the world's configuration in an artistic work. That is to say, our recognizing the participatory nature of spectatorship—its experiential quality as well as relevant subjective differences—is necessary for a proper understanding of how a film or television program can shape our thinking. It demonstrates how such potential is dependent not just on the work's relation to the world in its artistic transformation of the world, but on the work's relation to the spectator, too. To adapt Ricœur's comments: "It is the reader [spectator] who completes the work inasmuch as . . . the written work [film/television program] is a sketch for reading [spectating]" (1984, 77). Within the framework of threefold mimesis, it is the spectator who completes the configuration of the world that occurs in the work—piecing its different elements into a single, unified whole, making sense of it via this process, and, in so doing, affording an opportunity for that work to inform how the spectator sees and understands the world and their place within it.

The primary aim of this book is to systematically express this kind of attentive, active spectatorship. By articulating in language the experiences of a variety of films and television programs, and by establishing the connection between the worlds of the metaphysical screen and philosophy, the present work seeks to show how such artworks can inform thinking about the ordinary world and our place within it. In extending the insights of Ricœur, Alberto Baracco notes: "The long path of Ricœur's hermeneutics . . . always implies a direct involvement of the interpreter in the process of interpretation. . . . Interpretation acts as a mediation between the interpreted world of text and the world of the interpreter. On the other hand, understanding the world of text is always also for the interpreter a new understanding of herself/ himself" (2017, 118). Analysis, interpretation, and critical appreciation are the means by which the spectator articulates the understanding they have drawn from an experience with the metaphysical screen. This relies on an active spectator and their history, emotions, beliefs, and presuppositions about the world and so forth that they bring with them to any experience with a work of art. In refiguring such an experience—in seeing the world anew in terms of an artwork, whether one accepts the perspective on, attitude toward, or interpretation of the work's subject—is to potentially garner a new understanding not just of the world but of oneself and one's relation to the world.

Each of the chapters in this book is anchored in a particular metaphysical concept, though it should not be assumed, for example, that a film considered in the following chapter, which deals with free will and causality, would not just as easily sit alongside a television program in the chapter examining personal identity. The chapters are not meant to be de facto concrete delineations between concepts, but have been arranged so as to best structure the book: while they are internally coherent and can exist individually, taken as a whole they reflect a fuller picture of what I have termed the metaphysical screen. The films and television programs I explore throughout this book have been selected as clear examples of works that engage with metaphysical concepts (rather than borderline cases). In no way is the present book intended to be an exhaustive account of the concepts that populate the metaphysical domain of philosophy. Instead, I have chosen to consider certain concepts and certain ways in which they are made present through the metaphysical screen.

In writing about the significance of art to the way in which we think and contemplate existence, Iris Murdoch suggests that "metaphysical images, in their travels from obscure books through religious and aesthetic imagery into the daily consciousness of all sorts of people, undergo, in this 'do-it-yourself' process, many changes and reveal many ambiguities. Ambiguity, or call it flexibility, belongs to these curious processes" (1993, 504). Murdoch's comment highlights that across a range of artistic and creative pursuits, metaphysical images and ideas are revealed in new ways precisely because they have undergone some sort of transformation, being revealed anew to those who are attuned to their presence. As I highlight throughout this book, artworks that explore these metaphysical ideas can disrupt the preconceived ways in which we may think (if at all) about such concepts. It is the artistic transformation and remaking of such ideas that enable spectators of the metaphysical screen to notice them in a renewed sense, to wonder about them and their place in reality, and to potentially shape and inform spectators' understanding of them. The metaphysical screen does not just invite but demands close attention and appreciation. Championing the importance of art, Jacques

Barzun suggests that "art is an extension of life. Art uses the physical materials of ordinary experience... and puts them together in such a way that the sensations they set off arouse our memories of living, add to them, and thereby extend our life" (1989, 74). It is in giving proper attention to artworks such as those of the metaphysical screen that we can wonder about the world in new ways and contemplate the nature of our existence in the light of art.

2

Can Lola Choose?

Causality, Contingency, and Narrative Form

IN JACO VAN DORMAEL's *Mr. Nobody* (2009), Nemo Nobody (Jared Leto) is the last remaining mortal human on earth. His memory is fading, though at the invitation and provocation of a psychiatrist and journalist, Nemo recalls for them and us, the spectators, turning points in his life. These involve his parents' divorce and the various women whom he loved. Somewhat understandably given his advanced age, Nemo offers contradictory statements and variations on the events that were so central, so formative, to his existence. These fallible memories are interwoven with speculations about multiple possible futures—we often see what might have happened should a relationship have worked out differently, for example. Moreover, this emphasis on choice and free will, wherein the film gives weight to the causal possibilities that follow on from such decisions, is counterbalanced by the ways in which Nemo is a victim of chance and coincidence, the unplanned and unexpected often intervening and undercutting the decisions he tries to make. The film examines these metaphysical ideas through flashbacks, multiple timelines, possible futures, and specific types of narrative, as well as in concert with a range of other philosophical themes.

Nemo's story, then, is told as a complex narrative that is used as a means of drawing out its metaphysical emphasis on the limits and scope of free will, the influence of chance, and the way in which we anticipate causally connected effects of our actions. In Nemo, as is the case with many characters in films and television programs, the impression is given of his deliberating and acting freely in the narrative world in which he exists. This film, along with the other works considered in this chapter, provide a means of thinking about the ways in which the narrative form of films and television programs dictates, binds, and shapes the representation of free will that characters seem to possess. In animating examples of acting in a world, the works considered show us a range of ways in which we, too, can think about how we act in the world, how we deliberate on and speculate about the future, and how we navigate causality and contingency in our lives.

Any narrative film or television program will show us, more or less implicitly, characters making decisions or acting in the narrative world they inhabit. Here I am concerned with different types of complex narratives and how they present varying (and contested) understandings of causality (and related ideas of contingency, determinism, fatalism, and free will). While for certain scholars, as Matthew Campora points out, "complex structures often hide classical stories" (2014, 35), this is not to suggest a superficiality to classical narrative storytelling techniques but to consider how different types of complex narratives explicitly inform the way in which free will is explored in a work. Furthermore, the distinction between classical and complex narrative is more nuanced than a mere clear-cut demarcation suggests (Thanouli 2009). Given the interests of this chapter, classical narration's use of familiar storytelling conventions of film and television to meet spectators' expectations of coherence, linearity, and story logic is of less relevance than the ways in which complex narration challenges these expectations in various ways, innovating in the use of style and narrative form.

Both broad forms of storytelling involve the aspects of narration outlined by David Bordwell. Narration is "the process whereby the film's syuzhet and style interact in the course of cueing and channelling the spectator's construction of the fabula" (Bordwell 1985, 53). The narrative of a work, then, involves the arrangement of the plot (syuzhet) into a film or television program's story (fabula), and the narration of the work is simply that narrative mediated by style. Complex narratives such as *Mr. Nobody* showcase a range of ways (as mentioned earlier) in which works can manipulate the interplay of syuzhet and fabula to present different dimensions involved in the ideas of free will, causality, contingency, and chance. My interests in this chapter primarily concern narrative form, and how there is an intersection between the conventional and the complex, whereby complex narrative forms often innovate by repurposing familiar conventions. After considering at greater length the complexities of complex narratives, I will examine how complex narratives such as forking-path and multiple draft, spatial convergence, multimodal, and time-travel narratives each provide a different kind of examination of free will. I conclude with an analysis of parametric narration; however, I will identify certain problems with Bordwell's formulation of this term, and instead adopt Kristin Thompson's term *parametric form*—thus allowing parametric principles to occur through style or, in this case, narrative form.

Forking-path narratives proceed "from a fixed point—the fork—and purportedly present mutually exclusive lines of action, leading to different futures" (Bordwell 2002, 89) to strike a balance between paths and between repetition and change, making contingent events available to spectator experience (rather than merely following one path of action and leaving contingent events as possibilities optionally explored in the imagination). From the perspective of the filmmaker, in what Karen Pearlman refers to as the recombinative logic of film editing, "the director makes choices from among the variations offered to him by the editor. The editor makes choices from among millions of possible combinations of the material of what to present to the director" (2009, xxviii). Therefore, forking-path narratives can be seen to concretize a few more possibilities than a classical narrative. In showing different outcomes to the spectator, this narrative form highlights how events are contingent on prior actions or events, retroactively demonstrating how a causal chain can function. Forking-path narratives also present certain events as necessary and develop a deterministic flow to how the story unfolds. The point where the narrative forks, for example, is necessary for any event to occur in the story, as are events that remain consistent across each path. Furthermore, and contrary to Bordwell's claims (as will be noted later), I suggest that the variations of each path in a forking-path narrative lend a stronger sense of reality to possibilities and contingent events, precisely because they are shown and incorporated into the work's narrative. While one path (usually the last) will seem the most real, or legitimate, the alternative paths still retain a sense of significance for spectators—either in an epistemological sense (where the variety of differences between paths provides a greater degree of knowledge about the narrative or narrative world) or merely on the level of an enhanced sense of possibility itself. There is a "recombinative logic" that is at play in the forking-path narrative form; while the form implies that each path is an ontologically separate world, there is a sense in which the spectator unifies the information of separate paths into a single story-world.

The spatial convergence narratives I consider in this chapter suggest not just determinism but a sense of fatalism. I use *spatial convergence* as a catch-all term for a variety of storytelling techniques identified by other scholars: hub-and-spoke plots (Berg 2006), converging fates plots (Bordwell 2006), network and mosaic narratives (Parshall 2002), and modular or database narratives (Cameron 2008). The common feature is that such narratives have a form that spatially limits and intersects otherwise disparate lives of individual characters. These characters are brought into contact in a way that operates in a fatalistic sense—their intersection and interaction appear to unfold outside their control. Then, I will show how the *Fargo* universe, which I consider as an example of multimodal storytelling, develops its narrative across multiple modes (and in a nonlinear sequence). This foregrounds causal chains and places demands on spectators to seek connections across the film and the first two seasons of the television program.

Whereas the fatalism of spatial convergence narratives suggests that cause and effect exist outside the agency of individuals and that things unfold as they would regardless of the best efforts or intentions of characters, time-travel narratives explore determinism through a strong emphasis on free will and agent-driven causality. Time-travel narratives explicitly explore our capacity to act and deliberate on potential future actions. Therefore, they reinforce that certain events and outcomes are contingent on the choices of individuals. Furthermore, these narratives highlight that such free will rests on a deterministic understanding of the world, where causal chains unfold across time because of the decisions of central characters.

The final section of this chapter will address parametric form. Bordwell argues that this mode organizes "film techniques in patterns that may create an ongoing spectatorial engagement independent of narrative action" (1989, 271). Films such as Robert Bresson's *L'Argent* (1983) adapt parametric principles as a way of unifying aspects of several of the complex narratives addressed throughout the chapter; Luis Buñuel's *The Phantom of Liberty* (1974) uses parametric principles to exploit and break down our regular expectations of how cause and effect function. The film builds an expectation of causality as one vignette transitions to the next, yet within each vignette there is a total breakdown in causality that plays with our expectations developed out of both the narrative form and our experience of the ordinary world.

Complex Narratives and Their Metaphysical Concerns

There is a superabundance of terminology one has to hand when looking to categorize the variety of complex narratives across film and television. The following is an incomplete list: forking-path (Bordwell 2002), multiple-draft (Bordwell 2002; Branigan 2002), mind-game (Elsaesser 2009, 2014), modular (Cameron 2008), puzzle plot (Buckland 2009, 2014), network (Bordwell 2002; Parshall 2002), mosaic (Bordwell 2002; Parshall 2002), and converging-fates narratives/plots. As Campora notes, "The problem ... is that with each new analysis comes a new label for the film" (2014, 5). Maria Poulaki makes an admirable effort in drawing out common features across different types of complex narratives, suggesting that they "have a nonsequential temporal and spatial structure; they also tend to contain multiple levels of reality and different but parallel and interconnected stories, with chance, coincidence, or fate often becoming central forces for the plot development" (2014, 36). Films as artistically different as *Pulp Fiction* (dir. Quentin Tarantino, 1994) and *Mr. Nobody* ably demonstrate these features. Furthermore, Poulaki argues that "the stories of puzzle films self-reflexively draw attention to their own piecemeal textual structure, which, like their characters, follows nonlinear, reiterative steps from one spatiotemporal unit to the other" (36) and that "contemporary puzzle films are complex from a narratological perspective. Their 'stories' remain deliberately and emphatically open, rather than closed in the beginning-middle-end schema" (37). In considering parametric form in the final section of this chapter, I will reveal how a complex narrative can draw attention to its own narrative form despite following a relatively simple and linear narrative trajectory. Warren Buckland highlights similar features in puzzle plots (on his terms an especially complex form of complex narrative) that "blur the boundaries between different levels of reality, are riddled with gaps, deception, labyrinthine structures, ambiguity, and overt coincidences.... In the end, the complexity of puzzle films operates on two levels: narrative and narration. It emphasizes the complex telling (plot, narration) of a simple or complex story (narrative)" (2009, 6). The comments by Poulaki and Buckland ably describe how the complexity of certain films derives from their content and narrative form.

In the context of television, Jason Mittell adopts a historical poetics that "situates formal developments within specific historical contexts of production, circulation, and reception" (2006, 30), casting a much wider net to develop his understanding of the causes of complex televisual narrative than I do here. For Mittell, such causes are not merely related to narrative structure, style, and content but develop out of cultural, historical, industrial, and sociological factors too. As a result, Mittell's concerns are much broader than my own, and his articulation of complex narratives within contemporary television involves factors that move beyond the interests of this chapter. However, Mittell does offer some isolated analysis of formal features, suggesting that complex television maintains a balance between traditional, immersive storytelling and the discursive narrative techniques "needed to achieve each show's complexity and mystery" (38). Therefore, spectators engage in "noting usage and violations of convention, chronicling chronologies, and highlighting both inconsistencies and continuities across episodes and even series" (38). This is in part due to medium-specific features of television narrative whereby there is a complexity involved in the balance struck between innovation and coherence at the episode-to-episode level, as well as on a more long-term scale across seasons (38).

As alluded to earlier, Mittell also considers the comprehension of complex televisual narratives, identifying occasions of "narrative special effect," which draw spectatorial attention "to the constructed nature of the narration [asking] us to marvel at how *writers* pulled it off" (2006, 35). In television programs such as *Lost* (2004–2010), which culminate in a substantial plot twist, spectators are arrested and required "to reconsider all that we've viewed before in the episode" (35). This point again underlies the emphasis on spectatorial engagement with complex narratives in television, especially through "detailed dissection of [narrative] form" to address "complex questions of *plot and event* in addition to storyworld and character" (38). Mittell, too, illustrates the connection between complexity and narrative.

However, while this approach informs the one I develop here, it is important to note that for contemporary television series such as *Twin Peaks* (1990–1991, 2017), *True Detective* (2014–2015), and *Black Mirror* (2011–2014), there would be a great deal missing in analyses that examined only plot and storytelling. Instead, addressing narrative and stylistic form alongside content enriches our interpretations of complex films and television programs, as well as those that are somewhat problematic. For example, the themes of unstable and changing identities in the television program *Quantum Leap* (1989–1993), whereby the contingent quality of the protagonist's identity is a key narrative device (in combination with elements of time travel), appear novel and innovative at first, but, due to the requirements of network television, develop into a redundancy that drives spectators' expectations as to how such a device will function. Nevertheless, given that the concerns of this chapter regard the ways that complex narratives provoke consideration of different ideas surrounding causality and free will, it should not be surprising that innovation and complexity at the level of narrative form are the predominant forces for such metaphysical exploration.

It is important to note that none of the scholars mentioned thus far claim that complex narratives are so as a result of total incomprehensibility. As Buckland notes, "A puzzle plot is intricate in the sense that the arrangement of events is not just complex in Aristotle's use of the term (in which events are interwoven), but is entangled" (2014, 5). While there is no guarantee that narrative closure can be achieved with these sorts of storytelling practices, given that they will often remain open and perplexing, it is equally important not to conflate narrative openness with incomprehensibility. A degree of sense can be made with additional effort, and this can lay a solid foundation for the interpretive work required to contemplate ways the epistemological gaps of complex narratives may be filled. The main point is that spectators need to work harder to comprehend and make sense of their aesthetic experiences of complex narratives across film and television.

Isolating the different elements of narrative assists in our developing a better understanding of how complexity works at the level of narrative form. Bordwell, for example, draws upon Russian formalism to defend an account of narrative that rests on three central concepts—the fabula, the syuzhet, and style. He argues that "presented with two narrative events, we look for causal or spatial or temporal links. The imaginary construct we create, progressively and retroactively, was termed by formalists the fabula (sometimes translated as 'story'). More specifically, the fabula embodies the action as a chronological, cause-and-effect chain of events occurring within a given duration and a spatial field" (1985, 49). In articulating the distinction between the fabula and the syuzhet, Bordwell notes that "the syuzhet (usually translated as 'plot') is the actual arrangement and presentation of the fabula in the film" (50). Bordwell argues that " 'style' simply names the film's systematic use of cinematic devices" (50). Therefore, the fabula is the story that can be presented and arranged in a variety of ways, and such arrangement is the syuzhet. Furthermore, this arrangement is mediated stylistically by the filmmakers' use of mise-en-scène, cinematography, sound, and so forth. In the case of complex narratives, not only are spectators often dealing with conceptually and aesthetically intricate or dense stories, but structurally there is also a great deal of reformulation and innovation at the level of the syuzhet.

An important underlying assumption of Bordwell's approach is that all "filmmakers are spectators" (2008, 137), in that they exist in the same world of ordinary experience that spectators inhabit, drawing from that world to create and inform their art. This means that according to Bordwell's account there is a shared understanding underpinning the norms and conventions of narrative film. The spectators' expectation of conventions and norms, and the degree to which these expectations are not met, is part of what makes comprehending such stories harder cognitive work for spectators. Nevertheless, both spectatorial and creative reliance on cinematic (and televisual) narrative conventions enables spectators to make sense of challenging stories constructed by filmmakers and television showrunners that would otherwise be incoherent. As Bordwell notes, "We're guided through the games of gap making and gap filling by genre conventions, the redundancy built into mainstream storytelling principles, and our familiarity with adjacent traditions.... As the zone of indeterminacy widens, however, our reliance on classical closure wanes, and we must call on more rarefied comprehension skills to play with the ambiguities the films offer" (2002, 82). In aesthetic experiences with complex narratives, spectators are required to navigate narratives that make creative and productive use of such "zones of indeterminacy," making the jump, so to speak, from potential incomprehensibility to openness, and to contemplate how the expression of various dimensions of free will, causality, contingency, and chance in works of film and television aligns with spectators' own experience of the ordinary world.

Multiple Drafts, Forking Paths, and the Experience of Possibility

Forking-path narratives are particularly adept at foregrounding the dynamics between causality and contingency. The balance between repetition across multiple paths and differences among paths is the key feature that influences how this type of complex narrative form explores contingency, causality, and necessity. In doing so, it masks to a degree the contingent nature of certain events by repeating them in multiple paths.

Bordwell identifies seven conventions of this type of complex narrative: they are linear, the fork is signposted, the paths intersect eventually, they are unified by traditional cohesion devices, they run parallel, the final path presupposes the others, and the last one taken is the least hypothetical (2002, 92–100). Naturally, some films play with these conventions more than others. He concludes that we "might better describe [forking-path narratives] as multiple-draft narratives, with the last version presenting itself as the fullest, most satisfying revision" (102). Indeed, if we consider a multiple-draft narrative in these terms, each subsequent draft presents a refinement of ideas over the course of multiple drafts, whereby the final draft is the most coherent. Spectators may even be epistemologically more fortunate than the central characters often are in such a narrative form, as we have the benefit of having experienced and therefore remembering each draft, whereas characters in the film may not.

Edward Branigan takes the term *multiple-draft* in a much broader direction, and instead recommends retaining "the name 'forking-path' narrative as a way of marking a conservative, generic form of narrative (as exemplified by the films Bordwell discusses)" (2002, 108). There's something to Branigan's point: despite the drafting mechanism Bordwell identifies in forking-path films, the idea of multiple drafts more clearly fits works such as *Groundhog Day* (1993) or more recent examples such as Doug Liman's *The Edge of Tomorrow* (2014). In both cases, the central character(s) actively draft their actions in pursuit of some goal, fail at a given obstacle, edit, and redraft their actions until they achieve their given goal. This is not to say that a forking-path mechanism is not at play in these two works and other works like them, but rather the drafting aspect is given much greater emphasis; indeed, it is often a matter of emphasis rather than strict demarcation in the case of forking-path and multiple-draft narratives.

In *Groundhog Day*, TV weatherman Phil Connors (Bill Murray) is sent to Punxsutawney, Pennsylvania, to cover the annual festivities surrounding the eponymous event. Much to Phil's dismay, he is trapped on that day, being made to repeat it indefinitely. Phil is aware that he is living the same day over and over (as spectators are aware), though this knowledge is not shared by coworkers Rita Hanson (Andie MacDowell)—also Phil's love interest—or cameraman Larry (Chris Elliott). The film works as a kind of parable, where we track Phil's growth in virtue, witnessing how he uses his privileged knowledge for selfish and hedonistic means before falling to suicidal despair and then slowly developing a sense of charity (in his attempts to save an elderly homeless man who is fated to die on that day regardless of Phil's repeated attempts to avoid such an end, for example), which culminates in his authentic declaration of love for Rita (in contrast to prior attempts that sought just to win her over for an evening). Having developed his moral character and genuinely expressed his feelings for his coworker, Phil wakes together with Rita on the day after Groundhog Day, and the hellish, repetitious existence Phil had suffered is condemned to the past. The film, then, shows us Phil explicitly drafting his actions to various ends, and it is only once he is enacting his will to the right ends that his life can continue beyond the day in question.

A similar dynamic is at play in *The Edge of Tomorrow*, in which we follow Major William Cage (Tom Cruise), a public relations officer who is made to join a frontline assault against alien forces invading Earth. On the initial landing—a disaster with substantial casualties—Cage manages to explode an alien enemy and is covered with its blood, apparently to his demise. He does not die, though, and wakes up the previous day in the same spot in which he found himself on the first draft. Much like Phil, Cage is initially bewildered, and day after day (draft after draft) finds himself in the same frontline assault, getting slaughtered along with his fellow soldiers, and waking once more. (The film's alternate title—*Live. Die. Repeat*—aptly summarizes Cage's experience.) It is only once Cage discovers that much-celebrated soldier Sergeant Rita Vrataski (Emily Blunt) has the same condition as he that they can begin to work together, again over many successive drafts, to enact the plan that will save the world.

The forking-path mechanism is implicit in both films—there's a point at which each character makes a decision; if it's the right one, they continue, and if not at some point along the path, they will be condemned to repeat the day in which they find themselves. But the films emphasize more, and explicitly, the mechanism of drafting—that Phil, Cage, and Vrataski have an end in mind to which they are actively working toward, and it is a matter of discovering how to go about succeeding in fulfilling that end. Because of this aspect of endless repetition, the films present the view that characters are enacting their agency, their will, to discover or unveil the one path, and that errors in discovering the correct path need to be redrafted.

This is not exactly what is at play in forking-path films. Bordwell gives sustained attention to two works: Tom Tykwer's *Run, Lola, Run* (1998) and Krzysztof Kieślowski's *Blind Chance* (1987). The former is an account of Lola's (Franka Potente) three attempts to obtain 100,000 DM for her boyfriend in twenty minutes. In retelling the same narrative strand three different times, the film captures the dynamics between causality (particularly through causal chains) and contingency. It balances recurring elements across paths, such as characters and scenarios, and the variety of effects the outcomes of these scenarios and interactions with these characters have in influencing the ultimate outcome of each path. However, there are offshoots that briefly depart from the central narrative. For example, in the first path, Lola runs into a woman with a baby carriage—Lola's story briefly stops, and spectators are shown the woman stealing a baby, after having lost custody of her own child. In the third path, Lola avoids the woman—again Lola's story stops, and, flashing forward, this time we see the woman join a church and devote the rest of her life to God.

The latter film, though different, still sits firmly within the forking-path narrative form. *Blind Chance* follows Witek (Bogusław Linda) and his attempts to catch a train. Whether or not Witek collides with (and depending on his reaction to) a man drinking beer just before he reaches the platform influences whether he manages to catch the train and, if not, what happens following his missing the train. In the first scenario, Witek misses the man drinking beer, manages to catch the train, and subsequently joins the Communist Party. In the second scenario, Witek collides heavily with the man, continues on his way, and has a second collision—this time with a railway guard. Witek misses the train, is sentenced to thirty days of community service, and joins an anti-Communist resistance movement. The final scenario sees Witek avoid a collision with the man drinking beer, apologize for the near miss, and, by deciding to catch his breath, he misses the train. He eventually gets a teaching position at a medical school, and he distances himself from and is apathetic toward political causes. The film is also more fatalistic than *Lola* (which fits with its social and political concerns, in addition to its philosophical ones): one of the opening scenes depicts Witek screaming, and upon the conclusion of the film, we see the plane he manages to catch explode, suggesting that it didn't especially matter how events unfolded in between.

Despite the vast trough between the concerns of each film—one a hyperkinetic action-adventure, the other a solemn art film that captures the national anxieties related to how post–World War II Communist Poland is to emerge from its ideological and societal oppression—the similarity in narrative form dictates that both films ably highlight the dynamics between causality and contingency. The forking-path narrative form achieves this through a reliance on the recombination of familiar story elements such as characters and scenarios across multiple paths of the same narrative. By retaining familiar scenarios across multiple paths yet altering the outcomes, the forking-path narrative form foregrounds the sense of causality and the necessity of a specific event to generate a specific cause, as well as how, alternatively, a minute difference between similar events can render substantially different outcomes. It also highlights the contingent nature of events that, were they to occur in a simple, singular, and linear narrative form, would be taken as definite and irrefutably determined. Instead, forking-path narratives allow an experience of alternatives and possibility and thus lend a definite sense of reality to these alternatives (contrary to Bordwell's skepticism surrounding the limited number of paths).

The syuzhet of forking-path narratives actively works against any sense of realism drawn from and applied to our own world of ordinary experience, given the logical impossibility of contrasting events all occurring in the one story-world. Furthermore, the narrative form of *Lola*—where the obtrusive stylistic tenor, seen for example in rapid camera movement alongside animated sequences, and Lola's apparent knowledge of previous paths—ensures that the film works as an interesting blend of multiple draft and forking-path narrative conventions. *Blind Chance*, with its ties to Polish history and its more naturalistic and unobtrusive stylistic telling of the story, still retains the "antirealist" form of the forking-path narrative, though in a subtler way. Because its mood is anticipatory (future facing), each possibility is not considered retrospectively (as in *Lola*); rather the different alternatives are all possible precisely because they have not yet occurred—the drafting mechanism Bordwell identifies is much weaker or even nonexistent here, as compared to *Lola*.

Furthermore, by incorporating alternative possibilities, both films highlight how the variation of a single event can generate substantially different effects. In a manner shared with spatially convergent narratives, these events are given an inflated sense of causal power. However, in contrast to these narratives (as will be seen in the section to follow), this causal power is diminished somewhat by a series of events that are shown to alter the life course of the central characters (at least for a time). The causal power of the event of Witek's catching the train, for example, is weakened somewhat by his reaction and interaction with the man drinking a beer, as well as how he reacts once he misses the train in two out of the three paths. In *Lola*, Lola's reaction to a dog as she bursts out of her apartment, and her boyfriend's success or failure in convincing a blind lady to lend him her phone card are two similar examples. The films considered in this section show that there is a softer sense of causality in forking-path narratives. The causal power of a single event is shown to be a deterministic necessity. At the same time, forking-path narratives open an experience of possibilities by repeating familiar scenarios and interactions but variably changing outcomes.

Spatial Convergence and Fatalism

In concretizing contingency, forking-path films presuppose the free will of characters to make decisions to varying degrees. In a contrary way, my discussion of what I term spatial convergence narratives will illustrate how a different subset of complex narratives foregrounds the metaphysical idea of fatalism. I have arranged this section into three degrees of spatial convergence, as per the degree to which a sense of fatalism is present. For the most part, the style of the films in this section is subordinate to the syuzhet—it is largely the narrative form that generates the variable senses of fatalism across the films discussed.

Certain films in the oeuvre of Robert Altman are clear illustrations of the soft case for spatially convergent films. They offer a distinct spatial context and derive their complexity by interweaving subjective plotlines. Rather than creating a strong fatalistic sense, they demonstrate what Bordwell terms a sense of "sheer contingency" (2006, 98). *Nashville* (1975) boasts a cast of twenty-four characters whom we follow across five days in the lead-up to a political rally. Across these five days, characters' stories casually overlap and intersect, and there is a limited sense of fate for much of the film. Instead, the sense of contingency, through the casual interactions and subsequent loss of contact, is more prominent. The spatial convergence occurs precisely because the film is framed and set in a spatially stable environment. This is reinforced stylistically by the omnipresence of country music that acts as a sonically unifying feature of the film—not only are many of the characters country musicians and singers, but country music is also the draw card that unites the disparate characters in the final scenes of the film. Other Altman films—such as *Short Cuts* (1993) and *Prêt-à-Porter* (1994)—adopt similarly stable environments as spatial contexts in which the lives of disparate characters unfold and interweave. These films treat their spatial context as a microcosm of something greater and broader, yet by featuring ensemble casts of characters, they demonstrate the complexity of narrative form and the prominence of contingency even within this smaller space.

In moderate cases, rather than a contained spatial context serving as the primary convergent device, there is an event that acts as a prism through which the lives of characters momentarily intersect. In Michael Haneke's *Code Unknown* (2000), a brief event toward the start of the film provides it with the momentum to follow each of the character arcs involved. There is minimal interweaving throughout the film, and the event is presented in an incidental fashion and is not revisited. Anne (Juliette Binoche) walks along a street in Paris with her boyfriend's younger brother, Jean (Alexandre Hamidi). Anne departs, and Jean throws rubbish at a homeless woman, whom we later learn is Maria (Luminiţa Gheorghiu). A young man named Amadou (Ona

Lu Yenke) witnesses the act and confronts Jean. The momentum of the story is generated from this one event, where Anne, Jean, Maria, and Amadou are transiently connected, and the rest of the film deals with the effects of this particular moment. The coincidental quality of the event coupled with the deterministic trajectory of the rest of the narrative provides the subtler, but distinctly fatalistic quality of the film. As spectators, we recognize that this initial event is key to determining the trajectory of the rest of the film and links the otherwise disparate character arcs. This association is helped through the unobtrusive cinematography—each self-contained character vignette is shot almost in a single take and divided by a cut to black that acts as a dividing line between each arc. The sense of coherence that is constructed by the spectator—the attempts to unify the purposeful and deliberate fragmentation of the film's style and narrative form—traces back to the initial event in the film, which serves as the only point where each character arc intersects and from whence we derive the sense of fatalism. Each arc, too, is developed in a minimally parallel fashion, and there is a stronger sequential rather than simultaneous arrangement. This forms the stories as largely discrete, as opposed to the web of the Altman films discussed earlier. Having been disparate prior to the event, the characters are only transitorily aware of one another, and then they continue to be disparate. The sense of fatalism therefore is gently brought to the surface at the point of the causal event and then runs as a current underneath as the audience experiences its subtle effects. An incidental causal event is also at the heart of another film, Lawrence Kasdan's *Grand Canyon* (1991), which differs in that it maintains the contact between the central characters of the narrative.

In *Grand Canyon*, Mack's (Kevin Kline) car breaks down after a basketball game in a dangerous part of Los Angeles. He calls for a tow, but while waiting he is put into an uncomfortable position by would-be muggers. The tow truck driver, Simon (Danny Glover), arrives and talks the muggers out of committing their crime. Mack is appreciative; he later seeks out Simon, and the two become friends. Meanwhile, Claire (Mary McDonnell), Mack's wife, and Mack's friend Davis (Steve Martin) have existentially transformative experiences of their own. While out jogging, Claire hears and discovers an abandoned baby. Meanwhile, Davis is shot when a mugger attempts to steal his watch. A producer of ultraviolent action films, Davis adopts a philosophical and contemplative perspective, and devotes his life to eliminating violence from the cinema. These central stories operate as the nexus—Simon and Mack, Davis, and Claire—through which the spectator has access to other tangential plots. The unexpected quality of the causal events helps to reinforce a moderate sense of fatalism—Mack's car breaking down would ordinarily not put him in danger, but he had found himself unexpectedly in a dangerous neighborhood, and thus he needed to draw upon Simon's negotiation skills when Simon was called to tow Mack's car. Claire had gone running hundreds if not thousands of times along the same street until she chanced upon an abandoned baby. And Davis likely would not have adopted his philosophical outlook unless he had been on the end of a violent act himself. (His aggressive chastisement of an employee for cutting out a "money shot" of blood and brains prior to this incident is evidence of this.) There is a clear link that is developed in each arc, whereby characters are lacking something meaningful in their existence, and experience an event that reorients their stagnant lives with a sense of purpose or a renewed outlook. The fatalistic quality embedded within the unlikeliness of each causal event leads to a renewed appreciation for their existence. This reaches a poignant culmination in the final scenes of the film, in which Mack and Simon and their families make a trip to the Grand Canyon (fig. 2.1). Whereas sheer contingency brought the characters of *Nashville* into

Figure 2.1. Fate unifies in *Grand Canyon*. *Source:* Kasdan, Lawrence, dir. *Grand Canyon*. 1991. Beverly Hills, CA: Starz/Anchor Bay, 2012. Blu-ray Disc, 1080p HD.

one another's lives, the characters of *Grand Canyon* seem to intersect due to fatalistic forces outside their own control. The various parallel stories converge in the final moments of the film and, combined with the chance nature of their causes, convey a clear and moderate sense of a fatalistic universe.

One brief final example of moderate fatalism is that of Paul Thomas Anderson's *Magnolia* (1999). It opens with a monologue that primes the audience to attribute the events that follow to more than chance—to forces beyond the characters' control. Each of at least six central plots are developed in a parallel syuzhet, though they also stand alone as coherent stories. The opening monologue of the film deals explicitly with anecdotes that reference fate, chance, and causality. This contextualizes the events of the film that follow. Later in the film, these ideas are revisited in a moment of stylistic obtrusiveness that, while logically impossible (or at least extremely unlikely), unambiguously unites the characters of the film. Partway through *Magnolia*, spectators are treated to a sing-along of Aimee Mann's "Wise Up" where the camera pans and tracks slowly toward each character as they sing, in sequence, a line or two from the song. Rather than the sheer contingency of the Altman films mentioned earlier, there is a stronger deterministic bent to the film that, due to Magnolia's opening monologue, attains a quality of fatalism too. The web-like quality of the film is complicated further because the causes and effects are given an equal balance, and we see how characters are pulled together into unified subplots and pushed away into their own isolated plots. The ambiguity surrounding events that act as causes and those that act as effects highlights the complexity of causal chains.

Certain films of Alejandro González Iñárritu display a strong fatalistic view of the world. I will focus only on *Babel* (2006) in this section; however, his earlier films *Amores Perros* (2000) and *21 Grams* (2003) operate in similar territory, though to a slightly weaker extent. Through a complicated and nonlinear syuzhet cut across three seemingly separate stories, we come to realize that the central event at the start of *Babel* connects them all. In Morocco, a goat herder buys a new rifle and gives it to his two sons. One of the boys fires it from a vantage point on the hilltops down at some cars on the roads below, convinced that the shots will not make the distance. They later find out that the bullet ripped through the window of a bus full of tourists, hitting Susan (Cate Blanchett), a woman who is on holiday with her husband Richard (Brad Pitt). They had left their children in the care of their regular nanny Amelia (Adriana Barraza). To both look after the children and make it to her son's wedding in Mexico, Amelia takes the children with her across the border. Amelia has a problem upon trying to reenter the United States. In Japan we follow deaf high school student Chieko Wataya (Rinko Kikuchi). Chieko is approached by police, who are interested in talking to her father. She eventually invites one of them up to her and her father's apartment, assuming that it is regarding her father's alleged involvement in her mother's suicide—a problem that has come up before. Instead, the officer is interested in a hunting trip her father had taken in Morocco, many years earlier, and in particular a rifle he gave as a gift to his hunting guide, the man who had sold the rifle to the goat herder.

The scrambled syuzhet serves the narrative's interests regarding fate and the expansive effects of a single cause. Furthermore, there is stylistic unity, largely through cinematographic technique, that connects each story arc to the event. An abundance of film grain, and a drained, unsaturated color palette (offset only by differences in situational contexts—by the strobe lighting in a Japanese nightclub or the extravagant dress of the Mexican wedding, for example) illustrate how the style of the film supplements its narrative form to underscore the metaphysical content. The effects of the shooting reach from Morocco to Japan—though we are only aware of the direct relevance of the Japanese thread to the shooting in that thread's final moments. Furthermore, the decision of Richard and Susan to take the trip lands, in a sense, their children with Amelia in Mexico. The scrambled, nonlinear (and "modular") sequencing of the film's syuzhet further complicates the temporality of the different causes and effects. The web of plots is tangled, yet the mood is orderly rather than chaotic. The form of the film appears exceptionally deliberate, and each thread concludes rather coherently, despite the crosscutting that takes spectators across the globe. Despite the ambiguities between cause and effect, the chance-like quality of the causal event that propels the film forward—the shooting—has a strong fatalistic bent. The doubt cast on the rifle's capabilities, the clear failure of Richard and Susan's hopes for the trip, and the young boy's poor shooting technique casts the event not as sheer contingency—as developed out of nothing—but as sheer fatalism, as though nothing else could have occurred. This sense is further illustrated in that the different factors of a single event, through the confusion of cause and effect, have a global reach. While the web is difficult at times to navigate, one cannot doubt the concreteness of the connections among all the different threads. In a similar fashion to *Grand Canyon*, the conclusion of each thread seems to have renewed the lives of the characters involved: Chieko gains closure and a sense of closeness with her father; Susan is expected to recover, and her relationship with Richard appears calmer and open to regeneration through the trauma they experienced together. There is a question regarding Amelia; due to the problems with reentering the US, she is deported to Mexico. However, given the fatalism of the rest of the film, there is an implied optimism in her story, not because of luck or chance or her capacity to make good decisions, but because she could not possibly be anywhere else, and therefore she is where she is required to be—with her cherished family.

Spatial convergence narratives in a variety of ways foreground the metaphysical idea of fatalism. The interrelation between narrative form and style can use a microcosmic setting to explore a weak sense of fatalism that largely emphasizes sheer contingency, as in the example of *Nashville*. It can adopt a more moderate sense of fatalism wherein the management of different character arcs in films such as *Code Unknown*, *Grand Canyon*, and *Magnolia* operate to wrap chance events in existentially transformative and fatalistic outcomes for characters. Or, in the case of *Babel*, a strong sense of fatalism can be developed through narrative form to entangle cause and effect at a global scale. Although possessing important differences, each example illustrates how the spatial convergence narrative form, supplemented by style, makes the metaphysical concept of fatalism central.

Multimodal Complex Storytelling and the *Fargo* Universe

The *Fargo* universe is explored across a film (1996) and a television program (2014, 2015, 2017, 2020), operating as an instance of complex storytelling via the multimodal form through which the story-world is created, and especially through the medium-specific form of the television program. This interaction of features affords the *Fargo* universe across each of its instantiations that I consider here (for the sake of space I do not address the third [2017] and fourth [2020] seasons) a novel presentation of contingency and causality.

The original film, set in 1987, follows the investigation of a series of homicides that unfold because of car salesman Jerry Lundegaard's (William H. Macy) attempted kidnap of his wife through the services of Carl Showalter (Steve Buscemi) and Gaear Grimsrud (Peter Stormare), two criminals for hire. Season 1 of the television program *Fargo* occurs in 2006, where a violent and mysterious man named Lorne Malvo (Billy Bob Thornton) drifts through a small Minnesota town and meets Lester Nygard (Martin Freeman). The second season of the television program is set in 1976 and follows Peggy Blumquist (Kirsten Dunst) and her butcher husband, Ed (Jesse Plemons), and their attempts to cover up and move on from the accidental hit-and-run of Rye Gerhardt (Kieran Culkin), the son of a local crime family. Relatedly, local sheriff Hank Larsson (Ted Danson) and state trooper Lou Solverson (Patrick Wilson) attempt to make sense of a multiple homicide that took place at a diner that is adjacent to the hit-and-run.

In the film and each television season, there is an event that generates the momentum of the rest of the story. In the case of the film, a state trooper pulls the two kidnappers over (with the car salesman's wife in the boot of their car) on a lonely highway for a minor infraction. After a failed attempt at bribery, one of the kidnappers murders the state trooper and two eyewitnesses. These homicides subsequently involve police chief Marge Gunderson (Frances McDormand), who investigates the murders and follows the evidence back to the car salesman. In season 1 of the television program, a chance meeting between Lester and Lorne in a hospital, after Lester has had an altercation with his old high school bully and Lorne has had a minor injury from a car crash, leads Lorne to murder the bully. In the second season, Rye Gerhardt attempts to extort a judge at a quiet roadside Waffle Hut. When the meeting does not go according to Gerhardt's plan, he murders the judge and multiple Waffle Hut employees, is severely injured himself, and staggers out onto the road, where he is hit by a car.

Each of these key events suggests an enhanced degree of contingency. In and of themselves (regardless of the contextualizing circumstances), each event only slightly deviates from a plan, or an understanding of how things may have ordinarily gone. That is to say, the events, as they unfold in the *Fargo* universe, seem to function as an exception rather than a rule of ordinary or expected experience. A minor traffic infraction could easily have been prevented, the encounter in the hospital could easily have been a polite conversation between strangers, and the conversation between Gerhardt and the judge could have gone much more peacefully. Key events possess a "slightly off" quality that generates the causal chains that lead to such violent and troubling effects. This slightly-off quality is created by the discrepancy between how things were planned (or how they might be expected to ordinarily proceed) and how the events actually unfolded. There is a sense, therefore, in which these events are similar to the fatalistic causal events in the spatially convergent narratives discussed in the previous section.

The development of the *Fargo* universe began with the film and then after a hiatus continued through the seasons of the television program. However, the sequence in which the narrative events unfold begins in the second season in 1976, followed by the events of the film, which take place in 1987, and concludes with the events of the first season in 2006. There are references across these that not only unify the story-world and enrich our experience of it but reinforce the temporal reach of causality whereby the events in one influence and shape events and characters in the others. Therefore, spectators who attempt to unify the individual instantiations that create the *Fargo* story-world must rearrange and develop a macro-level narrative across seasons and the original film—as we would in a single film or television program with a complex and nonsequential narrative form. We may recall that Mittell places a great deal of emphasis on televisual narrative complexity emerging out of surprising plot developments and twists. However, he also identifies that complex storytelling requires spectators to notice continuities across multiple episodes and seasons, and that the onus is, in a sense, on spectators to comprehend stories and retain the stability of a story-world across such an expansive narrative arc.

This is further complicated in the multimodal story-world of *Fargo*. For example, spectators who have seen the film will recognize the satchel of money that the "Supermarket King" Stavros Milos (Oliver Platt) finds on the side of the road in a flashback sequence in season 1, providing him with the capital necessary to care for his family and start his supermarket business. Similarly, in season 1, Molly Solverson's father, Lou—who runs the local diner—is one of the lead officers who attempt to deal with the widespread violence that culminates in the Sioux Falls massacre in the second season (an event that is sporadically referenced by a much older Lou in the preceding season). If we consider the development of the *Fargo* story-world as a singular rich plot, we can see how the nonsequential development of this narrative (the syuzhet) is scrambled as it extends from the film and throughout the television programs. The multiple fabulas within each instantiation exist as standalone stories but interweave to enrich our understanding of this broader fabula.

The work required of the spectator to sustain narrative coherence not just across a season but across multiple modes of several seasons and a film is considerable. However, the unifying role of style across these different instantiations motivates spectators to assimilate the narratives into a single fabula. The combination of the mood created by the contrast of small-town manners and large-scale, spiraling violence, and small but iconic world-building details (such as accents, setting, and sweaters) cast across the backdrop of the stark and harsh snow-swept setting, signals to the spectators that despite the changing suite of characters, the different time periods, and the nonlinear development of the *Fargo* universe, the narrative events all belong to a single story-world. Stylistic decisions also help with the construction of the fabula—the color palette and music combined with details such as the use of period cars and fashion and the political and social backdrop place the second season of the television program firmly before the events of the first season and the film, for example.

The episodic quality of the television program directly influences how causality and contingency are explored across the story-world. To continually develop the interwoven *Fargo* universe, the television program cannot afford to both sustain the momentum of the narrative that develops from the key event of each season and continually revert back to the key event that generated the initial narrative momentum. Instead, narrative development through television manages individual, episodic components that serve to sustain a much larger and longer narrative than can a typical film. Therefore, rather than continually revisit the key event from multiple perspectives, the television program instead combines smaller causal chains across episodes that develop the temporal expanse of the narrative that began with the key event and eventually concludes in the final episode. The medium-specific demands of the television program that require episode-to-episode narrative coherence as well as comprehensible narrative development across seasons are further complicated in the case of *Fargo*, given that each season uses a discrete cast of characters that can exist on their own terms. The references we recall from season 1 as we are watching season 2 serve as subtle reminders that these events are enriching our understanding of a single, unified story-world, and this gives the actions and events a causal weight. We know some of the effects they are to have because of our experience with the first season and the film.

The representation of causality and contingency in *Fargo* is made complex by the development of that story-world across both film and television. Such a scenario poses a particular kind of challenge to spectators, in that to unify a macronarrative that factors in each instantiation of the *Fargo* story-world, we must be attentive to the causal chains that develop across the film and seasons of the television program. Subtle stylistic touches and world-building techniques in *Fargo* assist spectators in this task and demonstrate how multimodal storytelling can shape the presentation of and interplay between contingency and causality.

Free Will and Determinism in Time-Travel Narratives

The *Fargo* universe poses multiple challenges to spectators, not least due to its variable setting in time and the fact that due to the order of each instantiation's release, the causal chains that are developed are done so out of temporal order. Moving back and forth through time is the hallmark of time-travel narratives, and here I am concerned with how this complex narrative form establishes the agency of the individual through their capacity to enact change. The traversal through time embarked on by the central characters of these works rests on a deterministic understanding of the universe, and the high stakes of their choices inflate the sense of free will attributed to the individual. Although we aren't confronted with choices on the scale that the protagonists of time-travel narratives often are, the process of deliberation and our understanding of it is similar. Moreover, the sense of determinism is reinforced by the time-travel component of these narratives. That is, there is an assumption that the character's deliberate choice to act in a certain situation will unfold a causal chain that will achieve their goals.

There are also intellectually challenging features that further complicate these types of narratives, as manipulating time inevitably introduces the problem of paradoxes. This is part of what makes these narratives uniquely challenging to spectators. Furthermore, because of the idea of time travel itself, these works will often have different versions of the same character concurrently occupying the screen. In highlighting the capacity of agent-generated change, time-travel narratives open and make available to the spectator's experience the idea of contingency.

In Rian Johnson's *Looper* (2012), Young Joe (Joseph Gordon-Levitt) is a looper, who is tasked by a powerful crime gang that uses the technology of time travel (outlawed in the future) to make hits and dispose of bodies. When loopers retire, and as a means of protecting their employers, they kill their older, future selves, thereby closing their own "loop." One evening, Young Joe's friend Seth (Paul Dano) tells Joe that he (Seth) was sent his (Seth's) future self to kill, but he (Seth) decided to let him live. Before he ran away, he informed his younger self that in the future a person named the Rainmaker will eliminate all crime gangs and close all loops. There is a great deal of intricacy and density in the fabula of *Looper* for spectators to digest. In terms of syuzhet composition, there is minimal jumping back and forth, and the story unfolds linearly, though in "chunks"—we start with Young Joe, watch as he becomes Old Joe (Bruce Willis), and only then do we jump back in story time to Young Joe again, at which point the syuzhet continues in a linear fashion. The mechanics of time travel are also simplified, to the point where there is no exposition or attempt to address potential paradoxes; spectators are merely required to "keep up" with the intricacies of the narrative.

At the heart of the story is Joe's free will. In contrast to the spatially convergent narratives discussed earlier, *Looper*, as with many time-travel narratives, gives free will a central conceptual role in how the narrative unfolds and concludes. This is somewhat creatively reinforced by the noir-like character of the film, most clearly realized in the use of voiceover. As impressive as costuming and personal special effects are in providing Joseph Gordon-Levitt a degree of likeness to Bruce Willis (fig. 2.2), the disembodied voiceover serves to underpin the challenging choice that faces Joe. Joe's sense of free will is explicitly embodied in his consideration of whom he will allow himself to become—there is a sense of deliberation in that the disembodied

Figure 2.2. Continuity across time in *Looper*. *Source:* Johnson, Rian, dir. *Looper*. 2012. Sydney: Roadshow Entertainment, 2014. Blu-ray Disc, 1080p HD.

voiceover is a stylistic embodiment of the idea of free will itself, and it gives us insight into Joe's mind and the reasons for his ultimate decision. The causal power of this deliberation is fully crystallized in the film's tense final showdown.

Young Joe not only has the capacity to choose how to avert the very real crisis in the future but also understands that his actions generate the causal chain that will shape how the future develops. The stakes are unfamiliar to us in the sense that we are not acquainted with such choices in the domain of ordinary experience. However, the decisions laid out before characters resonate with us not because the stakes are something we deal with day-to-day but because we understand what it is to deliberate—what it is to be presented with an important and difficult choice whereby we negotiate possible outcomes contingent on the decision we make. Furthermore, we are given concrete experiences of a possible future (one that is to be prevented), and this possible path of time, contingent on the decision of Young Joe, is given the weight of reality in the context of the narrative.

Working similarly, Terry Gilliam's *12 Monkeys* (1995) follows James Cole (Bruce Willis), who is sent back in time to help uncover information regarding a virus that has wiped out much of humanity and forced the survivors to live in challenging conditions underground. He is troubled by memories and vivid dreams of an airport shootout he witnessed as a young boy, seeing a man get shot and killed. As

Cole jumps back and forth through time, with repeated attempts at finding those responsible for unleashing the virus, he finally ends up at the airport, this time not as the child witness but as the adult victim of the shooting. The story recursively winds back to an earlier point, from a different perspective of the same character from a different point in time. The film concretizes the cause-and-effect chain that has generated the final showdown, and in doing so operates in a similar way to *Looper*. Furthermore, as the setting of the film is principally in the future that is to be avoided, Cole's actions and decisions throughout the film are given a weight equivalent to that of Joe's in *Looper*. Cole's deliberation and actions are thus made more substantial to spectators, as we have experienced the possibility, contingent on Cole's actions, that is to be avoided at all costs.

Many of the observations made in the previous section about the *Fargo* universe and its use of television's medium-specific characteristics are relevant to *Dark* (2017–2020), a time-travel narrative streaming series, and its exploration of free will and causality. The opening voiceover in the first episode sets the tone of the series well: "We trust that time is linear. That it proceeds eternally, uniformly. Into infinity. But the distinction between past, present, and future is nothing but an illusion. Yesterday, today, and tomorrow are not consecutive; they are connected in a never-ending circle. Everything is connected." Set in the German town of Winden, initially in 2019, the series follows an increasing number of disappearances occurring in the local forest. In just the first series, the timeline expands to the years 1986, then 1953, and in the final episode a glimpse of the future in 2052. As it turns out, the nuclear power plant of Winden has a wormhole, whereby characters travel back and forth through time. The series' second season has seen time continue linearly, so 2019, 1986, and 1953 become 2020, 1987, and 1954, with the introduction of another timeline in 1921. To add to the density of timelines, *Dark*'s third season compounds the complexity with the inclusion of a parallel world, including some overlap with the aforementioned timelines in 2019 and 2052 as well as a new timeline set in 1888.

The extraordinary temporal expanse of *Dark* is possible because of the expanded duration that is afforded by the medium of television. It makes the fullest possible use of narrative time to traverse both temporal settings and multiple worlds. However, this increase in complexity requires the series to assist spectators in keeping up. As seen with *Looper*, the movement through temporal settings means that spectators are dealing with multiple versions of the same character, in terms of both age and versions across multiple worlds. A moment toward the end of episode 3 of the first season assists spectators with such complexity and helps to establish a sense of causality, continuity, and connection: the episode is set primarily in 1986, early in the wormhole's (largely) accidental discovery by a limited number of characters. A musical montage involving split screen shows the younger and older versions of characters juxtaposed with each other in sequence (fig. 2.3).

This extended moment of the episode gives us an opportunity to reflect both on the status of the characters in 2019 and on the small glimpses we have received of what they were like as children (or younger adults, depending on the character) in 1986. Moreover, *Dark* has provided spectators a hint as to the history of the relationships between characters, many of which involve pivotal events from the earlier time period that reemerge and are shown to underscore relationships in the 2019 temporal setting. For example, in 1986, one character's lie involving witnessing the rape of another by a troubled and already disreputable adolescent boy (who later becomes a police officer in Winden and whose son goes missing) simmers beneath the surface before explicitly being brought to the foreground of the

Figure 2.3. The past and present displayed at once in *Dark*. *Source:* Odar, Baran bo, dir. *Dark*. 2017. Los Gatos, CA: Netflix, 2017. Stream, 2160p UHD.

three's adult relationship in 2019. The use of split screen provides a stylistic convergence of space and time—spectators are presented with two appearances of one character at different times in their existence, the sense of continuity and causality is established by the connections and comparisons spectators draw as motivated by the series.

By jumping to and from various temporal settings, *Dark* emphasizes causal chains and free will in a way consistent with time-travel narratives. We are given the opportunity to construct the causal chains (when the series doesn't explicitly do so for us), building the connections between events in one time period with events or effects in another. As the temporal reach extends across multiple temporal settings and multiple seasons, the stretch of the causal chains in both directions becomes greater. The temporal and causal stretch is paired with the series' showing of characters actively using the wormhole to jump between temporal settings for various ends and intentions—we see them using the knowledge they have of their original temporal contexts to act in other ones. The form of time-travel narratives transforms free will and deterministic causality, offering often subtle examinations of both. The balance between causal chains and the deliberation of free will is developed primarily through narrative form and supplemented by style to reveal how characters explicitly understand their own agency in the context of the determinism of the story-world they inhabit.

Questioning Causality through Parametric Narration

Bordwell suggests that "parametric narration establishes a distinctive intrinsic norm ... [and] develops this norm in additive fashion" (1985, 288). How, then, can parametric narration—or, as I will suggest in a moment, parametric form—potentially involve ideas of contingency, free will, and causality while operating as a type of complex narrative?

Bordwell's emphasis is on the role of style in the parametric narrative mode. He clarifies that "a film's stylistic patterning splits away from the syuzhet when only 'artistic' motivation can account for it" and that the spectator "must take style as present for its own sake, aiming to become palpable as such" (280). Elsewhere, Bordwell clarifies that style has four functions—denotative, expressive, symbolic, and decorative (2005, 34). Per Bordwell, parametric narration utilizes style largely in the fourth sense whereby it "can work somewhat on its own. It creates discrete moments and broader patterns that engage us for their own sake, coaxing us to discover or notice fine differences" (34). He also suggests that parametric narration can be "thought of as a highly organized decorative stylistic execution" (35). There is an issue with Bordwell's strict connection between parametric narration and style.

As I have mentioned, Bordwell formally defines narration as "the process whereby the film's syuzhet and style interact in the course of cueing and channeling the spectator's construction of the fabula" (1985, 53). How is it, then, that in the mode of parametric narration, style can both exist for its own sake and fulfill its narrative function? Instead of parametric narration, Kristin Thompson uses the term *parametric form*, which she suggests is "governed by a structuring principle in which artistic motivation becomes systematic and foregrounded across a whole film" whereby "artistic motivation ... creates patterns that are as important or more important than the syuzhet structures" (1988, 247). I will develop Thompson's formulation here as a means of productively exploring how parametric principles operate at the level of narrative form.

L'Argent adopts certain parametric principles that offer a way to reflect on contingency, free will, and causality. *L'Argent*'s narrative form and use of parametric principles is not completely dissimilar to such films as *Tales of Manhattan* (1942), *Winchester '73* (1950), and *The Earrings of Madame de . . .* (1953). In each of these, one object in the film works as an organizing principle of the narrative (in the first a tailcoat, the second a rifle, and the third a pair of earrings) to connect different stories and characters. (*Tales of Manhattan* is an anthology film, for example, whereas *The Earrings of Madame de . . .* is much more firmly centered on the earrings and their importance to Comtesse Louise de . . . [Danielle Darrieux] rather than as a means of examining other characters.)

L'Argent uses a counterfeit 500-franc note as the organizing object—at least initially. The film begins with Norbert (Marc Ernest Fourneau), a young man who is looking to collect his allowance from his father. After receiving his allowance, he asks his father for even more money, telling him he needs to repay someone from school. His father denies him, so Norbert eventually acquires a counterfeit bill from a friend and goes to a shop, purchasing a photo frame to receive authentic change. The store manager subsequently uses the bill with some other counterfeit bills to pay a heating oil deliveryman, Yvon (Christian Patey). Yvon innocently tries to pay for his meal at a restaurant with a counterfeit bill, though it is picked up and he is arrested. From there, the film shifts from following the counterfeit note and instead examines the effects of its having passed through the hands of multiple people—mainly Yvon, but employees at the aforementioned shop and, briefly, Norbert too.

The use of parametric form in both style and narrative in the first part of the film ably illustrates what has been covered in this section so far, as well as being an inventive means for *L'Argent* to examine causal effects and the contingency of events as established through and because of parametric form. Stylistically, close-ups on the counterfeit bill (especially when passing hands) works both to embody the theme of causality and contingency as well as to serve narrative functions within the film (fig. 2.4). It triggers an understanding that we are to move to the next part of the film—the next aspect of the narrative—to examine the causal effects on whoever has come into possession of the bill. In these sorts of films—as with those briefly mentioned earlier—the organizing object operates as a moveable point of spatial convergence where we examine the spread of cause and effect

Figure 2.4. The counterfeit bill in *L'Argent*. *Source:* Bresson, Robert, dir. *L'Argent*. 1983. New York: Criterion, 2017. Blu-ray Disc, 1080p HD.

that it generates. Through the combination of narrative and stylistic form, *L'Argent* also emphasizes the idea of contingency—the bill could have been passed to anyone, for whatever reason. The stylistic device of the close-up of the bill is then transferred to other objects once the film shifts its narrative focus in the latter part: the bill that was the trigger for the events that transpire, its enhanced causal power signaled by the use of close-up, is substituted by other objects that become the means by which characters (especially Yvon) enact their agency in the world of the film.

L'Argent also magnifies causal effects in the way in which it leaves parametric formal principles behind. Having established the corruptive influence of money and the multiple, accumulative effects of one deed, the film plunges deeply into the causal scope and limits of this deed, exploring the interplay between the effects of outside circumstances and the extent of an individual's agency—especially by giving most of the film's duration in this second part to Yvon's moral decay and descent as circumstances and his own actions conspire against him. Yvon spends multiple stints in prison, his daughter dies while he is inside, and he attempts to kill himself, before finally being released from prison and murdering multiple people. The key point as this relates to free will, causality, and contingency is that Yvon's predicament is shown through the film's balance of parametric form and more conventional storytelling to involve a combination of the ideas addressed thus far. The sheer contingency that the counterfeit bill would fall into his possession is paired with the effects this has in his innocently trying to pay for a meal, unaware of its inauthenticity, and the multiple flow-on effects this has on his life. There is an emphasis, then, on causal chains and an undermining or diminishing of his agency from this perspective. However, Yvon is also shown to have choices as to how to respond to his circumstances—what to do once he leaves prison (each time), whether he kills the multiple people that he does. Here, his agency is given the greater central focus. The film's poetic and thematically rich quality, then, derives from a combination of formal elements, not least its balancing of parametric and more conventional narrative form.

As the first part of *L'Argent* suggests, parametric patterns generated out of artistic motivation can exist in the syuzhet—there is no need for parametric principles to exist solely in the domain of style. Nor is it a necessary condition for parametric principles to be persevered with throughout the entirety of a film. As Thompson cautions, parametric form "need not detract from the narrative.... If we cooperate and follow these stylistic patterns as well as ... the narrative, our perception of the film as a whole can only be more complete" (1988, 250). The analysis of Buñuel's *The Phantom of Liberty* to follow will demonstrate how a pattern established consistently across a film in the syuzhet operates on parametric principles, and that in paying attention to such patterns at the level of narrative form in tandem with the fabula (the level of content), we can derive a richer cinematic appreciation.

In his discussion of parametric narration, Bordwell also cautions against the tendency for interpretations of such films to resist the idea of parametric principles existing for their own sake (1985, 282–83). Although in light of Thompson's comment about how such principles at the level of form can enhance the content of a film, and especially because parametric principles seem so novel, it is worth exploring whether or not they can—as in the case of *The Phantom of Liberty*—enhance and magnify a theme of a film. I do not claim that Buñuel's riffs on cause and effect are the sole or intended thematic preoccupation of the film—there are other obvious themes at work. (For example, vignette 4 has clear sociopolitical motivations, and there is a thread of sexual taboos running throughout the film as well.)

The Phantom of Liberty operates as an instance of complex narrative, exploiting the audience's ordinary expectations of cause and effect through a parametric narrative form. Stylistically this is a restrained film, and with no stylistic obstacles to negotiate, the pattern of the narrative form dominates particularities of plot and character. Furthermore, the casual and free-associative tenor of the film located in the patterned narrative form—as one vignette transitions to the next—is contrasted within each vignette in which there is an event that breaks down our expectations regarding how causality functions. *The Phantom of Liberty* consists of a series of vignettes, each of which is largely linked by a chance encounter between characters (except for two transitions—from the introduction to the first vignette, and from the seventh to the eighth). Table 2.1 provides an overview of the film from the perspective of its narrative form.

The transition from one vignette to the next develops a casual, causal flow that reinforces the expectations of cause and effect developed not just out of our experience with films and television programs but out of the domain of ordinary experience that we inhabit day-to-day.

Table 2.1. An Overview of *The Phantom of Liberty*'s Parametric Narrative Form

Vignette	Vignette Overview	Breakdown Event	Transition Sequence
Introduction	A historical scene based on a story by a Spanish romantic writer, featuring French troops executing rebellions and desecrating a church.	The captain falls in love with a statue, and in caressing and attempting to seduce her (the statue), he is knocked unconscious by the statue of her husband.	The story is being read in a park by the nanny of two children.
1	The children are playing on a slide. They are approached by a man who gives them photos, and he tells them not to show any adults. The children and nanny go home, and one of the children immediately shows her parents the photos—they abhor and are aroused by their contents. Previously the husband and wife had been discussing how tired and exhausted the husband had been, and how he should go and see a doctor. The husband mentions that he has not been sleeping well.	(a) When the parents are perusing the photos, they comment on how disgusting many of them are; the photos are of French architecture. (b) While restless and trying to sleep, the husband sees (not dreams) a cockerel, a postman, and an emu in his bedroom.	The husband goes to the doctor, and a nurse requests permission for immediate leave to visit her sick father.

continued on next page

Table 2.1. Continued.

Vignette	Vignette Overview	Breakdown Event	Transition Sequence
2	The nurse drives to visit her father, but due to bad weather and a road being closed off, she must stop at a small hotel for the night. Other guests include a group of Carmelite monks, a flamenco dancer and guitarist, a milliner and his assistant, and later a young man and his aunt conducting an incestuous affair.	(a) On the way to visit her father, the nurse passes a tank occupied by three soldiers who are hunting foxes. (b) When the aunt exposes her naked body to her nephew, her body is that of a young woman.	The next morning, a man waiting for a bus asks the nurse to give him a lift into town, as the bus won't arrive for a couple of hours. She obliges him, and we find out that the man is a professor at a police academy.
3	The professor arrives at the academy and attempts to lead a class on the relativity of taboos, morals, and laws. He is constantly interrupted, either by the antics of the officers or by their being called away to address a variety of crimes.	The police officers act like poorly behaved children—writing obscene statements on the chalkboard before the professor arrives and pinning something on his coat when his back is turned.	The professor brings in a senior police officer to assist in controlling the class, and he provides an anecdote to help illustrate his point.

Vignette	Vignette Overview	Breakdown Event	Transition Sequence
4	The anecdote involves the professor and his wife attending a dinner party with friends.	The social expectations and taboos are inverted. The party is seated on toilets around the dinner table; they openly use them, and discuss defecation and human waste. A young girl is chastised for speaking freely about being hungry. The professor excuses himself and asks a nearby maid, privately and quietly, where the dining room is. He is directed there, and sits in a private room to have his meal.	We return to the classroom, where the final two police officers are called away to duty. They pull over a man for speeding, who states he is on the way to an important doctor's appointment.
5	The man visits his doctor; he is told to cut back on cigarettes and that he has cancer.	Upon finally telling the man his diagnosis, the doctor offers him a cigarette.	The man returns home after the appointment and tells his wife that everything is fine. They receive a phone call from their daughter's school informing them that she is missing.

continued on next page

Table 2.1. Continued.

Vignette	Vignette Overview	Breakdown Event	Transition Sequence
6	The parents and the girl's nanny arrive at the school to discuss their daughter's disappearance with the headmistress and the girl's teacher. Dissatisfied with the response of the school, they go to the police to file a missing person's report.	(a) While in the classroom, the girl is clearly physically present, and is even interacted with. (At one point she is told not to interrupt.) (b) The parents and nanny take the girl to the police station. One of the officers looks at her and asks her questions so as to fill in the details of the report. Another officer, a sergeant who is tasked with leading the investigation, looks at the girl in detail to help with his enquiries.	The sergeant is chastised for his shoes not being polished. He goes to have them polished. Another man is also having his shoes polished there.
7	We follow the other man to a vantage point in a high-rise building. He takes a sniper rifle out of a case he is carrying, and begins to unload at random on people in the streets below. He is taken to a court where he is tried, found guilty, and sentenced to death.	Once the sniper has been sentenced, he is released and his handcuffs are removed; the officers guarding him shake his hand, offer him a cigarette, and light it. The jury and public in the courtroom mob him and shake his hands, and on his way out of the court, some people ask for his autograph and treat him like a celebrity.	A voiceover takes us back to the parents where the missing girl has been "found." They are in the police commissioner's office to hear the good news. The commissioner is interrupted for his next appointment and asks his secretary to take care of it.

Vignette	Vignette Overview	Breakdown Event	Transition Sequence
8	The commissioner arrives at a bar, where he waits for some acquaintances. A woman walks into the bar, and the commissioner is struck by how closely she resembles his deceased sister. The commissioner recounts a story of one of the last times he saw his sister. He is called away to his family plot at the cemetery. He is initially not allowed in, but he provides his credentials as police commissioner and visits his sister.	(a) The call the police commissioner receives is from his deceased sister. She is even able to verify certain details of the story the commissioner has just recounted to the lady at the bar. In the mausoleum, his sister's hair is hanging out of the coffin, and there is even a phone next to it. (b) In spite of commissioner's providing his credentials, the guard at the cemetery had requested reinforcements, and they refuse to believe he is the commissioner, charging him with desecration.	The commissioner is treated dismissively and disrespectfully by officers at the station. He continues to maintain that he is the commissioner. The "real" commissioner has requested to see him. Officers still treat him roughly, shoving and pushing him to the "real" commissioner's office.
Conclusion	The first commissioner and the second commissioner have a conversation, discussing ideas and systems of crowd control. They also talk about the zoo. They decide to go to the zoo, where there is an unseen riot going on. Both commissioners direct officers to use force to control it.	In spite of the first commissioner's dismissive treatment, and implicit conclusions that he is insane and deranged, once in the office he and the second commissioner treat each other like old friends and conduct their conversation cordially and warmly.	The film concludes.

For example, the transition from vignette 1 to vignette 2 has the audience follow a man to a doctor's appointment, where a nurse at the surgery requests time off to visit her ailing father. We then leave the man's vignette and follow the nurse as the central character in the next. Once we identify the pattern (this likely occurs early on), our expectations for the film are entrenched. In vignette 2, for example, we are surprised when the nurse drives past a tank manned by soldiers hunting foxes. However, in the breakdown event of vignette 7, we are not necessarily surprised that it occurs (as we are by now accustomed to this part of the pattern), but we remain surprised by precisely *how* our expectations of cause and effect break down in the film. Such events, in their absurdity and randomness and pulled straight from the imagination of the director, destabilize us—and yet once they have occurred, the film continues in a common causal flow once more.

Our surprise is further enhanced by the ordinariness and familiarity of the settings and characters: hotels, schools, and courtrooms, and teachers, nurses, doctors, and parents all feature. Furthermore, the simplification of the narrative (in one sense), whereby the syuzhet and the fabula are aligned and expressed through an unobtrusive filmmaking style, further strengthens the expectations of cause and effect. Unlike the characters of the film, who remain deadpan and largely unsurprised by the destabilizing events of each vignette, the audience may expect a sudden breakdown in cause and effect (having detected the pattern) and are left to make sense out of precisely how such regular causality has been violated. Therefore, when in vignette 6 parents and police are looking for a missing girl with whom they are openly interacting, our expectations of cause and effect drawn from the world of ordinary experience and reinforced by the pattern of the narrative are completely shaken. While we can expect causality to break down, we cannot possibly know how (at least on first viewing of the film).

Both *L'Argent* and *The Phantom of Liberty* extend Bordwell's (1985) original formulation of parametric narration, and I have demonstrated how parametric principles can be incorporated as patterns in both the fabula and the syuzhet—as parametric narrative form. Through the range of complex narrative forms I have addressed in this chapter, complex narratives as a whole illustrate how films and television programs can artistically explore the metaphysical concepts of causality and free will, and related ideas of contingency, determinism, and fatalism. Forking-path films develop a balance between repetition and change, making contingent events available to spectator experience, whereas spatial convergence narratives can create a sense of fatalism to varying degrees—including soft, moderate, and strong cases. The multimodal storytelling universe of *Fargo*, in its development of a story-world across film and television, and especially given the medium-specific narrative form of television, functions as an example of complex storytelling. In this case, spectators are required to trace causal chains across individual instantiations to create a macronarrative that involves the film and multiple seasons of *Fargo*. Time-travel narratives manage both the determinism of the universe and the free will of characters, whereas in my reconceiving the idea of parametric narration as parametric form, films such as *L'Argent* and *The Phantom of Liberty* examine more freely the idea of causality and agency.

Despite the shared preoccupation the complex narrative forms I address here have with free will and causality, they do not aspire to solve a particular philosophical problem. After all, the different complex narrative forms I have considered adopt contradictory positions on these metaphysical concepts. Treating different kinds of complex narratives in the implicitly comparative way I have suggests the importance of being attuned to the inextricability of form and content, as well as the particular ways certain films and television programs artistically transform the same content in different ways. But in examining them in tandem, we accumulate a suite of experiences that enable us to consider whether a particular metaphysical system artistically explored in a work functions in the world of ordinary experience, or indeed whether it illuminates something of our own sense of free will and causality.

3

Is Shane Virtuous?

Goodness and *Telos* in the World of the American Western

Sam Peckinpah's *The Wild Bunch* (1969) follows an aging group of outlaws on what is purportedly their final heist. Their leader, Pike (William Holden), is seeking retirement, and his right-hand man, Dutch (Ernest Borgnine), and the rest of the bunch are only too happy to lend their support to his cause, motivated as they are by the promises of riches of their own. They are relentlessly tracked by another group led by former member—Pike's former partner in crime—Deke (Robert Ryan). The wild bunch operates throughout the film as a rambling, traveling community—they are men who are joined together with a shared purpose, a shared set of values, and a shared understanding of how to attain the ends to which they are drawn. The bunch led by Deke is a community of its own, too—their purpose, values, and ends run up against those of Pike's, given that Deke's task is to eliminate the group that has formed around his former partner. While initially there is a kind of rough charisma to Pike's group and a nobility to Deke's, as the film goes on and desperation, violence, and self-interest start to overwhelm the motivations of each community, they grow less and less disparate, the harsh conditions of the world of the American Western wearing on them, the shared history between Deke and Pike making the interests and purpose of each group less communal and increasingly personal. Each hyperviolent gunfight reduces the fragile human assistance lent by their respective band of supporters, and an absence of virtue and goodness becomes apparent as the film draws to a close.

In this chapter, I am concerned with how the characters that populate the American Western show goodness, virtue, and *telos* (purpose, or the ends for which something is done); how the apparent goodness is complicated by the violent world of the West; and the ways in which certain heroes of this world can bring goodness to life. The works I consider throughout are concerned with maintaining a balance between the shared social space of a particular community (such as a town) and the individual existence of certain characters.

Given the global and longstanding popularity of the Western, which has resulted in culturally specific versions of the genre seen in, for example, the kangaroo Western, the spaghetti Western, the sauerkraut Western, and the curry Western, my focus here is limited to that of the American Western. The historical connection of the genre to America is not a controversial one: André Bazin, for example, argues that "the Western is rooted in the history of the American nation" (1998, 49), and film scholar Jim Kitses suggests that "what gives the form [of the Western] a particular thrust and centrality is its historical setting" (1998, 60).

Generically, the American Western possesses a preoccupation with questions regarding virtue, goodness, and telos. These ethical questions presuppose a metaphysical understanding of the concepts I am focused on in this chapter. Charles Taylor argues that "philosophical theory has explored this [the goodness of different ways of being] in the language of virtue," yet "even more important for our moral consciousness has been the portrayal of good and bad lives in exemplary figures and stories" (2014, 9). Taylor's comments allude to two important points. First, what is central to my approach here is the way the artistic exploration of these concepts allows spectators an opportunity to consider in a new way how goodness, virtue, and telos function in the world of ordinary experience. Second, the artistic exploration of virtue in the American Western enables spectators to consider the nature—or metaphysical quality—of virtue, goodness, and telos.

Scholarship on the genre has pointed out its richness in style and thematic concerns, particularly in terms of how Westerns explore sociohistorical issues such as industrialization, the treatment of Native Americans, representations of men and women, and the examination of the frontier myth. Furthermore, the dominant structuralist account of the genre seeks to demonstrate the ways that the Western is ordered under a master opposition of civilization and wilderness as the key to the genre's thematic structure (Kitses 1998; Wright 1977). Other accounts have aimed to illustrate archetypal characters and their place within the genre. Certain scholars have also sought to establish a connection between the genre and myths in a range of ways: national myths (Pippin, 2010) and myths of Ancient Greece and Rome (Day 2016; Winkler 1985). My emphasis on the metaphysical concerns of the genre complement these other accounts of the American Western.

The philosophical territory I work in throughout this chapter is drawn from the work of Alasdair MacIntyre and Iris Murdoch. The former explicitly explores how goodness, virtue, and telos are given unity in the narrative shape of our existence, and it is through Mac-Intyre's insights that I develop the connection these concepts have to the individuals that populate the Westerns (and, by extension, the world of ordinary experience). By adopting MacIntyre's notion of practices—of which the western town or community is one example—I also examine the shared or social context of goodness, virtue, and telos.

For Murdoch, as Floora Ruokonen explains, the "picture of human beings [is] a being structured by the idea of the Good" and that Murdoch "presents her picture through a description which starts with basic human experience and proceeds from there to metaphysical concepts intended to illuminate the nature of the experience" (2008, 79). The approach I take in this chapter mirrors these general comments, and I will give a more thorough explication of Murdoch's understanding of the Good in later sections.

The shared social context of a practice (such as a town or community) in combination with the characteristic setting of the American Western creates what Noël Carroll (2002) calls a "wheel of virtue" that allows spectators to consider the interplay of virtue and vice both within a character and among multiple characters. The individual context affords an examination of the telos of the Good and how it is given formal expression in various films through the subjective experience of certain characters. The world of the American Western is, however, a notably violent one, so the place of violence in both the social and individual contexts bears consideration. The American Western's preoccupation with violence complicates the presence of goodness, virtue, and telos, but works of the genre also offer some ways in which violence can be nullified through practices such as communities as well as the friendship of characters.

Goodness, Virtue, and Telos

The Western is typically treated as manifesting a dichotomy between civilization and wilderness. In *The Wild Bunch*, we could even recast both Pike's and Deke's groups as relying more and more on the techniques of the wilderness to achieve their ends. Here, though, I am interested not so much in the historical setting of a nascent community as it relates to the standard view of the genre, but rather the ways in which this setting in combination with other generic markers brings out its distinctive concern with the metaphysical concepts of goodness, virtue, and telos through an interplay of the individual and the community.

In *After Virtue*, wherein he examines ancient and classical ethics in light of nineteenth- and twentieth-century moral philosophy, MacIntyre argues that virtues "are to be understood as those dispositions which will not only sustain practices and enable us to achieve the goods internal to practices, but which will also sustain us in the relevant kind of quest for the good, by enabling us to overcome the harms, dangers, temptations and distractions which we encounter, and which will furnish us with increasing self-knowledge and increasing knowledge of the good" (2007, 219). I understand virtue, therefore, as a class of dispositions (for example, courage, fortitude, and diligence) that furnishes an individual with a number of possibilities: through virtue we achieve the goods internal to practices (which I will define in a moment); through virtue we overcome harms and challenges (physical, intellectual, and moral, for example); it is through virtue that our lives are ordered to the Good; and it is through cultivating virtues and acting virtuously that we come to understand and know the Good. In the context of the American Western, one way in which spectators can consider the metaphysical idea of the Good is by considering the extent to which characters act virtuously, and, in considering such actions, contemplate what it is to act with or possess virtue in light of the narratives experienced onscreen. Furthermore, we can consider how a film or television program artistically explores goodness and telos—the latter of which in this context regards the extent to which, or whether or not, an existence is ordered toward the Good through the cultivation of virtues. As I will illustrate later, telos is also often visually represented through what I term the telos shot.

As with virtue—wherein particular virtues relate to each other insofar as they are dispositions of the same class—we can say that particular forms of life, or practices, have their own group of internal goods that are themselves illustrations of the Good. According to MacIntyre, a practice is "any coherent and complex form of socially established cooperative human activity through which goods internal to that form of activity are realized in the course of trying to achieve those standards of excellence which are appropriate to, and partially definitive of, that form of activity" (2007, 187). One such practice is the establishment of society—a town, for example. One of the generic features of the American Western is its setting of the town or society in a state of becoming—that is to say, not yet established—or under threat. Therefore, the practice is given an opportunity to exist, or it continues to exist insofar as the virtues of the people within it overcome any potential harms or dangers. Considered another way, arguably a practice such as a town, city, or society is always in a state of development, and it is through virtue that it can exist, allow for the attainment of goods internal to that practice, and enable the flourishing of individuals.

To consider a brief example: John Ford's *The Man Who Shot Liberty Valance* (1962) depicts the small town of Shinbone constantly under duress by Liberty Valance (Lee Marvin) and his gang. When Eastern lawyer Ransom Stoddard (James Stewart) stands up to Valance consistently throughout the film—despite being completely ill-equipped in his technical proficiency with a gun—he shows the virtues of courage and perseverance. The film renders the notion of virtue in a complex way, however. After all, it is not Stoddard but Tom Doniphon (John Wayne) who in the end kills Valance unseen from a shadowy corner of the Shinbone streets, and Doniphon's unacknowledged act enables the town's existence to continue. It is Stoddard's participation in this lie that provides him with a glowing political career, and marriage to Hallie (Vera Miles), the woman Doniphon loves. Spectators, then, can consider the extent to which the virtue of courage is manifest in certain characters, as well as how it allows for the consolidation of the community—the practice—of the town of Shinbone to exist, precisely through the courageous acts of those who exist within it. At the same time, it contrasts such images and acts of courage with complicity in falsehoods that is suggestive of a kind of cowardice. Stoddard's initial courage is matched with Doniphon's and contrasted with Stoddard's cowardice in capitalizing on the outcome of Valance's death.

In the Western, then, virtues enable not just the continuing of social communities but the goods internal to such communities—stable living, safety, friendship, and peace, for example. As MacIntyre argues: "Every practice requires a certain kind of relationship between those who participate in it. Now the virtues are those goods by reference to which ... we define our relationship to those other people with whom we share the kind of purposes and standard which inform practices" (2007, 191). The practice of community building in the town in the American Western, for example, will only exist because of the virtuous acts of its members—the townsfolk. But the practice can also only exist insofar as the townsfolk have a shared understanding of the character of that practice—what sort of town Shinbone will be, say—and therefore a shared understanding of the virtues required in achieving that practice and the goods internal to it. In the case of the American Western, spectators can consider different instances of the one virtue—Stoddard's courage compared to Doniphon's, for example—and the ways in which each contribute to the practice of Shinbone. Furthermore, in contemplating both examples of courage, spectators can consider what is common to them, thereby developing an understanding of that particular virtue (courage) as well as virtue itself. Because of the nature of a practice, virtue has a social dimension—and while certain central characters (Stoddard and Doniphon, for example) lend themselves to consideration, all characters can be interrogated. For example, Hallie's limited role in terms of screen time is no less deserving of consideration. The cumulative contemplation of these different instantiations of virtue can foster a holistic appreciation of that virtue or even virtue itself, as well as the connection between virtue and a particular practice.

What I have been describing thus far in terms of the embodiment of virtue across a cast of characters can be given further clarity through a wheel of virtue. In such a case, Carroll argues, "A studied array of characters... both correspond and contrast with each other along the dimensions of a certain virtue or package of virtues" (2002, 12). The American Western's artistic exploration of goodness, virtue, telos, and practices enables spectators to consider how the same virtue differs or is the same across characters, especially insofar as they contribute to a practice such as that of a social community.

The social dimension of goodness, virtue, and telos is afforded consideration by the context and setting provided by a particular practice. In terms of the individual, MacIntyre suggests that what coheres virtue, goodness, and telos in an individual's existence is the narrative shape of that existence: "The narrative... in which the human life is embodied has a form in which the subject... is set a task in the completion of which lies their peculiar appropriation of the human good; the way towards the completion of that task is barred by a variety of inward and outward evils. The virtues are those qualities which enable the evils to be overcome, the task to be accomplished, the journey to be completed" (2007, 175). What makes the connection between goodness, virtue, and telos intelligible for a particular person is the narrative form of life—that a person's existence has some end, some point to which it is ordered. Virtue, because it is ordered toward the Good, furnishes us with the ability to overcome harms and challenges and continue on our teleological path—to recognize our end and complete the journey, as MacIntyre states.

In *Liberty Valance*, the bulk of the film is told in flashback, as we see the events that led not just to Stoddard's career but to his reason for returning to Shinbone (the death of Doniphon). Audiences are shown that Shinbone does not just exist but is a flourishing town. The particular narrative of Stoddard's life reinforces the idea of telos by showing the end at the start—we see the direction toward which the bulk of the story is headed. The film's rich exploration of virtue is conducted through the contrasting narrative lives of Stoddard and Doniphon and concludes with a challenging note: the much-celebrated Stoddard is only so because of the actions of Doniphon, the actions that went and continue to go unheralded. Where Stoddard failed in skill, Doniphon succeeded. The film does not just depict the social nature of the virtues required to overcome harms, thereby ensuring the continuing practice of Shinbone. Through its narrative form, *Liberty Valance* also expresses the narrative that unifies the concepts of goodness, virtue, and telos in the individual context, contrasting the lives of Stoddard and Doniphon.

Virtue itself has a shape, a direction that is governed by a conception of the Good. MacIntyre argues that "it is in looking for a conception of *the good* which will enable us to order other goods, for a conception of *the good* which will enable us to extend our understanding of the purpose and content of the virtues, for a conception of *the good* which will enable us to understand the place of integrity and constancy in life, that we initially define the kind of life which is a quest for the good" (2007, 219). In sum: it is a conception of the Good that orders the understanding of virtue, whose telos is the pursuit of such goodness, and which is continuously refined through our experience of life—as our lives go on, we become better equipped to understand what constitutes a particular virtue, which feeds our understanding of the Good to which virtue is directing us. A practice such as a town has a shared understanding among its members of how to achieve the goods internal to the practice. These internal goods develop and refine our understanding of the Good. The narrative shape of a human life is another means by which we better understand the Good, insofar as cultivating virtues enables us to overcome harms and obstacles in the pursuit of our individual telos.

In Fred Zinnemann's *High Noon* (1952), we follow Will Kane (Gary Cooper), who, on his wedding day, is informed that a man he helped put in jail, Frank Miller (Ian MacDonald), is due to arrive back in town on the noon train to exact vengeance on Kane. Despite reservations expressed by his wife, Amy (Grace Kelly), Kane attempts to recruit some deputies to help eliminate Miller and his gang. For various reasons, however, some decide not to help; others agree to help, but eventually retract their assistance. All recommend that Kane and his wife avoid confrontation and leave town instead. At one point in the film, a former romantic partner of Kane's, Helen Ramirez (Katy Jurado), says: "Kane will be a dead man in half an hour and nobody's gonna do anything about it. And when he dies, this town dies too." What is at stake could not be made clearer—the existence of the town depends on the courage of Kane and his willingness to confront the past. Ramirez, however, is not optimistic: after all, should Kane die, the only people left to defend the community are those cowardly individuals who would not stand up to Miller and his gang in the first place.

Early in the film, Kane and Amy, upon learning of Miller's imminent return, do act on the advice of the other townspeople and pack up and ride a wagon out of town. They are silhouetted against the landscape, traveling to the left of screen, minute against the vast backdrop of nature. The film is iconic for its use of time: its repeated close-ups on clocks and watches and its narrative unfolding almost in real time provide an important narrative context for this shot. Kane is attempting not just to escape but to also undo the past, to go back in time and act more decisively—maybe to shoot Miller when he had a chance, maybe to muster better evidence so that Miller wouldn't walk free as he does now. But Kane, realizing the folly of his actions, decides to return to town and confront the circumstances that await him.

Amy initially does not help her husband—refusing to be part of violence and killing, wanting instead just to leave—until the penultimate showdown. Kane is trapped in the street, pinned down by Miller and his last remaining gang member. Amy is in a building, witnessing things unfold. She has a change of heart and for the sake of her husband picks up a gun and shoots the henchman. Amy and Kane's courageous actions are not solely individualistic affairs—their courageous behavior not only has effects for themselves and each other but for the continuing existence of the town. Furthermore, as noted earlier, virtuous acts are in service to the internal goods of the practice of the town. In *High Noon*, the town continues to exist despite the widespread cowardice of many of its members, because two individuals—with different motivations—cultivated the virtue of courage to overcome an array of harms and dangers.

There are similar dynamics at play in the George Stevens film *Shane* (1953). In this film, the titular character (Alan Ladd) drifts into a small community of homesteaders under threat from landowners who want them off the land. Shane moves in with the Starrett family, consisting of Joe (Van Heflin), Marian (Jean Arthur), and their son, Joey (Brandon deWilde). He decides to help ward off the increasingly violent and oppressive actions of Rufus Ryker (Emile Meyer), who has enlisted the help of gun-for-hire Jack Wilson (Jack Palance). The outcome is much the same as that of *High Noon*—Shane faces Ryker and Wilson alone, after various other homesteaders who initially pledge their help have either been killed or have chosen to leave. Shane ensures the existence of the town by overcoming obstacles, danger, and the failings of others. In one of the most iconic shots of cinema, Shane leaves in much the same way as Will and Amy Kane do at the end of *High Noon*. After eliminating Ryker and Wilson under the watchful eyes of Joey, Shane says: "Joey, there's no living with... with a killing. There's no going back from one. Right or wrong, it's a brand. A brand sticks. There's no going back." Shane's actions and statements explicitly register the complication violence brings to the world of the American Western.

Prior to the final showdown, Joe is willing to face Ryker and Wilson himself—he is courageous to a fault, as such action would unquestionably result in his death, calling to mind Stoddard's attitude in *Liberty Valance*. Joe is devoted to his wife and son, and he is invested in the practice of building the social community of the homesteaders. In one chaotic scene—a bar fight, earlier in the film—he stands side by side with Shane in an act of friendship as they hold their own, well outnumbered by the Ryker gang. Joe's virtue is largely uncomplicated, yet, lacking the technical ability of Shane that allows for the removal of the obstacle threatening the social community, he is not the hero of the film and seems even more virtuous as a result. The wheel of virtue is relevant here, as it was in the case of *Liberty Valance* (and to a less complex extent, *High Noon*) in that it enables spectators to compare how courage (and other virtues) are embodied in Joe and Shane. Furthermore, contemplating Shane in relation to Joe helps to clarify the ambiguity of Shane's virtue, seen in, for example, his relationship with the Starrett family.

Shane and Marian have a mutual admiration for each other, and there are suggestions of romantic feelings between the two as well. Joey idolizes Shane, and Shane even replaces the boy's father in certain important ways—not just in his technical skill as a gunfighter capable of protecting the family, but in his ability to pass this skill on to Joey. In terms of virtue, though, Shane exists in Joe's shadow. Shane is second to Joe in his willingness to defend the community, in devotion to Joey, and in caring for Marian. Joe is the exemplar of virtue—in certain instances, as mentioned, to a fault—that Shane is measured against. Part of what makes the film so compelling is that it is the ways in which Shane is limited in virtue as revealed through a comparison to Joe that enable him to overcome the potential harms threatening the existence of the community.

This is not to say that Shane is unvirtuous—after all, he is tender, courageous, and resilient. The ambiguity attached to Shane is not just explored through character and narrative in the ways outlined earlier but through elements of the film's style, too. His glamorous costume offers one interesting example. The buckskin cowboy getup he is wearing when he first rides into the homestead is untouched and impeccable, as are the clean and proper clothes he wears for much of the rest of the film. These elements are at odds with his existence as a drifting gunslinger, a man who seems to live his life from town to town, engaged in the act of killing. This glamorous, performative quality of Shane's costume is also adopted in adoring close-ups of the character. In comparison, Joe's dirty clothing is worn to the point of ruin, a testament to his hard work and investment in the social community. It is only when Shane's contributions merge with Joe's—working in the homestead, for example, or during the aforementioned bar fight—that Shane's appearance becomes, paradoxically, unclean with virtue.

Shane is also engaged in the practice of building a social community of which he is only transiently a part. He arrives without much explanation and leaves in much the same way. This final point is especially significant if we recall the claim made earlier regarding the importance of the shared understanding of virtues in informing practices. Shane's transient presence in the community, along with the other details just mentioned, complicate his virtuous qualities. The wheel of virtue places him as less virtuous than other characters, especially Joe, and certain stylistic features only enhance his ambiguities. Shane, therefore, is a compelling paradox through which the film provides a rich exploration of the relation of goodness, virtues, and practices.

Shane's ambiguity as a character is not replicated in the characters of the Delmer Daves film *3:10 to Yuma* (1957). Dan Evans (Van Heflin) plays a farmer suffering through a drought. In order to get enough money to buy access to a stream for his cattle, he agrees to escort the recently captured criminal Ben Wade (Glenn Ford) to the 3:10 train going to Yuma. Although there are several volunteers initially willing to help, in much the same way as in *High Noon* and *Shane*, they fall away for various reasons, with the exception of the town drunk, Alex Potter (Henry Jones). Even Mr. Butterfield (Robert Emhardt), the wealthy businessman who employs Dan, and whose carriage Wade and his gang held up, pleads with Evans to save himself and let Wade go free, promising to pay him anyway. There are several key moments in the film that reveal the relationship between virtue and goodness in the social context of a practice.

In one scene, Wade has dinner at the Evans's family ranch, with Dan's wife, Alice (Leora Dana), and his two sons present. Wade is incredibly charismatic and polite, and there is an unexpressed romantic dynamic between him and Alice. It is clear that Alice is unimpressed, disappointed, and doubtful of her husband's capacity to get their family and property out of their problematic state—in short, to contribute to the practice of sustaining the homestead. Wade, despite his predicament, is confident, in control, and wealthy—the sort of man who could not only solve the problem but would likely be able to avoid it in the first place. Wade drifts into the orbit of the Evans family in much the same way Shane does with the Starretts. Wade, too, not only mirrors Shane in this way but does so in the confluence of his attributes; he is technically competent, for example, and possesses those virtuous traits just mentioned, though he is also a known murderer and thief. While Wade could, in theory, contribute to the Evans's social community—indeed, he continuously attempts to bribe Dan throughout the time he's captured—it is difficult to believe he would go through with his promise.

For Dan to compromise the virtuous path would also, in all likelihood, ensure the demise of the practice of sustaining the homestead. As noted earlier, virtue allows obstacles to be overcome—in the case of *3:10 to Yuma*, the virtues of perseverance, courage, and honesty allow Dan to resist the temptations presented to him. However, through the wheel of virtue, the courage of Dan can be compared to the courage of another character—the drunk, Potter. Potter initially volunteers to help, simply to help (as compared to Dan, who volunteers for money)—his courage is present from the start. By contrast, Dan's courage is something that develops throughout the film as it is gradually tested, refined, and cultivated, thereby allowing him to act with greater courage, overcome greater harms and dangers, and resist greater temptations. It is in acting virtuously that he witnesses the farm-saving rains at the film's conclusion while he rides the train with Wade to Yuma. Film scholar Douglas Pye also highlights the freedom in Dan's chosen course of action to see his agreement through to the end in spite of promises that he will be paid regardless. However, Pye incorrectly claims that there is in the film some implied causal relationship between Dan's actions and the turn in the weather (2014, 253). Such a connection is inferred by Pye, rather than implied by the film, but Pye's comments afford a final consideration before moving on, and that is with regard to the role of luck.

Dan's virtue did not *cause* the rain, as Pye suggests; rather, his persistence with virtuous action allows him to witness the weather turn for the better. The weather might not have turned—furthermore, Dan might have taken the money and run, placing his trust in Wade and his gang not to kill him, and he might or might not have been killed. These contingent events point to how cultivating virtue enables one to continue along the teleological path of the Good. The idea of luck (or fortune) is one that can be drawn out through our appreciation of these events. In *High Noon*, Will Kane hears a member of the Miller gang break a window as he is attempting to stalk Kane through town. Kane thus gains an early advantage in the fight. In *3:10 to Yuma*, a herd of cattle crosses a road, obscuring Wade and Evans from the view of Wade's gang as they get closer to the train, so that Evans can make good on his promise to escort Wade to prison. These small, serendipitous moments demonstrate how fortuitous contingent events are not, as some sort of reward, caused by the Western hero's cultivation of virtue as they pursue the Good. Rather, they are events that allow the Western hero to display their own virtue—they are moments that provide the Western hero the opportunity to continue cultivating virtue in the pursuit of the Good, and often to ensure the continuing existence of a practice.

In laying out an account of goodness, virtue, and telos, I have outlined an understanding of how these concepts are expressed in the individual context of a person's existence. Predominantly, though, I have provided a sustained examination of how goodness, virtue, and telos are manifest in a typical practice of the American Western, that of the town or homestead. The analyses have demonstrated that, through the wheel of virtue, spectators can consider not just the variable embodiment of virtue across a cast of characters but how the common features of particular virtues reflect the nature of virtue itself; in so doing, spectators can consider how virtue functions in the world of ordinary experience too.

Cinematic Form and Teleological Experience

One clear way the American Western presents the experiential dimension of telos is through what I term the telos shot, whereby the small silhouette of the character is overwhelmed by the backdrop of the landscape in which they are situated. Such a shot embodies the very purposive nature of the character's experience (fig. 3.1). Although I have emphasized the social context of goodness, virtue, and telos thus far, it is worth noting that the films analyzed in detail to this point also make use of the telos shot.

However, there are more ways than this single stylistic technique through which the teleological experience of characters is conveyed to spectators. Westerns such as Don Siegel's *The Shootist* (1976), Andrew Dominik's *The Assassination of Jesse James by the Coward Robert Ford* (2007), and Kelly Reichardt's *Meek's Cutoff* (2010) demonstrate how the genre can use cinematic form to present the teleological experience of characters. To this point, I have shown how witnessing characters' pursuit of the Good through the cultivation of virtues in the social context of a practice can refine our understanding of goodness. I have also illustrated a cursory connection between the telos of our existence and the notion of the Good as ordering that telos; in this section I will develop such a connection in greater detail.

Figure 3.1. A telos shot from *High Noon*. *Source:* Zinnemann, Fred, dir. *High Noon*. 1952. Chicago: Olive Films, 2016. Blu-ray Disc, 1080p HD.

Curiously enough in the context of this section, Iris Murdoch—whose work I will adapt here—states that a fundamental assumption of her argument is that "human life has no external point or τέλος [telos]" (1997, 364). However, Murdoch's comments are at least suggestive of a relation between telos and goodness, even if she stops short of arguing (and, indeed, cuts off any consideration of the argument) that goodness is *the telos* of human life. Ruokonen summarizes the development of Murdoch's argument as follows:

> In human life there is a sense of moving either to the right or the wrong direction. This sense involves an idea of goodness which we think to be more than just a projection of our own evaluations on neutral circumstances, since having a sense of direction means having a sense of scales and distances independent of ourselves.... In any given area of life, the idea of a scale, an order of merit, leads in turn to the idea of perfection.... This idea of perfection, also called the Good, is necessary for all thinking. It unifies our experience, makes it in fact the experience of a person, and hence is a necessary condition of us having a vision of ourselves or the world in the first place. (2008, 79)

The MacIntyrean idea of telos—that of a task to be accomplished or a quest to be completed—can be located in this summary of Murdoch's thought. The Good provides our individual existence with a sense of direction and a scale or metric by which we examine the extent to which we are on the right path—the degree to which we are appropriately directed toward the completion of our particular task or narrative quest. The Good is also the apex of the scale of goodness—the Good is goodness perfected. However, such an understanding of the Good implies the possibility of accomplishing a task or completing a narrative quest imperfectly. As MacIntyre argues, "Quests sometimes fail, are frustrated, abandoned or dissipated into distractions, and human lives may in all these ways also fail. But the only criteria for success or failure in a human life as a whole are the criteria of success or failure in a narrated or to-be-narrated quest" (2007, 219). Therefore, whether we accept, like MacIntyre, or reject, like Murdoch, that the telos of our existence is the attainment of the Good, the synthesis of the insights of both philosophers allows for the conception of narrative quests and tasks that are not ordered toward the Good, but still retain the narrative shape of a quest or task. However, in such cases, there will be a privation of virtue insofar as there is a lack of goodness. As Murdoch suggests, the "Good is mysterious because of human frailty, because of the immense distance which is involved" (1997, 381). What is critical is that the very notion of the Good—as with the very notion of telos (and as with the notion of virtue as understood through the wheel of virtue discussed earlier)—offers a lens through which we can examine how characters in the world of the American Western understand their telos and whether or not, or the extent to which, such telos is ordered toward the Good.

To refine her understanding of our relation to the Good, Murdoch draws on Plato's analogy of the cave. In particular, she argues that "when Plato wants to explain the Good he uses the image of the sun. The moral pilgrim emerges from the cave and begins to see the real world in the light of the sun, and last of all is able to look at the sun itself" (376). Murdoch makes the further point that "the sun is seen at the end of a long quest which involves a reorientation (the prisoners have to turn round) and an ascent. It is real, it is out there, but very distant" (376). Finally, Murdoch notes that "Plato's image implies that complete unity is not seen until one has reached the summit, but moral advance carries with it intuitions of unity which are increasingly less misleading. As we deepen our notions of the virtues we introduce relationship and hierarchy" (378). This last point echoes the MacIntyrean claim that the cultivation of virtue enables us to deepen our understanding not just of virtue but also of goodness, insofar as virtues are ordered toward goodness. Furthermore, Murdoch's point highlights how certain virtues are required in overcoming particular external harms and dangers, as well as our own particular shortcomings and frailties.

The Shootist follows J. B. Books, a cowboy dying of cancer, played by John Wayne in his final film role, as he too was dying of cancer. Books attempts to go out on his own terms, in a way appropriate to the narrative of his life as it has been written thus far. This doubling between film world and real world is evident from the opening montage. With voiceover narration providing a history of Books, a stream of images of Wayne in earlier films—black-and-white and color—shows the history of the actor as much as the persona he brought to the Western. After this is a long telos shot of Books on horseback, riding slowly from the horizon toward the screen, clearly representing in visual terms his embarking on a narrative quest that just so happens to be his final chapter (fig. 3.2).

Books confirms his diagnosis with the town doctor (James Stewart), and in a later conversation, the doctor tries to convince Books that a man with his courage should not waste away in pain and unconsciousness in a bed. It is interesting to note a connection in the film to *Liberty Valance*—Books teaches Gillom Rogers (Ron Howard), the son of the owner of the hotel where he is staying, how to shoot, as Doniphon tries to teach Stoddard how to shoot in *Liberty Valance*. Books arranges for a final showdown in the town hotel and kills all the outlaws who have been hunting him, eventually meeting his demise as the bartender shoots him in the back with a shotgun. After watching the events unfold, Gillom enters the hotel, picks up Books's dropped gun, shoots the bartender, and throws the gun away.

Books's narrative ends not just as he wanted but as the direction of his entire life demanded. It is unclear whether or not Books's end was at one with the Good—he is a dying old man, so the virtue of courage was not enough to overcome this particular harm. However, the reflexive use of both the history of John Wayne and the genre of the American Western frames the entire film, so there is a sense in which Books's narrative quest—his telos, the task he is to complete—is to die

Figure 3.2. A telos shot from *The Shootist*. *Source:* Siegel, Don, dir. *The Shootist*. 1976. Hollywood, CA: Paramount Pictures, 2001. DVD, 480p SD.

in a way that does justice to his own life, to the life of the man who brings him into existence in the film (John Wayne), and to the life of the genre itself. This is not to say that if Books had accepted his diagnosis and died quietly from cancer, he would have been demonstrating cowardice. Rather, the film's expression of telos shows that the particular end to which Books was pointed was inextricably tied to the world of the American Western. The reflexivity of Books's telos that is developed throughout the film illustrates his awareness of his own narrative, as well as his willingness to participate in it. The telos of the two central characters in *The Assassination of Jesse James by the Coward Robert Ford*, however, could not be more unequivocally divorced from the Good.

The film follows Robert Ford's (Casey Affleck) ingratiation into the gang led by Jesse James (Brad Pitt). Ford drifts in and out of James's social orbit throughout the film. He idolizes James, but the trajectory of their relationship builds toward Ford's shooting Jesse in the back in his own home for fame and repute. Much of Ford's remaining life is dismal and depressed, and ends in his being murdered in a bar. Despite space given to other members of the gang, the film focuses largely on Ford and James. As with the films considered thus far, *Jesse James* uses telos shots to convey the experience of the narrative quest—but the existence of Ford and James is in total ignorance of the Good. In fact, the virtue wheel at play in *Jesse James* reveals a privation of virtue and goodness (fig. 3.3).

Figure 3.3. A telos shot from *The Assassination of Jesse James by the Coward Robert Ford*. *Source:* Dominik, Andrew, dir. 2007. *The Assassination of Jesse James by the Coward Robert Ford*. 2007. Burbank, CA: Warner Bros. Pictures, 2007. Blu-ray Disc, 1080p HD.

Jesse James notably foregrounds the sensory experiences of characters. The opening monologue of the film, delivered through third-person voiceover (a somewhat unique selection for the genre), describes James in sensorial terms: we hear how James's children "knew his legs, the sting of his moustache against their cheeks" and that "he had two incompletely healed bullet holes in his chest and another in his thigh. He was missing the nub of his left middle finger and was cautious, lest that mutilation be seen. He also had a condition that was referred to as 'granulated eyelids,' and it caused him to blink more than usual as if he found creation slightly more than he could accept." James's presence is given a weight of detail by the unnamed narrator—it establishes both the textural, embodied aspects of his experience as they are experienced by others, and how he experiences his own embodied self. This is further established in more poetic terms, when again in voiceover we hear, "Rooms seemed hotter when he was in them. Rains fell straighter. Clocks slowed. Sounds were amplified." The voiceover establishes the effects of James's presence, the draw he has for all those who encounter him. The virtue wheel, then, is in a sense rigged toward his behavior, at least for characters. Other members of the gang, James's family, and especially Ford define their existence, their telos not toward the Good but toward James. Their virtues (or "virtues"), then, are at least initially ordered toward James's ends, and not the ends shaped by the Good.

The voiceover at the start sets up the film as concerned with the experiential dimensions of its characters' stories, especially with regard to James and Ford. The magnetism James possesses is what captures Ford and draws him along to his demise even after James's death. This is reinforced by the aforementioned telos shots scattered throughout the film and the contemplative and lingering cinematography that foregrounds fine details of the world that struggles to contain James's magnanimous presence—shots of fingers grazing tips of wheat and hovering shots of dust motes floating in air are atypical of the American Western, but serve to reinforce the experiential dimension (rather than the purely plot-related one) of its central characters.

All of these artistic features foreground subjective experience as an important way through which the stories of its two central characters are told. The question remains, though, as to how the film conveys the experience of telos, and how the privation of goodness and virtue is artistically explored as a result. At the simplest level, the character of Ford is often explicit about the ends for which he strives:

for example, he attempts to get close to James and his gang and to have a larger role in his gang; and he kills James for money, fame, a legacy, and other material rewards. James's motivations, though, are less than clear. He is haunted by the specter of death—he is unwell, the color drained from his face, and with a darkness under his eyes. The psychological toll also escalates as the film progresses—his paranoia heightens, his behavior is less controlled, and he is more prone to outbursts and threats. Although he is materially affluent, James seems to be ignorant of the light of the Good, his actions lacking the ordering (or teleological) relation of virtue to goodness.

Ford's actions, despite showing that he is also trying to achieve certain ends, reveal an absence of virtue. His sense of telos—ultimately, to found his legacy as the man (the hero, even) who killed Jesse James—is not motivated by virtue or goodness. Instead, Ford enacts his telos in the interests of a certain self-perception of the narrative he desires his life to have, in a way not dissimilar to Books in *The Shootist*. The toll of a self-defined telos divorced from the Good is written on James's and Ford's bodies—the former's in the impenetrable opacity of his facial features, the latter's through the dismal depression that characterizes his existence after executing the murder. Their skill as outlaws substitutes for the virtuous disposition required to continue on the path of the Good, to put such skill in the service of the Good. The mise-en-scène and cinematography of the telos shot, the use of voiceovers, and aspects of performance cinematography all combine to foreground experience, to reveal the effects of a privation of virtue and goodness, and the misguidedness of their telos anchored in that which should be overcome.

Ford enacts his telos through the violent act of murdering James. In the Wild West, violence is a way of enacting justice—and there is a touch of justice in Ford's killing. After all, James has taken a number of lives and robbed countless trains and banks; however, any sense of justice seems incidental to Ford's motivations for fame and a legacy. Any sense of justice is also removed given the context of the killing—Ford shoots an unarmed James in the back in his own home, with James's young children nearby. Afterward, Ford tries to capitalize on and grow his fame through increasingly embellished public retellings of the events. Ford's demise harkens back to Shane's caution that a man who kills is a changed man, even a marked man. Violence hasn't been used to overcome potential harms in Ford's case, and the telos of Ford's existence is unhinged from the Good toward which it should be ordered.

Thus far I have shown how the American Western artistically explores the metaphysical concepts of goodness, virtue, and telos in both the social context of a practice and the individual context of a narrative quest. In this section, I have emphasized the latter context, demonstrating how the American Western can examine the relation between telos and the Good, particularly through formally representing the experiential dimension of characters' existence. As the analysis of *Jesse James* illustrated—and as has been alluded to throughout this chapter—the metaphysical concepts of goodness, virtue, and telos can become unhinged or separated from one another, and one way this is most readily seen is through the enactment of violence.

In *Meek's Cutoff*, we follow a lost group of settlers and their guide as they struggle in the desert, lacking basic supplies and in a search for water. The group captures a Native American; due to the kindness of some of the settlers, his life is spared, and he agrees (or so he claims) to lead the settlers to water. Certain members of the group act virtuously despite the nonguaranteed nature of the reward that has been promised. The virtues of kindness, even friendship and community, are present despite the fact that there is no formal social community to speak of. The promise of the practice of building and maintaining a social community is dependent on their survival, so the telos of the group is clear, and the collective experience of this telos is only made clearer through the use of telos shots (fig. 3.4).

Elena Gorfinkel suggests that *Meek's Cutoff*'s "slow aesthetic" of landscape and people serves to "index or to unravel the already frayed bonds that draw people together and apart, in impoverishment and in rituals of the everyday, in relations of dependency and debt" (2015, 123). The weight of the group's predicament is felt in the uncomplicated aesthetic of the film, in the long and lingering shots of the harsh environment, and in the characters' ragged and weathered faces.

Any violent act toward the Native American would result in almost certain disaster and death for the group. However, that the film does not depict a physically violent act does not mean that there is no violence. While the settlers ensure the best possible treatment of the Native American and guarantee his survival, the guide of the group, Stephen Meek (Bruce Greenwood), treats the man harshly, particularly in his use of language. For example, Meek describes the

Figure 3.4. A telos shot from *Meek's Cutoff*. *Source:* Reichardt, Kelly, dir. 2010. *Meek's Cutoff*. Brooklyn, NY: Oscilloscope Pictures, 2011. Blu-ray Disc, 1080p HD.

Native American and his way of life as that of a savage, claiming that hell is full of Indians and that even other Indians hate his kind. Therefore, in the section to follow, my consideration of how violence complicates the ways in which the American Western can examine the metaphysical concepts of goodness, virtue, and telos needs to go beyond acts of violence typical for the genre (such as shoot-outs). Furthermore, I need not just to consider the range of violent acts but also to be sensitive to the ways in which such acts are represented in both film and television.

Violence as an Obstacle to Virtue and Goodness

The world of the American Western is an inherently violent one, so it is worth considering how violence complicates the genre's preoccupation with goodness, virtue, and telos in both the individual and in the social context. If violence is one means of overcoming or responding to harms or obstacles, an act of violence may in certain circumstances be a virtuous or honorable act that aims to achieve the Good. Furthermore, as MacIntyre notes, "It is through conflict and sometimes only through conflict that we learn what our ends and purposes are" (2007, 163–164). Virtues help us to refine and develop our understanding of goodness, and they enable us to overcome obstacles—often through conflict of some kind—further revealing the telos of our existence and the extent to which we are ordering it toward the Good. MacIntyre argues that "it is in the course of the quest and only through encountering and coping with the various particular harms, dangers, temptations and distractions which provide any quest with its episodes and incidents that the goal of the quest is finally to be understood. A quest is always an education both as to the character of that which is sought and in self-knowledge" (219). Therefore, not only is it in the overcoming of various obstacles and dangers that we learn the virtues necessary to overcome such obstacles—overcome in the pursuit of the Good—but also that the quest itself becomes intelligible through the overcoming of such obstacles. The two key points here are that, first, conflict is necessary to the understanding of ends—it makes ends intelligible, as it does with regard to the nature of virtue and the Good—and, second, that this is an experiential process, whereby such education occurs not through abstract contemplation of contingent or possible events but through the lived engagement with such obstacles, harms, and dangers. However, this is not an outright justification of violence—after all, conflict and the like can be overcome in various ways, many of them nonviolent—yet violence seems in the American Western to be the necessary pathway to overcome conflict.

The place of violence as a means of overcoming obstacles is further complicated in the American Western because the spectator must consider the act itself contextualized by the narrative, and the stylistic representation of that act. Stephen Prince argues that film violence is "the stylistic encoding of a behavioral act. One can, therefore, examine the behavior or its stylistic depiction" (2006, 11). The inextricability of form and content is a significant reason that one should pay attention to the way violence is represented as a means of understanding the significance of the act itself. A nuanced understanding of a moment of violence and the means by which it is represented is important to our consideration of how such a moment is related to goodness, telos, and virtue. For example, while the original *3:10 to Yuma* lacks the visceral, cannibalistic brutality of *Bone Tomahawk* (2015), the stringing up and hanging of a man in a hotel lobby that takes place in the earlier film is still an inherently violent act despite its restrained stylistic representation, especially compared to the full-blown gore of the later film. Prince further notes that violence is "enacted . . . through a deliberate orchestration of camera positions, lighting, editing, and sound" (11). Cinematic and televisual violence, therefore, is not just a matter of measuring the volume of blood spilled or considering the extent of its depravity. Rather, what is required is a sensitivity to how all the elements of style in the context of the work's narrative shape the violence of the act, its representation, and how it fits within that work's depiction of goodness, virtue, and telos. The earlier analysis of Ford's murdering of James in *Jesse James* is a good illustration of this point.

There is a historical dimension that should be addressed in terms of the place of violence and its representation in the American Western. Lee Clark Mitchell considers the shift in American cinema to a more explicit representation of violence. He argues in terms of the Western that "not only did violence no longer offer moral resolution, it also served only marginally as closure to Western plots now loosely defined" (1996, 224). In the transition from what is commonly understood as the classic Western—the films of John Ford and Anthony Mann from the 1940s and 1950s, for example—to the revisionist Westerns of the 1960s and 1970s, the connection between violence and narrative develops a different meaning. Mitchell doesn't deny that classical Westerns were violent—even in the few examples considered here, I have shown that they are—but rather that violence came to mean something different, both in terms of its place within a narrative and how violent acts were represented. Whereas violence in the earlier films helped, in the language of this chapter, to overcome obstacles and define understandings of the Good and one's telos, the violence in later films (such as *Jesse James*, and the threat of violence in *Meek's Cutoff*) does not tend to have those earlier films' educative, even noble function.

Whether or not we accept Mitchell's distinction, the emphasis on violence and its representation and the connection between violence and narrative are important. In Clint Eastwood's *Unforgiven* (1992), for example, violence is central to the narrative unity of Will Munny's (Clint Eastwood) life and to the quest he is on. The film is also an excellent example of how violence complicates goodness, virtue, and telos. Throughout the film, Munny consistently speaks of who he was and what he did in his past—the awful, violent acts he committed and in particular the women and children he hurt and men he killed. The Munny of the past is in stark contrast to the timid Munny who is remembering the man he once was. In the final gunfight of the film, however, Munny undergoes an extraordinary transformation into the man he once was, whereby the stories previously told become a story relived.

The purpose—the telos—of Munny's narrative quest changes as the film unfolds. It begins as a journey to kill two men responsible for cutting the face of a prostitute so as to gain the monetary reward on offer. It concludes, instead, with the revenge killing of Little Bill Daggett (Gene Hackman), the deceptively cruel and nefarious sheriff of Big Whiskey. Daggett not only killed Munny's friend Ned Logan (Morgan Freeman) but also dealt a vicious beating to Will in an earlier scene in the film. The film's final moment of violence—the moment when Munny and Daggett square off—is significant in terms of the narrative unity of both men's lives, though particularly Munny's. We learn in the film that Daggett was told in horrid detail of Munny's former exploits and that he was untroubled. In a sense, we can understand Daggett as the man Munny once was. Paradoxically, to kill the past, Munny must also and once again become this previous version of himself. The history of violence is unearthed from beneath a weight of technical incompetence—at the start of the film, Munny can't shoot a pistol and struggles to mount a horse.

Eastwood's performance is categorically exquisite, especially in how he transforms into the aged harbinger of violence. Munny's violence is accompanied by terror and doom; Daggett's acts of violence are delivered with pleasure. Two moments illustrate once more Shane's prescient comment about the effects of violence on men. There is the final showdown between Munny and Daggett, and there is also an earlier moment in the film when Munny's riding companion, the Schofield Kid (Jaimz Woolvett), is excitedly telling Munny of the first man he has killed—the second outlaw responsible for harming the prostitute. What begins with giddy pleasure and pride quickly turns into the Kid's sobbing, shaking meekness. Learning a lesson similar to Robert Ford's, the Kid does not find glory in the act of killing, but an existence-shattering act that defies all romanticism: "three shots and he was taking a shit."

Unforgiven—perhaps not entirely unintentionally—also shares something with Eastwood's directorial Western debut, *High Plains Drifter* (1973). In that film, Eastwood plays the Stranger, an ethereal character who emerges out of the horizon and happens upon the lakeside town of Lago, dealing out violence in a variety of ways to townspeople complicit, as we find out, in whipping a US marshal to death. The Stranger's first act is the murder of three men who taunt him; his next is the rape of a townswoman in the livery. The Stranger is employed to protect the town from criminals—the men who actively whipped the marshal to death as the town looked on. In anticipation of their arrival, the Stranger instructs the townspeople in defense, though they are hopelessly inadequate, and a number who actively double-crossed the criminals are gunned down in the final standoff. The Stranger, though, dispatches of the criminals. One is whipped to death in the street—represented only through the sounds of screams and of the whip cutting the air while the remaining townspeople cower inside as they hear the man die. Another criminal is hung to death with a whip. The final criminal is beaten to the draw by the Stranger and gunned down.

The Stranger is a skillful man in overcoming harm, but he is not virtuous (as his opening acts demonstrate), and the violence he inflicts on others is divorced from goodness and virtue. However, his violence is not random—the marshal's whipping reinforces this. The violence is presented viscerally, experientially—for example, shaky POV shots imaginatively place spectators in the shoes of the marshal as he is whipped to death. Furthermore, the soundscape of the film is sparse and silent, though it is punctuated with musical sound effects that can jar. These sound effects are paired with a soundtrack that is reminiscent of a wailing ghost. Whereas the violence at the conclusion of *Unforgiven* in one sense allows the practice of Big Whiskey to continue—whereby justice is dealt both to the men responsible for the harm of the prostitute and to the man (Daggett) unwilling to mete out comparable justice to such men—there seems to be little contribution to the practice of Lago in *High Plains Drifter*. Although using different language than that developed here, Rich Hutson sees instead that *High Plains Drifter* flips the tension of community and individual seen in *High Noon*, arguing: "*High Plains Drifter* presents a portrait of a community that has an amazingly rich and complicated resonance," and what is notable in the film is its "devastating portrait of a frontier community, despite the perspective of the film forcing spectators to be on the side of the isolated drifter, the catalyst, if not the destroyer, of a corrupt social entity" (2007, 101). This complements an observation by Lea Bandy and Kevin Stoehr, in that "Eastwood tended toward characters who were *anti*heroes, driven toward revenge and killing for reasons that had little to do with building or defending a growing civilization" (2012, 243). For the reasons noted, this is arguably truer of *High Plains Drifter* than *Unforgiven*; the Stranger's use of violence for its own sake, at times and in ways that please him, underscores his privation of virtue and the separation of his telos from the Good, despite the limited good perceived by Hutson.

To be sensitive to the connection between violence and narrative requires us to be sensitive to possibilities for how stories can be told—the way in which the medium-specific features of film and television might dictate how the presence of violence shapes the artistic exploration of goodness, virtue, and telos. For that reason, I turn now to the television program *Deadwood* (2004–2006) and consider in greater detail how violence complicates the examination of goodness, virtue, and telos in the social context of a practice. Deadwood is a place of flux and transition, a social community in the very process of formation. As Jason Jacobs notes, "*Deadwood* is a return to first principles, to a point of origin where the fundamentals of societal organisation are worked up and lived out" (2012, 65). The program follows a wide cast of characters whose lives influence and intersect each other in a variety of ways. The narrative capacities of television are suited to the quantity of character arcs and their development, and through the world building that accumulates across episodes and seasons, spectators are immersed in the social locus of the program.

The medium-specific temporal form of television allows *Deadwood*'s violence to accumulate across the expanse of the program. Spectators are treated to standard fare for the American Western—fistfights, shoot-outs, and hangings. There are also primitive medical procedures depicted in shocking detail (such as the passing of kidney stones and the removal of bullets from people both dead and alive), suicide and suicide attempts, stabbings, a plague of smallpox, and the addictive consumption of opium. A reverend suffers from seizures, a Black man is tarred and feathered in the street, a man attempting to smuggle gold out of a mining town has it forcibly removed from his rectum. The son of one of the main characters gets hit by a wild horse and eventually dies, a man's eye gets ripped out in a fistfight in the street, and a man gets spat on in a ritual of humiliation. This is not to mention the steadily rising body count across the program's seasons.

Many of these acts are clearly violent. Others have an enhanced sense of violence through their representation—the camera's unflinching depiction of the reverend's seizures, in tandem with the actor's full-bodied performance, lends this example its violent quality. The inherently violent world of *Deadwood* contextualizes moments as having a violent tenor simply because they are placed in a setting—in a town—that is not yet a practice. For example, in "A Lie Agreed Upon, Part I" (S02E01), Seth Bullock (Timothy Olyphant), the sheriff of *Deadwood*, and Alma Garrett (Molly Parker) are engaged in an act of lovemaking. It is not so much the act itself—enthusiastic though the participants are—that suggest its violence. Instead, it is seen when the camera cuts away to the dining room below Alma's bedroom, where flakes of paint are shown falling from the ceiling onto Alma's adopted daughter, Sofia (Bree Seanna Wall), as she is being tutored. Even the opening credits of the show forecast the violence about to unfold—a chicken is slaughtered, there are pools of blood, a corpse lays in the street, and a man painfully removes the gold from his tooth (Jacobs 2012, 12–14).

Deadwood's use of style is important, because in considering the connection between violence and narrative, we must be sensitive not just to the violence itself but how it is represented. As alluded to earlier, the camera does not shy away from these moments—that they are presented at all, without cutting, is significant. Just as characters cannot escape the extraordinary violence made ordinary by its frequent presence in the community of Deadwood, so too are spectators not afforded relief in the camera's shying away from the existence of such acts. *Deadwood* uses style not just to unflinchingly portray violence but to present the experiential effects of violence too. For example, in one scene, the legendary Al Swearengen (Ian McShane), proprietor of the Gem Saloon, punches another man in the face; a shuddery zoom brings spectators into tighter proximity with the violence being shown. In "Suffer the Little Children" (S01E08), Cy Tolliver (Powers Boothe), the owner of competing saloon the Bella Union, repeatedly knocks, beats, and breaks the skull of a girl who had tried to swindle the Union's hostess out of jewelry. This gruesome scene is not merely shown; it unfolds in slow motion—the camera not just reflecting the proximity of the act but reveling in it and elongating its duration. Proximity rendered visually through style is appropriate for a program whose central theme is community.

As mentioned earlier, violence can be present not just in physical acts but in dialogue and communication too, and it is this latter kind of violence for which the program is especially notable. In "Reconnoitering the Rim" (S01E03), a well-orchestrated symphony of profanity escapes from Wild Bill Hickock's (Keith Carradine) mouth in a tight close-up as he puts a drunken poker opponent in his place. His lips fill much of the screen as he speaks the commanding, measured words, the proximity of the spectators to the violence on screen rendered inescapably intimate through performance, cinematography, sound, and editing.

The program's iconic use of dialogue is intrinsically tied to violence. As Ina Rae Hark notes, "it is important that these curses do carry a palpable threat, for the more violence with which a *Deadwood* character freights his or her language, the more likely it will be that this violence remains discursive and does not spill over into action" (2012, 33). This is not to suggest that the language is nonviolent, but rather that the creative use of verbal threat and discourse between characters serves to limit and temper physical violence, displacing the potential for it into language. However, simultaneously, given that such language is ever-present in *Deadwood*, it also serves to reinforce that so too is violence and the threat of violence. Not all characters reach Swearengen-esque heights of poetic verbal perversity. Seth, for example, is closer to a Clint Eastwood–style cowboy, in that he says little. His tension, though, runs high, and he is set off into destructive violent rages at a moment's notice. As Hark notes, "everything that is emotionally alive in Seth Bullock is so wild and dangerous that he must, essentially, lay it to rest in the most respectful manner possible" (53). There is purpose in his posture, in his gait, and in his glare—he feels justified in his raw brand of justice even prior to wearing the sheriff's badge in Deadwood.

It does not take much for the red mist to descend on Seth—he is both proactive in his violence, as in the case when he beats Alma's father, leaving him spitting his own teeth onto a floor, and ably reactive, as when he beats a Native American who has ambushed him for traipsing through a burial ground. This fistfight in particular is vicious, with Seth beating the Indian's face with a rock well after he has lost consciousness and died. Again, the camera does not shy away, alternating between the Native American's face and Bullock's, reiterating not just the proximity of the characters but the proximity and intimacy of the violence. The narrative of *Deadwood* unfolds among the town of Deadwood's attempts to become an established social practice. Both the narrative and style of the program reinforce the omnipresence of violence. In Deadwood, a town lacking a telos ordered by the Good, violence cannot help but erupt as the most prominent individuals in the town fight to maximize the advancement of their own interests. This also underscores an observation of MacIntyre's: "We human beings are vulnerable to many kinds of affliction and most of us are at some time afflicted by serious ills. How we cope is only in small part up to us. It is most often to others that we owe our survival, let alone our flourishing, as we encounter bodily illness and injury, inadequate nutrition, mental defect and disturbance, and human aggression and neglect" (1999, 1). It is no wonder that in the town of Deadwood—a town still nascent, undergoing formation and establishing its identity and shared understanding of values and goods—the afflictions of others (often due to the violence of the world in which they find themselves) often overcome the still underdeveloped sense of community. There are moments, though, when friendship and community, goodness and virtue, do shine through.

Deadwood uses the temporally extended narrative form of television to temper the moments of violence with moments of tenderness and, indeed, goodness. As with violence, the relationships and even friendships between characters also rest on characters' proximity to one another. Such character development is achieved not just narratively but through visual techniques, such as the prominent use of rack focus. Jacobs notes that "the camp functions analogously to the technique [of racking focus] as a contextualizing plane for the characters we follow and occasionally those background figures will snap into focus and claim their own space" (2012, 68). This is true, but I would argue that racking focus does more than this. It affords spectators a visual means of linking characters' narrative arcs and so tethering characters not necessarily in terms of space but in terms of shared experience and meaning. Early in the program, for example, a rack focus shifts from Trixie (Paula Malcolmson), who is talking to Al on the balcony of the Gem, to Alma in the neighboring hotel, looking out of her window, forecasting the relationship that flourishes and erratically ebbs and flows between Trixie and Alma as the program develops, as well as the parallels of their individual storylines.

If the connections between characters can often be competitive and violent, there are perhaps as many that exemplify the virtues of friendship and companionship. After beating the Native American, Bullock is happened upon by a recent acquaintance, Charlie Utter (Dayton Callie), an old friend of Wild Bill's, who reveals why Bullock was attacked. The two men lay the man in his grave, according to his customs and rituals, with care and respect. Throughout the program there is also friendship in the relationship between Seth and his business partner and coowner of their hardware store, Sol Star (John Hawkes). There is friendship, too, though of a different kind, between Seth and Al. One of the most compelling friendships in the show, though, is between Charlie, Wild Bill, and Calamity Jane (Robin Weigert), which continues after Wild Bill's death. Emerging out of the neighboring woods in a characteristic drunken stupor, Jane finds herself at Wild Bill's graveside and talks to him, updating him on what has been happening in the town. In a later moment, both Charlie and Jane find themselves there, talking to Wild Bill, irritating each other as the closest of siblings do. Despite Jane's abrasive and antagonistic use of language and her erratic intoxicated behavior, in "Deep Water" (S01E02) and the aforementioned "Reconnoitering the Rim" she talks tenderly to Sofia after she has been rescued from outside of town following the slaughter of her family. In the earlier of those two episodes, Jane and Charlie sing "Row, row, row your boat" to her as the image fades to black.

These brief examples point to how *Deadwood* uses the temporally prolonged form of television to balance the privation of virtue and goodness with their presence—to balance violence with friendship. As Jennilyn Merten notes, "*Deadwood*'s varied scenes of intimacy temper the assault of brutality" (2013, 163). In no way is the program's use of style and narrative to balance the omnipresence of violence with love and friendship more powerfully presented than in the closing moments of "A Lie Agreed Upon, Part I," the opening episode of season 2. We watch Seth walk through town, his arms swinging through his purposeful stride in twilight, the warm copper hues of color filtering the image. In voiceover, we hear Seth narrate a letter to his wife, Martha (Anna Gunn)—in plainspoken detail, he describes the different woods and their use in the various structures of the house built for the Bullock family. Pine for the "sills, posts, floor joists, and rafters," spruce for the other framing. He describes the necessary reinforcement of different areas of the house, and the spacing between the boards that lay beneath the floors. The letter concludes with Seth speaking of the hope that he may be a good husband and father. This sequence is slow and poetic, the composition of the letter mirrored in the movement of Seth's walk through the town and his careful articulation in voiceover of the letter's contents. The beauty, simplicity, and promises of devotion in the letter find contrast not just in the emotionless rhythm of his speech, but in the adulterous affair that began the episode (and this analysis). There are many components that make viewing *Deadwood* a compelling experience, particularly regarding its complicated treatment of goodness and virtue, the role of violence, and the narrative expression of these concepts. Family and friendship—flawed and fragile though they are in *Deadwood*—act as small attempts to buttress the violence and threat of chaos. The town continues to exist at times because of, and at times despite, the violence. The goods internal to the practice of Deadwood are achieved only insofar as small virtues break through the muck and the blood of its foundations.

The American Western artistically explores the metaphysical concepts of goodness, virtue, and telos in both the social context of a practice and the individual context of a narrative quest. One of the typical settings of the genre—that of a town or social community—functions as a practice, the existence of which relies on the virtuous actions of some of its members. In this setting, moreover, the wheel of virtue is a device that allows us to consider the embodiment of a particular virtue in different characters as a way to enhance and refine our understanding of specific virtues as well as virtue itself. However, these practices are made up of individuals whose lives can be examined through the lens of a narrative quest with a particular purpose (telos, which the genre formally articulates through what I term the telos shot). Westerns can thus present the experiential dimension of a character's story and in so doing reveal a complexity and nuance to the ideas of telos, virtue, and goodness as they relate to the individual context of a particular character's existence—even a privation of virtue and goodness can crystallize our understanding of these concepts and their connection to telos. The omnipresence of violent acts and language in addition to how they are represented in the American Western complicates the genre's expression of the metaphysical concepts of goodness, virtue, and telos.

The world of the American Western is an inherently violent one, yet in the analysis of *Deadwood* that concluded this chapter, I demonstrated how a loving friendship is but one way that violence and individual frailties can be overcome. As Sue Matheson notes, "Love remains a constant feature in the Western, underpinning . . . characters' acts of social transgression and personal transformation" (2013, 3). In the struggles of nascent communities that populate the genre, made up as they are of characters who struggle to be virtuous and to pursue the Good in the face of great harms and dangers, the Western offers a rich examination and depiction of narratives that explore the place of goodness, virtue, and telos, and violence, friendship, and even love in the shared social environment of a town. The genre articulates the richness of human experience, and the struggle to find one's footing in the world, to identify a purpose, and to pursue it to the end.

4

How Does Julie Grieve?

Qualia and the Texture of Subjective Experience

In Lynne Ramsay's *We Need to Talk about Kevin* (2011), Eva Khatchadourian (Tilda Swinton) attempts to restart her life after her son, Kevin (Ezra Miller), murders several of his schoolmates and his father, Franklin (John C. Reilly), and younger sister, Celia (Ashley Gerasimovich). Swinton's performance imbues Eva with an emotional muteness and facial catatonia that alienates her interiority from the spectator as much as it isolates Eva from the world she inhabits in the film. Eva is at various moments pitied, angrily blamed for her son's actions, or cruelly humiliated by coworkers, neighbors, and people she encounters on the street. She often withdraws: physically from the world surrounding her, spending long stretches of the day and night in her darkened home, and mentally, as the film shows us, into her memories of the past and the recollections of her relationship with her son. Narrative, performance, and style—especially through the motif of the color red—work together to attempt to convey something of what it is like for Eva to subjectively experience the world around her. Part of this experience is contained through the alienated qualities of performance just mentioned; we are to gather that Eva's life is no longer an especially rich one. It is not one invested in the world around her, and the film slowly charts her attempts to reach an existential position where she can begin anew.

The opening flashback scene shows Eva participating in the La Tomatina Festival in Spain, soaked in the vivid, bright red of squashed tomatoes. The color red is established from the outset and revisited consistently throughout the film—Eva's face bathed in red light, the noticeably heightened red of such objects as toys, seats, posters, and tomato soup cans, as well as a spilled glass of wine that stains the carpet, and paint used to vandalize Eva's house and car. In these two final examples, the red's purpose in the film—narratively and in telling spectators something of Eva's experience of the world—is clear. Presumably those responsible for the paint, for example, could have chosen any color, but opted for red—the splattered pattern across the house and car calling to mind the blood her son spilled with his bow and arrow at the school and the Khatchadourian home. Given the film's strict association between the world of the film and Eva's experience of it, the use of red serves an expressive purpose, too. In the film's present, the red expresses the pervasive, nagging, haunting reminder of the past events that so shattered her world and the world of the community of which she is a part. In the film's flashbacks, which are presented as memories and so as past events imbued with the knowledge of the present, the red expresses forewarnings of the violence that eventuated.

Thus the film is attempting to communicate, through various stylistic, narrative, and formal devices, what it is like for Eva to experience her world—that is, what it is like to be a mother of a murderous son, to attempt to restart her life, and to try to draw meaning from her existence in the wake of such tragedy for which (at least from certain areas of the community) she is being blamed. These aspects of Eva's existence involve an inclusive understanding of the term *qualia*—the "what it is like" aspect of subjective experience. However, these brief comments on *Kevin* provoke certain questions: To what extent can works represent qualia, and which artistic capacities of films and television programs are central in doing so? How can spectators "verify" the authenticity of such a representation?

Kevin is an artistically sophisticated work that captures many of the interests of this chapter. It offers an opportunity to consider what qualia are, and how the phenomenal aspects of subjective experience can find their way into films and television programs by externalizing the "my" of an individual's interiority. Moreover, *Kevin* invites us to consider how works can offer a representation of a world via a character's experience of it. Although *Kevin* doesn't rely on POV shots, this technique is one (contested) way in which works can aspire to do this. However, one of the central concerns of this chapter is to go beyond the POV shot and to consider a range of artistic and formal ways in which films and television programs can represent the qualia of a character's experience. As I will show, this requires a more nuanced understanding of and attention to different dimensions of artistic realism—perceptual, subjective, psychological, and expressive—to appreciate the challenge to spectators in interpreting various aspects of a work as being connected to the qualia of a character's subjective experience (as opposed to artistic flourishes disconnected from such representational aims). These considerations form the basis of the remainder of the chapter, wherein I consider the ways that different dimensions of realism combine to represent the qualia of a character's grief, how the temporally elongated narrative form of television affords a different means of representing a character's subjectivity, and how animated works can operate both as a limit case of representing qualia and as having an artistically expressive freedom to represent, for example, the qualia associated with one sensory domain (taste or sound) through another (vision).

Qualia: What Is It Like?

In 1974, Thomas Nagel asked: "What is it like to be a bat?" The purpose of Nagel's question was to highlight the subjective nature—or quality—of consciousness. As Nagel argued, "An organism has conscious mental states if and only if there is something that it is like to be that organism—something it is like for the organism" (1980, 160). Nagel's comments implicitly address the concept of qualia, or the "what it is like" aspect of subjective experience.

Qualia are involved in any sensory experience (Wright 2008, 7), and as Michael Tye (2018) suggests, there are different ways in which the term is used throughout philosophy of mind; here, I am concerned with the most general sense, which is "the introspectively accessible, phenomenal aspects of our mental lives" or the "phenomenal character" of an experience (n.p.). I adopt this rather than other views of qualia, as it underpins my interest in how films and television programs can "externalize" or "bring out" what would ordinarily be the aspects of experience that are only interiorly, or subjectively, accessible, thereby making them available to spectatorial experience.

Qualia, in this inclusive view, refer to phenomenal features of an experience—that is, an experience's "feel" or "texture" (Kind 2008; Tye 2018). Amy Kind notes, "Qualia are often referred to as the *phenomenal* properties of experience, and experiences that have qualia are referred to as being *phenomenally conscious*. Phenomenal consciousness is often contrasted with intentionality (that is, the representational aspects of mental states). Some mental states—for example, perceptual experiences—clearly have both phenomenal and intentional aspects" (2008, n.p.). Both Wright and Kind note that qualia refer to the feel of some sort of experience (across all sense modalities), rather than referring to the object(s) of that experience. Therefore, when considering the qualitative nature of an experience, one is concerned not so much with the representational aspects of the object of the experience, but what it is like to experience that thing. As Kind notes, however, certain kinds of experiences will have both phenomenal and intentional (representational) aspects.

In this chapter, I am interested in how films and television programs can artistically realize the feel or texture—the phenomenal aspects—of a range of experiences. To take an example, I do not claim that what it is like for the central character in Krzysztof Kieślowski's *Three Colours: Blue* (1994) to experience grief is what it is like for all people to experience grief. Rather, in showing one way in which it is possible to experience grief—to show what it is like for Julie (Juliette Binoche) to experience grief via the artistic capacities of the film—is to provide spectators an opportunity to develop and refine their own understanding of what it might be like to experience grief at all. In watching films and television programs that artistically render characters' subjective experience, spectators can not only perceive a particular experience (such as grief) afresh but also grasp some of the invariant qualities of grieving, in addition to certain aspects of grief for characters in specific circumstances. Spectators can reflectively navigate the general features of a certain kind of experience (grief) and the particular (subjective) ways in which that is given expression in a film or television program. Part of the value of such reflection lies in the ways spectators can appreciate what it might be like for another person to experience something that is otherwise inaccessible given its subjective nature.

Implied in any consideration of qualia is the idea of embodied subjectivity. The quale of any subjective experience always involves a particular subject, and the phenomenal qualities of that experience are perceived through all sense modalities. Michael Tye notes that "the phenomenal character of an experience is what it is like subjectively to undergo the experience. If you are told to focus your attention upon the phenomenal character of your experience, you will find that in doing so you are aware of certain qualities. These qualities—ones that are accessible to you when you introspect and that together make up the phenomenal character of the experience are sometimes called 'qualia'" (2018, n.p.). So to focus on the phenomenal character of a subjective experience—an experience of grief, for example—is to emphasize certain aspects of that experience over others. It does not so much aim to answer the question, "What is grief?" but to answer, "What can it be like to experience grief?" However, it should be clear that an at least rudimentary answer to the first question is necessary in answering the second. In experiencing a certain character's experience of grief in a film such as *Three Colours: Blue*, spectators can consider the nature of grief in light of this depiction and navigate the dynamic between the general and particular mentioned earlier. Moreover, in considering the depiction of the character's grief, spectators can also consider the more fundamental idea of qualia itself.

Shaun Gallagher and Dan Zahavi suggest that the subjectivity of an experience constitutes the experience, in that "a minimal form of self-consciousness is a constant structural feature of conscious experience. Experience happens for the experiencing subject in an immediate way and as part of this immediacy, it is implicitly marked as *my* experience" (2012, 52). In the context of film and television, part of the challenge to spectators is to interpret how this "my" becomes "their"—that is, how it is that we understand certain stylistic, formal, and narrative attributes of a film or television program as representing the phenomenal qualities of a character's experience. Gallagher and Zahavi continue, arguing that "self-consciousness must be understood as an intrinsic feature of the primary experience.... It is tacit, and very importantly, thoroughly non-observational (that is, it is not a kind of introspective observation of myself) and non-objectifying (that is, it does not turn my experience into a perceived or observed object)"

(2012, 52). Self-consciousness is an important part of the subjectivity of experience because it reaffirms that a certain experience not only belongs to an individual but is distinctively or particularly that individual's experience. Even though two people might grieve the loss of the same person—two siblings grieving the loss of a parent, say—it is not the case that the qualia of that experience of grief will be the same for both parties. Nor is it the case that one can know what it is like for the other merely because their experience of grief is shared. In the world of ordinary experience, we do not have direct access to the qualia of another person's experience. However, this is exactly what films and television programs can afford in artistically expressing the "my"—the subjective, phenomenal features—of a character's experience.

Murray Smith connects art's capacity to represent qualia to its cognitive value. He suggests that "if art can provide us with knowledge, and if it is uniquely or especially well-placed to furnish us with particular kinds of knowledge, then phenomenal knowledge—knowing what it is like to perceive and experience from a particular point of view—must be a frontrunner" (2017, 118). While I am not concerned with the strong claim that art can uniquely produce certain kinds of knowledge, the aim of this chapter is to examine some of the ways in which films and television programs can shape our understanding of the concept of qualia itself, the invariant features of particular qualia, and certain ways in which these qualia are experienced subjectively.

There is a range of means by which films can aim to convey the qualia of a character's experience, in that the expression of the phenomenal features of a character's experience is tied to a work's interplay of form and content. Central to films such as Spike Jonze's *Being John Malkovich* (1999), Julian Schnabel's *The Diving Bell and the Butterfly* (2007), and *Kevin*, for example, is the means by which the subjective, qualitative experience of characters is realized through the formal properties available to cinema. The first two films notably use POV shots to function as the first-person perspective of given characters (the latter of which I will revisit later in this chapter), whereas *Kevin*'s use of color, performance, and narrative form as mentioned earlier expressively explores the shifts in Eva's relationship with her son and her experience of the world.

Evoking a character's subjective experience is not limited to the visual domain, as sound can also be effective in establishing a strong sense of a character's subjectivity. For example, in the Coen Brothers'

The Man Who Wasn't There (2001), Ed Crane's (Billy Bob Thornton) reflective voiceovers function to highlight that the film is not just a story but the story of a particular character, who, in recounting the narrative events of the film, imbues them with his subjectivity through the work's sonic form. Purely through retelling the events of the film, Ed provides spectators with a sense of what it was like to experience those events. This series of brief examples points to how the various elements of (in this case, cinematic) style establish a clear sense of subjectivity—the formal properties of these works establish as central to them the experiences of that world by the characters who exist within it, and thus the spectator's experience of the films' world is mediated through the subjectivity of the characters.

The subjective experience of characters is critical to a swathe of contemporary television programs, too, as seen in *The Killing* (2007–2012), *Breaking Bad* (2008–2013), *The Bridge* (2011–2018), *Top of the Lake* (2013–), *True Detective* (2014), *Mr. Robot* (2015–), *Atlanta* (2016–), *Legion* (2017–), and *Sharp Objects* (2018). As with the films mentioned earlier and those given more sustained consideration later, style, form, and narrative in certain television programs are used not just to artistically express what happens to a character in terms of plot points and narrative arcs but to artistically represent the phenomenal features of a character's experience of the world they inhabit. In the case of television programs such as those mentioned here, temporal prolongation acts in tandem with other elements of form to further enrich the representation of a character's qualitative experience of their world.

It is here that the second central idea underpinning this chapter—what I term the doubling of experience—is pivotal. I do not mean to suggest that the doubling of experience refers to two different kinds of experience that are at play. It refers, rather, to spectators' attunement to how the formal properties of a work are used to express the phenomenal qualities of a character's subjective experience. In understanding that such a work uses the subjectivity of characters to mediate the representation of the world, one can begin to see how more than just first-person formal techniques (i.e., POV shots and subjective sound) can be used to express the phenomenal qualities of a character's experience. If the narrative is preoccupied with the experiences of an individual—with Eva in *Kevin*, for example—then the story does not need to be told entirely through POV shots from

Eva's perspective. Instead, the range of formal techniques (such as flashbacks and the use of color) that are deployed in that film in tandem with the narrative give a sense of the phenomenal characteristics of Eva's subjective experience of the film's/her world. The doubling of experience therefore is not a literal doubling in the sense that we experience in an identical way what Eva experiences; rather it refers to the aspect of spectatorship whereby our spectatorial experience is of an experience that is being rendered through the artistic capacities of, in this case, film.

My understanding of the doubling of experience is informed by Smith's structure of sympathy, which he develops to examine questions surrounding cinematic emotion and character identification. The structure of sympathy involves a move from recognition to alignment to allegiance. Recognition regards "the spectator's construction of character: the perception of a set of textual elements, in film typically cohering around the image of a body, as an individuated and continuous human agent" (Smith 1995, 82). Alignment "describes the process by which spectators are placed in relation to characters in terms of access to their actions, and to what they know and feel" (83). As Smith notes, this is akin to literary theory's idea of focalization, whereby "narratives may feed story information to the reader [spectator] through the 'lens' of a particular character" (83). According to Smith, alignment is constituted by two components: spatiotemporal attachment, which refers to "the way a narration may follow the spatio-temporal path of a particular character throughout the narrative or divide its attention among many characters," and subjective access, which involves "the way the narration may vary the degree to which the spectator is given access to the subjectivities—the dispositions and occurrent states—of characters" (142). Finally, allegiance "pertains to the moral evaluation of characters by the spectator" (84), which relies on "the spectator having what she takes to be reliable access to the character's state of mind, or understanding the context of the character's actions, and having morally evaluated the character on the basis of this knowledge" (Smith 1995, 84).

Here, I am not so much concerned with the question of identification and the debate surrounding the extent to which spectators experience the emotions of screen characters, nor am I interested in claiming the extent to which spectators may have sympathy or empathy for screen characters. Rather, my interests lie in how the formal capacities of films and television programs can render the subjectivity of characters onscreen. I am therefore primarily concerned with recognition and alignment/focalization, constituted by spatiotemporal attachment and subjective access (insofar as alignment also involves recognition). In a film such as *Kevin*, for example, spectators identify Eva as Eva for the duration of the film (recognition). However, more than this—and, adapting Smith's structure to my concerns here—the film is also focalized through or aligned with Eva's experiences of the events and world of the film. In this way, works such as *Kevin* use the artistic capacities available to each art form to poetically or expressively convey the qualia of a given experience. This unity of form, style, and narrative expresses the phenomenality of the character's subjective experiences.

But how might spectators go about understanding certain elements of a film's style as representing that experience, as opposed to simply expressively disclosing the world of the film? How can films express something that is ordinarily attained by the subject's introspective attention, and why might this matter to film experience? These questions develop some of the concerns raised by Nagel (1980) in his philosophical discussion of what it is like to be a bat. Before returning to that paper, though, it will be helpful to consider an example drawn from the world of film to set up some of the possible limits of film's artistic capacities to express qualia.

In Hall Bartlett's *Jonathan Livingston Seagull* (1973), we follow the eponymous seagull as he is banished from his flock for behaving with concerning individuality—namely, by trying to fly at ever greater speeds, never seen by the other members of the flock to which he belonged. The film charts Jonathan's personal odyssey of self-discovery, far from his home flock and out into the reaches of the world. The film's virtuosic cinematography and editing, filming the movements of real-life seagulls to construct the story, helps to offset some of its more dated and hackneyed elements, such as its particular use of voiceover and occasional labors in narrative development. We see seagulls swooping and soaring in close-up and cast as specks across the endless hues of sunset skies and floating mounds of large, fluffy clouds. We also get occasional POV shots from Jonathan's perspective— trying to convey the speed and agility with which he slices through the coastal air.

The camera's movement in such POV shots aspires to convey something of what it is like to be, if not any seagull, certainly Jonathan. That is, in the use of the camera, the film looks to give us, the spectators, a first-person perspective of Jonathan's experience. However, this aspect of the film's cinematography is one that is noticeably "cinematic"—at points the footage is clearly sped up, working against the largely documentarian or naturalistic visual style of much of the film, such as the poetic long shots and close-ups that represent Jonathan and the other seagulls. At times, then, the spectator's attention is drawn to the cinematic means by which Jonathan's experience is represented, rather than to the representation itself. The means of expressing any particular qualitative aspects of Jonathan's experience in these moments thus work against the artistic conveying of such experience, so the representation is limited in its attempts at showing spectators what it is like for Jonathan to experience the world—his world. The artistic way in which the experience is intended to be represented undermines a realistic or authentic portrayal of the character's experience of the world (let alone what that might be like for a real-world seagull). The spectator's capacity to understand through these moments what it is like for Jonathan, then, is obstructed somewhat by the artistic means of their portrayal.

In considering the limits of how we might know what it is like for someone or something other than ourselves to have an experience of some kind, Nagel, again writing of bats, suggests that "in so far as I can imagine this [what it is like to be a bat] . . . it tells me only what it would be like for *me* to behave as a bat behaves. . . . I am restricted to the resources of my own mind, and those resources are inadequate to the task" (1980, 161). There is something of this idea underlying what Erica Fudge describes as "inevitable anthropocentrism," in that humans seek to understand nonhumans by humanizing (anthropomorphizing) them (2000, 5).

For David Herman, Nagel looks to provide a partial solution to the problem of other minds via an "objective phenomenology," or "a theory of what it's like to be a particular kind of creature based on the creature's physiological structure, perceptual capabilities, behavioral dispositions, and so forth" (2018, 214). Conceding the incompleteness (after all, according to Nagel completeness is not possible) of such an approach, Nagel suggests that his so-called objective phenomenology's goal "would be to describe, at least in part, the subjective character of experiences in a form comprehensible to beings incapable of having those experiences" (1980, 166). These comments capture how I understand films and television programs to express the qualia of various kinds of experiences. Given the adaptation of these ideas to the realm of film experience, I am not as concerned as Nagel with the question of incapability (though these concerns would apply to the example of *Jonathan Livingston Seagull*, likely with additional problems given Jonathan is a fictionalized, semi-anthropomorphized seagull). Rather, I would suggest that the kind of objective phenomenology Nagel articulates is what films and television programs do in representing the qualitative features of a character's experience.

A film can "describe"—expressively, if not naturalistically—through style and narrative an experience of grief, for example. Spectators can match up their own experiences with those depicted onscreen (should they have experienced such in their own lives), though not necessarily just to test and verify its legitimacy. After all, legitimacy is not necessarily the central question—for example, what it is like for one character to grieve as represented in a film may plausibly differ from what it is like for a spectator to grieve in the world of ordinary experience, without the cinematic representation being deemed inauthentic. More important, spectators can consider the dynamics between grief's general characteristics and its subjective embodiment in a certain character's experience as represented onscreen. While these sorts of considerations might unfold in the course of experiencing a particular work, spectators would likely work through such reflections after the fact.

Given the complexities involved in artistic expression, that representation's relation to reality, and the contingency of a spectator's taking up such considerations in terms of a character's qualia, it might be a step too far to expect a film to be able to convey what it is like to be a seagull. After all, despite *Jonathan Livingston Seagull*'s evocative attempts at showing the movement of gulls, the film is perceptually lacking in that the POV shots do not represent the ultraviolet vision of these birds. (Nagel [1980, 161] notes something similar regarding bats.) Moreover, the ways in which the reflexive cinematography draws attention to its own cinematic qualities rather than effectively representing the qualitative experience of the birds operate to prevent spectators from experiencing what it is like (even imaginatively) to be Jonathan (or a seagull). (Herman [2018, 217–21] addresses similar concerns as they relate to a piece of historical fiction and how it uses certain prosaic techniques to convey something of an eagle's experiences.) Despite the failure of POV shots in *Jonathan Livingston Seagull* to re-create the perceptual realities of a seagull, there is an intuitive sense that this stylistic technique is ideally placed to show spectators what it is like for a character to have some sort of experience. This view, though, is a contended one (Branigan 1992, 142–60), and certain scholars have expressed skepticism that POV shots can do anything other than show us the world of a film.

POV and Perceiving Characters

Delmer Daves's film *Dark Passage* (1947) is one notable example that features extensive use of POV shots for much of the film, showing the world of the film and its narrative from the POV of San Quentin prison escapee Vincent Parry (Humphrey Bogart). The film's opening scenes show the aftermath of the escape, with Parry stowed away in an empty barrel on the back of a truck leaving the prison. Using his weight to throw himself off, he rolls down a hill and under a bridge; he then stalks toward the road looking to hitchhike away from San Quentin, being careful to avoid the fleet of police motorcycles searing toward the prison as an alarm blares indication of his escape.

As Julian Hanich notes, the way in which a camera moves in combination with what it shows helps to establish something of the reality of a character's perceptual capacities (2011, 130–131). In this example, the POV shots are combined with camera movement as Parry makes his way to the road, the camera whipping left and right anxiously at the sound of sirens, prompting not just the notion of head movement but something of Parry's emotional state (something that was given extensive consideration in production [Sobchack, 2011, 72–74]). It is critical to note that the camera movement is contextualized by the narrative of the film; in a different narrative context, spectators may well be cued to associate a different emotional state to Parry's head movements as indicated by the camera.

Despite the POV shot's apparent primacy as a stylistic technique that represents the subjective experience of characters (there is an adjacent, well-traveled debate in cognitivist film studies regarding whether POV shots allow spectators to imagine from the "inside" of characters: for an affirmative example, see Smith 1997; for a skeptical view, see Choi 2005), certain scholars are skeptical. Gregory Currie suggests that in films, "What is depicted on screen is depicted as belonging to the world, and not to experience of the world" (2011, 42). Currie uses the POV shot to illustrate this point: "The images we count as PoV show us what the character's visual experience is *of*, and what a visual experience is of is part of the world that we experience" (42). Currie argues that "what is depicted in a film image, if it depicts anything, is always some aspect of the world and never any aspect of experience of the world" (41). In Currie's view, POV shots merely show the world of the work from the perspective of the character, and in showing the world, they do not show the experience of that world. Moreover, Currie suggests that "we may see what the character sees, and we may see things as they see them, having experiences ourselves which are relevantly like their own. But we do not see their seeing of it" (41).

Currie instead locates the peculiar contribution of a POV shot not so much in terms of how the world of a work is represented but rather that the world is unequivocally represented from the perspective of a character. He argues that "what is distinctive about them [POV shots] is not what they show, but what is communicated by the act of presenting them to an audience. By seeing the shot in a certain relation to other shots, and in the context of the narrative's development so far, I understand that I am to imagine that what is depicted is what is seen by the character, and seen by the character pretty much as it is depicted" (2011, 42). I understand Currie to mean that a POV shot is not distinctive because it shows the world—after all, on Currie's account, all kinds of shots show the world of the film, because that is all a shot can do. Rather, a POV shot is distinctive in Currie's view because it prompts a spectator to imagine that what is depicted is merely of the world from the perspective of a character, more or less as represented. However, is this all a POV shot does?

In Steven Soderbergh's *Contagion* (2011), we follow the progress of a highly contagious disease as it spreads across the world. Patient Zero, Beth Emhoff (Gwyneth Paltrow), has returned to Minneapolis from Hong Kong, stopping in Chicago on the way to engage in an adulterous tryst. Once home, Beth is in the process of succumbing to the then unknown virus. In her kitchen, we see her ailing face and then a POV shot, blurry in its lack of focus. This shot is certainly of the world of the film, and it is a shot of the world of the film from a particular character's perspective, but the world is not lacking focus— Beth's perception of it is. So in this particular moment it would seem that the POV shot is not *only* of the world, but clearly of aspects of a character's experience of it too. The POV shot is used in tandem with the narrative context of the film as well as Paltrow's performance of Beth to convey something of her experience, and, critically, this is incomplete. Spectators cannot experience all qualitative features of Beth's condition, although we may imaginatively (and speculatively) fill in the gaps with our own experiences of being unwell.

Another example: in *The Diving Bell and the Butterfly*, spectators are aligned—for much of the film through POV shots—with Jean-Dominique Bauby (Mathieu Almaric), a former editor of French *Elle* magazine who suffered a debilitating stroke, the main effect of which is locked-in syndrome. Jean-Dominique is able to understand what people say to him, but cannot move or express himself except through a system of blinks developed with his speech therapist. Again, we see various moments of shifting focus and other visual flourishes that indicate not just shots of the world from the perspective of a particular character but also what it is like for Jean-Dominique to experience the world. The use of cinematography attunes us not just to the world of the film but to Jean-Dominique's experience and seeing of the world. As noted earlier, POV shots are used with other techniques—at various points throughout the film, a lack of clarity in the aural domain represents Jean-Dominique's affected hearing, though as with the example from *Contagion*, the film cannot re-create the character's qualitative subjective experience in totality. In the context of *Diving Bell*, this is important, as such incompleteness motivates a particular kind of other-focused, spectatorial attention—it invites a response that is involved in the doubling of experience, which has a distinct ethical component. As Jane Stadler articulates, the film's reliance on POV shots "engages the film audience ethically, perceptually, affectively, and cognitively in perspective sharing, thereby communicating a compassionate vision of how Bauby sees the world and how he is seen by others. The range of aesthetic techniques allows subjective, experiential immersion as well as more reflective distance" (2013, 39). In using POV shots to express a character's experience of the world, a film relies on a designed use of form and content that is motivated by the nature of its narrative. As Edward Branigan notes, "A POV shot is subjective because we see space from the character's point in space. Since we are witnessing *what* a particular person sees in a POV shot, it is an easy step to represent *how* that person sees an object" (1984, 94). Currie is correct to note that what we see in a POV shot is a representation of the world of the film from the perspective of a particular character; however, the myriad ways such shots can be artistically realized and used in combination with other aspects of style and form indicate how such a shot can be both of the world and of the character's experience of the world.

Qualia and Dimensions of Artistic Realism

POV shots—in combination with other stylistic and formal techniques and the specifics of the work's narrative—are capable of representing elements of a character's qualitative subjective experience. They do so through a largely naturalistically motivated attempt to re-create the perceptual capacities of the character. This might be more (as in *Contagion* and *Diving Bell*) or less (as in *Jonathan Livingston Seagull*) successfully realized in a particular work. However, other formal or stylistic techniques that aspire to further externalize the subjective phenomenality of a character's experience will likely need to move beyond a naturalistic approach to representation toward that of an expressive one. The challenge to spectators then regards how we are to understand certain elements of a work's style and form to be conveying the qualia of an experience rather than functioning as a decorative or ornamental artistic flourish, for example. These issues are related to the myriad ways in which films and television programs are seen to be realistic. In the context of this discussion, I understand realism as it pertains to film and television as involving the use of style, form, and narrative in the representation of a work's world and the character's experience of that world. In my view, realism is not simply a way of establishing the likeness of a work's world to that of the ordinary world; rather, it involves the internal logic by which that work's world can operate. In the case of qualia, the stylistic, formal, and narrative means by which a work expresses and discloses aspects of its world also include the ways in which the work mediates such disclosure via the representation of a character's experience of that world.

There will be varying degrees of resemblance between a film's world and our own world, and that resemblance may be anchored in a kind of naturalistic, "documentary," or literalist use of style and form—simply showing things happening in a film world in a way purportedly verisimilar to how they happen in the ordinary world—or in attempting to expressively represent phenomenal features of experience. Films that take the expressive route can therefore be realistic in my sense of the term, though in a way that perhaps runs counter to common usage. The different ways in which films can be said to be realistic therefore necessitates a rich and multifaceted view of artistic realism. My focus will be on four dimensions: perceptual, subjective, psychological, and expressive realism.

Offering a simpler example than a film, Currie suggests that "the experience of recognizing a picture of a horse is in an important respect like the experience of recognizing a horse when you see one" (1995, 90). This holds for what Currie calls "naturally generative" depictions, which rely on our recognition of the thing being represented (88–89). This idea underpins perceptual realism in that there is an interplay between the means of representation on the one hand and the spectator's ability to recognize what is being represented on the other. POV shots from films such as *Contagion* and *Diving Bell* operate—in a perceptually realistic if experientially partial way—on an understanding of the ordinary operations of vision to then undercut them in various ways as appropriate to their respective narratives. On the other hand, *Jonathan Livingston Seagull* represents a failure to create a perceptually realistic depiction of a seagull's vision in its use of POV shots. For films that seek to represent the phenomenal aspects of a character's experience in an expressive way the possibility of perceptual realism is complicated by the filmmaker's attempt to represent something that isn't strictly speaking an object, as well as by the contingency of the spectator's drawing together different expressive properties of the film into an understanding that those properties do in fact contribute to the film's representation of, for example, a character's grief.

The second dimension of realism is subjective realism, which refers to a film that "represents the subjective perspective of its central character" (Campora 2014, 7). It is a "type of realism that approximates for the spectator something resembling the direct experience of a character in the film" (55). Regardless of how we interpret Campora's use of "direct"—whether in a strict sense confined to POV shots and subjective sound, for example, or in a more inclusive sense that involves other stylistic techniques, subjective realism does seem to allow for the representation of phenomenal, qualitative aspects of a character's experiences. Carl Plantinga also seems to be attuned to this point, in that he suggests that "a film is not only a way of seeing, but also a way of hearing, feeling, thinking, and responding. It presents not just a mental universe (of perception and cognition), but a holistic experience connected to the emotions, affects, and the body. It offers a particular experience of what it displays, of the fictional world presented. This way of experiencing mimics the phenomenological contours of conscious experience generally, and thus is complex and multifaceted" (2009, 49). Subjective realism as a dimension of artistic realism is more expansive than perceptual realism. It opens up the possibilities of expressively representing the phenomenal aspects of a character's subjective experience that may not be strictly perceptually accurate but nevertheless realistic. *Three Colours: Blue*'s use of blue works in exactly this way, as does *Kevin*'s use of red—it is not necessarily always the case that the use of color in each work is perceptually congruent with how the colors are being experienced by each character. Rather, the use of color is used expressively to represent some element of their experience of their world.

Psychological realism involves an "emphasis on the form of character, which . . . is inseparable not just from elements like dialogue and performance but from the ways that audiences attribute emotion, intention, consciousness, and more to a character" (Stevens 2015, 3). Kyle Stevens suggests we understand psychological realism as "a host of styles that makes available the attribution of minds, a means of thinking about perceived or imagined psychological objects, those feelings, thoughts, desires, etc. that only *ever* exist (or existed) in spectators' minds. It is about our familiarity with, and our estrangement from, kinds of relations" (2015, 17). Whereas subjective realism addresses primarily the representation of a character's phenomenal experience through form, style, and narrative, psychological realism emphasizes the ways in which spectators aim to identify certain artistic aspects of a work as specifically associated with a given character's experience. That is, it involves verifying the artistic aspects of a work as externalizing the "my" of a character's experience of the world in various ways. The attributed minds of characters are not just manifested through the bodily work of cinematic performance but can extend into representational aspects that stylistically mediate such performance to spectators as well. Encompassed in this understanding of the attributed mind are the phenomenal aspects of experience—the qualia of a character's experience of the cinematic world they inhabit.

Two examples will illustrate the connection between subjective and psychological realism. In Fritz Lang's noir film *Scarlet Street* (1945), we follow Christopher Cross (Edward G. Robinson), an undiscovered artist with remarkable talent, who falls for the film's fraudulent femme fatale Kitty (Joan Bennett). Cross has fortuitously met Kitty and misled her into believing he is a wealthy artist. The film follows Kitty and her temperamental lover Johnny (Dan Duryea) as they attempt to fleece Cross for all of his apparent money. Cross's obsession with Kitty, and Kitty's suggestion of her reciprocal feelings for him, result in his losing his job and his marriage. Finally "free" of it all, he declares his desire to have a future with Kitty, only for her to laugh manically at his folly. Cross kills her and frames Johnny, who goes to the electric chair.

Cross's days, though, are not characterized by relief or the prospect of a fresh start. Instead, he is haunted by his actions. In the film's penultimate scenes, Cross has checked into a cheap hotel. Entering the room, he is disheveled, lightly staggering as he takes off his coat and hat. As he turns off the room's light, he starts to hear loving, sing-song whispers echo between Kitty and Johnny from beyond the grave. Earlier in the film, Cross's overhearing of similar words had alerted him to their deceit. The flashing neon light outside the window beats away relentlessly as Cross checks behind the drawn bedroom curtain for a human presence, before lying down and mopping his brow with the back of his hand, the whispers now mocking him for inadvertently "reuniting" them forever. The use of lighting, voice—not just in dialogue but in tenor, timbre, and quality—and Robinson's performance of Cross are woven together to present what it is like for Cross to now experience the world. He cannot escape the regret of his past actions, and it colors and conditions his existence. Moreover, the designed and combined use of these different artistic devices clearly establishes that they are expressively associated with Cross's experience, despite a lack of complete perceptual fidelity.

In Charles Vidor's *Cover Girl* (1944), we follow dancer Rusty (Rita Hayworth), the star attraction at Danny Maguire's (Gene Kelly) nightclub, who enters a competition to be the newest cover girl of *Vanity* magazine. Winning the competition—and with newfound interest from the likes of manager Noel Wheaton (Lee Bowman)—Rusty, spurred partly on by Danny's pigheaded refusal to admit his feelings for her and to ask her to remain at his club, pursues her newfound fame and attention, leading to Wheaton's offering to marry her. Still wrestling with her diverging interests (professional and romantic), Rusty stands Danny up, failing to meet at a local oyster bar for one of their established traditions. Spectators are treated to the "Alter Ego" dance sequence from the film, in which Danny, walking the conspicuously empty nighttime streets, wrestles with his desires and potential courses of action. The film shows this not just through the intrinsically expressive qualities of Kelly's dance routine but via Kelly's performance against a second version of himself—transparent, ethereal, the embodiment of his alter ego. Trying to escape the translucent presence of his alter ego, Danny rushes by the closed shop-front windows as his alter ego is reflected in them. Rational as ever, the alter ego tries to reason with Danny: "You can't run away from yourself, you've got to make up your mind, and I'm going to see that you do it now."

What is it like to deliberate? The sequence, through dance and the stylistic touch of Kelly dancing alongside himself, wrestling through his skillful deployment of choreographed movement with different possible courses of action, looks to show us cinematically and expressively what it is like for Danny to have this experience. The ethereal alter ego sets the tone. Danny is wooden and mechanical while his ghostly presence, working as puppet master, moves first in their alternating routine, urging Danny to deliberation, before Danny, gradually reaching his decision, masters his alter ego. Eventually, the two Dannys are dancing in sequence before Danny freely expresses himself independent of the ego, chasing after his ghostly counterpart (fig. 4.1). Once again, we understand these different artistic touches as conveying something of the world via Danny's experience of it—city streets literally and conspicuously empty, suggesting metaphorically the emptiness of the world to Danny without Rusty's presence in it—as well as clearly associating it with a specific character (Danny).

The subjective and psychological dimensions of artistic realism expand the possible ways in which certain stylistic techniques can be used to express aspects of a character's experience. The representation of the world is stylistically "modified" to take on qualities of the character's subjectivity (Grodal 1997, 133). These dimensions of artistic realism evoke a host of similar ideas familiar within film

Figure 4.1. Danny's dance of deliberation in *Cover Girl*. *Source:* Vidor, Charles, dir. 1944. *Cover Girl*. London: Eureka Entertainment, 2017. Blu-ray Disc, 1080p HD.

and television studies: Smith's structure of sympathy, and especially the aspect of alignment mentioned earlier (1995); Branigan's notions of focalization and projection (1984); and George Wilson's indirect subjectivity (1988). What is important is that in expressively representing phenomenal aspects of a character's experience, works will rely on an expansive suite of stylistic and formal techniques to do so. As Maike Sarah Reinerth and Jan-Noël Thon note, "Media representations of subjectivity are thus *subjective* in the sense that they constitute instances of media attempting to represent experiences that are necessarily *exclusive to the inner realms of a character (or person)*, and they are *representational* because they attempt to medially transform the complex interactions of subjective intentional states into *intersubjectively comprehensible external forms of representation*" (2017, 3). Therefore, a work's expressive disclosure of its world can involve representations of the character's subjective experience of that world.

It is the task of the spectator to pay attention to the different stylistic and formal aspects of a work that function as representations of the phenomenal qualities of a character's experience, as opposed to those that are simply aspects of the external world. These spectatorial and interpretive nuances are especially important for films that deal with especially meaningful sorts of experiences—for example, grief, given that grief shapes our experience of the world and informs the meaning and value placed on people and objects within it.

In expressively conveying the qualia of a character's grief or deliberation or regret (or any other kind of experience), a film discloses its world through a character's experience of it. In doing so, there is also an opportunity to expressively portray the specific meaning or value that is inscribed in this experience: this is another way in which there is an interplay between the general features of a kind of experience and the subjective embodiment of it. The portrayal of experiential value and meaning—or, to put it another way, the artistic representation of the meaning and value inscribed in a character's experience—is the domain of expressive realism.

Matthew Flaherty identifies a tradition of literary works that emphasize not just the (first-person) experiences of characters but such characters' evaluative interactions with objects of significance in the story-world, and the attitudes associated with and invested in such objects. Works in this tradition stimulate critical reflection on the objects of the story-world and a character's value-laden experience of them (2019, 135–36). Inscribed in the literary (formal, expressive) portrayal of a character and their subjective experience of the world is that character's evaluations of objects within the world. The works Flaherty identifies aspire to convey not just a character's experiences but the texture of meaning woven into such experiences. *Kevin*, for example, does just this—the use of color filters and mediates Eva's experience of the world, and, through the heightened use of the color red, specific objects are imbued with a particular meaning for her.

In the domain of film studies, Marilyn Fabe uses the term *expressive realism* in a much less prescriptive sense. Considering *Citizen Kane* (1941), Fabe notes how Welles adopts a variety of Hollywood techniques and conventions in tandem with presumed tendencies in German Expressionism to externalize "the subjectivity of . . . characters by means of psychologically charged settings, acute camera angles, distorting lenses, and disconcerting camera movements" (2004, 92).

One such example Fabe provides is when Kane (Orson Welles) and his future wife Susan Alexander (Dorothy Comingore) first meet; she notes how the use of cinematographic and editing techniques show the couple falling in love, though in Fabe's view, "Their being so emphatically framed in separate shots as they speak to each other . . . suggests that each is off in a separate fantasy world, cut off from the other person mentally" (87–88). The value-laden experiences and the film's expressive representation of such experiences depict, according to Fabe, the qualia of their respective feelings toward each other.

The animated short film *Sound of Sunshine, Sound of Rain* (dir. Caroline Heyward, 1983) offers a further example. In it, we follow a blind boy, the film's animated visuals showing us what he hears. Cutting between external representations of the boy's world and "interior" or subjective visual representations of the sounds he hears, the film attempts to convey what it is like for him to experience the world. He tells us his mother's voice is "soft and warm, like a pillow," and as he wakes up at the start of his day, he tells us that he experiences the world through the sounds he hears: low, high, soft, and hard. The colorful and abstract shapes onscreen respond to the different types of sound, before coming together to, as he says, make a new sound. Eventually he informs us that his sister's heels begin "putting holes in what I hear," while onscreen the tapestry of shape and color is torn with holes—his sister's footsteps imprinting the boy's morning soundscape (fig. 4.2). This moment illustrates some of the ways films can aspire to express what it is like for characters to experience their world, and that in doing so, films often must go beyond a typical, or naturalistic, sense of realism—they must rely on subjective and psychological realism to convey phenomenal qualities of experience, and on expressive realism to imbue those qualities with certain values and meanings for a given character.

The Qualia of Julie's Grief

The interplay of subjective, psychological, and expressive realism can be better understood through a sustained analysis of how a film—in this case, *Three Colours: Blue*—represents the central character's experience of grief. Such a portrayal necessarily involves a reliance on stylistic and formal devices beyond POV shots (of which, in the film, there are

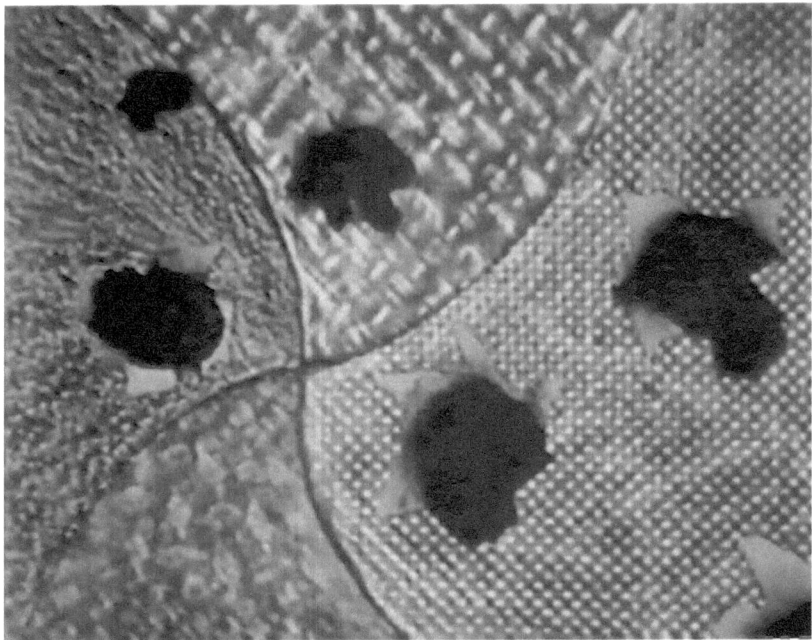

Figure 4.2. The look of sound in *Sound of Sunshine, Sound of Rain*. Source: Hayward, Caroline. dir. 1983. *Sound of Sunshine, Sound of Rain*. San Bruno, CA: YouTube, 2017. Stream 480p SD.

strictly speaking none), an expectation that spectators can parse the expressive rather than perceptually naturalistic use of the color blue, and the way in which grief is intrinsically a value- and meaning-laden experience that shapes how we understand the world we experience.

I will begin with two canonical articulations of grief within which I will situate the following discussion. The first is from C. S. Lewis, who writes of the grief he felt after the death of his wife, Joy: "No one ever told me that grief felt so like fear.... There is a sort of invisible blanket between the world and me. I find it hard to take in what anyone says. Or perhaps, hard to want to take it in. It is so uninteresting. Yet I want the others to be about me. I dread the moments when the house is empty. If only they would talk to one another and not to me" (2002, 657). The second is from Saint Augustine (2012), who writes of his grief after the death of his friend: "Black grief closed over my heart, and wherever I looked I saw only death. My native land was a torment to me and my father's house unbelievable misery. Everything I had shared with my friend turned into hideous anguish without him. My eyes sought him everywhere, but he was missing; I hated all things because they held him not" (*The Confessions* 4.4.9). In these two brief accounts, several similarities can be noted. First is the use of emotive and poetic language to try to capture the experience of grief: the attempts by both authors to render the "what it is like" of their experience of grief authentic and understandable through poetic expression ("an invisible blanket between the world and me"; "black grief closed over my heart"). Second, both examples hint at a background sense of disconnect between the individual grieving and the world—that they feel out of place or have a sense of nonbelonging is precisely because of the absence of the deceased. Finally, there is an ambiguity or tension between the absence and presence of the deceased person—that Lewis and Augustine see or sought the deceased person everywhere is a symptom of the deceased's absence.

Matthew Ratcliffe notes that grief is not "a state or episode but, rather, a process" (2017, 157). Furthermore, he argues that "other types of emotion are often integral to grief" (156) and that "the unity of grief... consists in what it recognizes, reacts to, and responds to: an all-enveloping, dynamic disturbance of life possibility" (157). There is, I suggest, an important twofold quality to the notion of life possibility and its connection to grief. The grief experienced in the wake of the death of an individual to whom we are close crystallizes that life ends—that we die. Grief is as much a process of working through this universal point as it is the more particular one related to the one whom we grieve. However, beyond this, grief also reveals that the existence of the deceased made a certain form of life possible—our existence had its particular kind of meaning precisely because that person existed and was a part of it, so grief is also a process through which we attempt to reconceptualize our own existence in light of the absence of the deceased.

Ratcliffe suggests further that grief "includes specifically directed intentional states, which have the deceased and one's relationship with her as their objects" (2017, 162). In grieving the deceased, therefore, we grieve not only them as individuals but the relationship with them that has been severed. Grief has an experiential dimension with two components—the deceased and one's relationship with the deceased—as its object. However, grief as an experience is not strictly perceptual. After all, qualia need not issue from perceptual experience. (Emotions and moods might be considered paradigmatic mental states that involve qualia, but do not involve perceptual experience.)

Moreover, I suggest that it is the disturbance of life possibility particular to grief through which its phenomenal qualities arise. The tension between presence and absence characteristic of the process of grieving creates the qualia of this experience. In writing about this feature of grief, Thomas Fuchs argues that "bereaved individuals experience a fundamental ambiguity between presence and absence, between the present and the past, indeed between two worlds they live in—an ambiguity which may also manifest itself in being painfully torn between acknowledgement and denial of the loss" (2018, 44). Fuchs also identifies certain features of grief I mentioned earlier: "Severe grief may also be described as a pervasive 'existential feeling' ... of not belonging to the world, of detachment and even of derealisation: everyday life seems empty, hollow and unreal; this reality is no longer one's own" (48). The tension between absence and presence manifests itself in an ambiguity—this ambiguity arises out of the process of grieving wherein we attempt to make sense of the disturbance and interruption of life possibility.

Fuchs (2018) alludes further to another central element of this aspect of grief—that of memory. Ratcliffe notes that "in grief, when past events involving the deceased are recalled, one remembers how things were back then, but in a way that is infused with one's current perspective, with the recognition of her subsequent death" (2017, 158). This is precisely the dynamic of Eva's experience of the world of *Kevin*—although her son is still alive, she is not just grieving the death of her husband and daughter but the form of life she had prior to the murders. The flashback scenes are imbued with her present (in the context of the film) experience of the world she inhabits. In this dynamic between past and present is the ambiguity of which Fuchs writes. In grief, there is a loss, of course, but not just a loss of an individual. There is an absence of possibility that is central to the absence of the deceased person. A loss in the possibility for meaning or the presence of certain kinds of value, the loss of the previous sense of meaning and value, and a loss of what could be in the world.

Implied within this cursory characterization of grief is its subjectivity. Grief is particular to the individual grieving because it reflects what was unique about the relationship the bereaved had with the deceased person. Relationships of any kind have a history and inform one's form of life. They characterize how one understands one's own existence, and each relationship an individual has with another has its own particularity in how it influences one's intelligibility of the world. Grief therefore involves both the bereaved and the deceased—an experience of grief is always an experience for and of someone. The variety of relationships one has will mean that the qualia of various experiences of grief (and even a single experience of grief across time) will differ.

The diversity of films that have grief at their center can be seen as pointing to the range of ways in which grief can be experienced and to the benefit of using artistic forms of expression in trying to capture something of grief. *Three Colours: Blue* explores the grief of Julie, whose husband and young daughter die in a car crash. Julie was in the vehicle, too, but she escapes with her life. Various elements of style, form, and narrative use the tension between presence and absence as a means of presenting the phenomenal qualities of Julie's grief, and how the grief for her daughter differs from that for her husband.

From the opening scenes of *Blue*, cinematography is used to amplify and give weight to seemingly small details—the world of the film is established through close-ups of ordinary and familiar objects and aspects of Julie's life, especially her daughter. The film presents elegant extended portraits of the car's wheels as they speed along the highway, of Julie's daughter playing with a piece of blue-and-silver foil out the window of the car, the foil moving chaotically through the air. Spectators also see oil dripping beneath the car, and Julie's daughter staring absently, her face moving in and out of shadow as the multicolored lights of a tunnel and other vehicles reflect off the car window. When the family stops for a quick roadside break, the camera shows fluid rhythmically dripping from beneath the car. Then, a close-up of a wooden toy being played with by a hitchhiker—a young boy—in a field fills the frame, and the camera slowly moves to reveal the car emerging in the background as it breaks through the heavy fog, itself filling the frame before speeding past. The boy's smiling face overwhelms the screen, before we hear screeching and a crash off-screen that signals the death of Julie's husband and daughter.

This sequence of close-ups establishes the setting of the film. It depicts as ordinary those things that, to Julie and her family, and to many of us, are recognizably ordinary. The family and the trip they are taking has a familiarity that is violently shattered upon the event of the car crash. In the images of Julie's daughter idly playing in the backseat, we are provided a glimpse of the blue that will characterize Julie's grief—though no such clue is given to the means by which her grief of her husband will be manifest in the film's sonic form. The opening scenes of the film show the comfortable, familiar world—the presence of those elements that shape Julie's particular form of life and give her existence the intelligibility that it had prior to the crash.

After the crash, Julie awakens in a hospital. An extreme close-up of her eye reflects the doctor standing over her, and he informs her of her husband's and daughter's deaths in the crash. Spectators see the anguish at the mention of her daughter break across Julie's face. She is provided a small handheld TV to watch her husband—a renowned composer—and daughter's state funeral. Under the hospital covers, she casts her finger over the tiny, pixelated image of her daughter's coffin. Extreme close-ups of Julie's lips trembling and tears rolling unsteadily down her cheeks fill the screen—the incessant rhythm of the car's wheels and fluid in the earlier scenes of the film are juxtaposed with the instinctual responses of her body.

The sequence of close-ups establishes Julie's subjectivity—her presence in the world of the film—and through external shots (though with an artful quasi-POV shot to begin the scene), spectators experience the world in terms of Julie's experience, her emotional tenor, and reactions. Her subjectivity therefore mediates (or focalizes/aligns) the spectator's experience of the world of the film and the film's narrative—we comprehend and understand them in terms of their significance to Julie, and the film is working in an expressively realist way to indicate for spectators the value and meaning to Julie of certain objects and aspects of the world. For example, attentive spectators will notice her response to her daughter's coffin and the lack of reaction to her husband's. While the commission of a state funeral for Julie's husband signifies his importance to the cultural life of the public, Julie's grief—understood through the subtle performative gestures and facial expression of Binoche—is much stronger for her daughter. This contrast in reactions and grief between the public and Julie in the narrative of the film assists in demarcating her subjective experience of grief from that of others.

As mentioned, Julie's experience of the grief for her husband is different than that for her daughter, and the film responds accordingly.

The grief for her husband is presented through a particular musical phrase publicly thought to be composed by her husband (though the film alludes to Julie herself being the composer). In one scene, Julie traces her finger over the composition of her husband's unfinished work, and the music plays as the camera follows the notes on the paper. As Irena Paulus and Graham McMaster note, the music of the film (and especially the main theme from which this phrase derives) "contributes to the experience of the music as a living being" (1999, 71). This is especially true for Julie's association with the music—it represents the resonance and memory of her husband's life and their relationship (despite the difficulties, of which there were several) and acts as a reminder of her grief.

The music also functions as a critical means by which the film artistically explores what it is like for Julie to grieve her husband. Beyond the previously mentioned scene, the musical phrase interrupts Julie's attention. Rather than prompting fond and heartfelt recollections, the music is violent, haunting, and jarring in its intrusion on her. It is not always clear whether the music is strictly subjective in the sense that Julie is hearing it in her aural imagination, or whether the film is deliberately creating an ambiguity in the music's dual role as both diegetic and nondiegetic sound. The tension between presence and absence that permeates the bereaved's experience of grief, that informs and shapes their experience of the world, here has a different nature compared to Julie's grief for her daughter (as will be seen in a moment). It is as though, through the use of music, spectators are shown that the absence of the husband, rather than being present everywhere, could be experienced at any time—it is not so much a constant condition of Julie's existence in the world as it is a contingent and random interruption that could strike at any moment.

Blue uses the color blue to denote the tension between absence and presence that is characteristic of Julie's grief for her daughter in a way different than that of the grief she experiences for her husband. The use of blue relies on a combination of subjective and psychological realism that is not perceptually realistic but is nevertheless used to expressively convey the qualia of Julie's grief. Blue is used in different ways throughout the film, varying from a permeating, omnipresent quality, immersing Julie in her environment, to highlighting specific objects and blue light itself. When Julie moves into her new apartment, she brings one blue object from her family's home with her: a kind of chandelier that hung in her daughter's room, referred to as the blue room. The placement of the chandelier in the foreground of the frame and Julie's positioning behind it amplifies the chandelier's importance as a site of meaning and memory (fig. 4.3). Julie's reaching out to touch the chandelier reasserts her longing for her daughter as well as the felt and experiential quality of grief. It shows us Julie's desire to reconnect to her daughter—to touch her, to assert her existence and presence.

The use of the color blue in this scene is extremely particular. In another scene, though, what it is like for Julie to grieve her daughter is different, despite also being expressed through the color blue. In this scene, Julie is diligently swimming in a public pool. Rather than blue being the notable feature of a particular object, here it envelops the entire setting, its different tones shifting as the interplay of light and water changes against Julie's movement through the pool. Color, setting, and performance harmonize to reinforce the suffocation of Julie's grief. In contrast to the earlier scene, here Julie is overwhelmed by blue—by the stylistic marker of her daughter's absence. Rather than reaching out to touch her daughter, to attempt to resurrect her presence, she cannot escape the reminder of her absence.

Figure 4.3. Julie grieves and remembers in *Three Colours: Blue*. Source: Kieślowski, Krzysztof, dir. *Three Colors: Blue*. 1993. New York: Criterion, 2011. Blu-ray Disc, 1080p HD.

Each of the scenes mentioned involve shots of the world, and none of them use POV shots. However, in the context of the film's themes and narrative, the use of color in *Blue* works as a representation of the phenomenal qualities of Julie's grief, of the different ways in which her experience of the world is mediated by the meaning associated with the absence of her daughter. The way in which *Three Colors: Blue* artistically renders Julie's grief through a reliance on subjective, psychological, and expressive realism provides spectators the opportunity to reflect on the nature of grief and what it can be like to experience grief.

Immersion in the Subjective: Qualia and Television's Extended Time

Blue emphasizes the different ways in which one character experiences grief. Television's extension of storytelling time allows for a greater depth of character development and therefore provides artistic opportunities for a more enriched sense of a character's qualitative subjective experience of the world that is developed across multiple episodes and seasons. Spectators can then be attuned to the temporal aspect of a particular mode of experience.

In *Rectify* (2013–2016), we follow Daniel Holden (Aden Young), who was imprisoned as a teenager for the rape and murder of his then sixteen-year-old girlfriend, Hanna (Madeline Taylor). He served twenty years on death row before DNA evidence led to his release and return to his hometown of Paulie, where he is tasked with clearing his name and readjusting to his life back in the world. Despite his exoneration, Daniel is still the main suspect in Hanna's death, with the district attorney pushing throughout the series for his reconviction. There are two seismic shifts in Daniel's existence—his conviction and transfer to prison and then his release twenty years later. Spectators are given access to the former only through Daniel's memories and descriptions. The show opens with the latter, and it is the latter that informs and generates the narrative momentum of the program across four seasons.

Rectify develops complex intersections of character, and the narration of the show does not solely orbit Daniel's attempts at (re)adjustment. After all, the shifts in Daniel's existence have also deeply affected his family, who are a close-knit unit that wants, but struggles, to fit Daniel back into the fold upon his release. Here, I am concerned with how *Rectify* explores Daniel's subjective experiences, particularly in terms of his readjustment to the world outside prison. The television program amplifies the ordinary aspects and details of the world to show what it is like for Daniel to process and reorient himself to existence out in the world.

Grief is central to the program. The Holdens have experienced a death of a kind—the ordinary trajectory of their son and brother's human life was lost to a twenty-year sentence in prison. Their experiences during that twenty-year period would not have been completely dissimilar to an experience of grief—Daniel's absence registered obviously in the sense that he was incarcerated and not in the world living an ordinary existence; his presence registered not just in his still being alive but in the objects left behind in the Holden household. Moreover, his presence is registered in his family's hope that their loss may only be transient and that he would one day be given his freedom.

Daniel also experiences a sense of grief for his own existence. He, too, grieves a loss of life, a loss of possibility—the loss of twenty years of his life. But, in a way, his time in prison gave him an opportunity to speculatively grieve his own impending death. We catch glimpses of this in flashback sequences, but it is in Daniel's comments upon his release that this is also clearly represented in the program. In "Sexual Peeling" (S01E02), for example, at one of the first family get-togethers after his release, Daniel is speaking to Tawny (Adelaide Clemens), the wife of his stepbrother. Daniel, in trying to relate the paradigm shift in his existence in terms that Tawny—and likely most spectators—will understand, says, "Now that I'm here in this world where everything's marked by hours or dates or events, I find myself in a state of constant anticipation. What it is I'm anticipating, I'm not always sure, nor is it necessarily a pleasant feeling." In prison, Daniel's existence was one conditioned by confinement and quite a different kind of anticipation—of his potential execution, and perhaps of a glimmer of hope that he might be exonerated. His life possessed the same ambiguous play between absence and presence that is characteristic of grief—he was still alive, of course, but in an impoverished way, in a way that kept the substantial possibility of his execution—the absence of his existence—at the forefront of his mind.

In the episode "Until You're Blue" (S02E09), Daniel is at his mother, Janet's (J. Smith-Cameron), house. Prior to the scene, his lawyer has informed him that the district attorney has offered Daniel a plea deal: the charge of rape will be permanently dropped, and in exchange Daniel will cop to the murder. If he accepts the deal, he will be banished from every county in the state of Georgia, save one. Daniel is sitting in his mother's bedroom across from her as she lies propped up in bed. He cannot bring himself to tell her of the banishment clause, and states simply that he cannot live at the house anymore. In a conversation regarding Daniel's concept of time preceding this moment (in the same scene), Janet asks Daniel if it remains the same concept as it was when he was in prison:

DANIEL: "Not anymore, the world has a way..."

JANET: "...of drawing you back in."

DANIEL: "In spite of one's best efforts."

He continues, explaining that he "gets bits and pieces as the days go by. Memories. The way the world was before I went away. And memories of the days since I've gotten out." This scene is helpful, particularly considered in light of the earlier conversation Daniel had with Tawny. Taken together, they clarify that as well as anticipation, Daniel has a reluctance and uncertainty about his existential situation. It speaks to, in a roundabout or tenuous way—as is often the case with Daniel's dialogue—the central challenge in front of him: to readjust to a world that is familiar yet changed. In the language of expressive realism, there is a reluctance or fragility that characterizes Daniel's value- and meaning-laden experience of the world. Having been released from prison, he is uncertain as to what can anchor his life. The conditions of his existence that are the bedrock of his qualitative experience of the world have suffered a monumental change—the phenomenal features of Daniel's experience are altered. A key element in Daniel's uncertain existence is that he has a foot in each of two worlds—the world of his prison cell and the world outside it. But this latter world is tinged with ambiguity due to the interaction of familiarity and difference.

What it is like for Daniel to subjectively experience the world, therefore, has certain key similarities to the model of grief outlined earlier. Daniel certainly has grieved the loss of his high school girlfriend, who was brutally raped and murdered, but instead what he seems to grieve most significantly is his relationship with the world he knew—the loss of twenty years of his life to jail. Part of the challenge of Daniel's readjustment is not so much dealing with people's opinions regarding his guilt or innocence but his working through grief of various kinds: an entanglement of grieving Hanna as much as his own life—the life he did have as much as the life he could have had. In one scene, in the attic of his mother's house, Daniel finds his Walkman and a mixtape his then girlfriend made for him. He finds his old clothes, and, aided by the memories contained within these objects, he is imaginatively and sensorially transported back to his adolescence—to the familiar world, the world he knew. He can feel the clothes on his skin that he wore then; he can hear his dead girlfriend's playful and loving voice. In this moment of expressive realism, draped in tangible signs of his past, he is reminded of the loss of possibility, constituted by the death of the girl whose voice he hears through decades-old headphones. The ambiguity of the world is presented through Daniel's experience of it, through the ways in which he tries to retain what it was like prior to his incarceration despite how it has changed since then.

Cinematography—especially through close-ups—is particularly important in conveying Daniel's experiences. In "Modern Times" (S01E03), for example, Daniel is in his bedroom in his mother's house. He is staring intently, consumed by a sliver of light that pushes through a slit in the curtains. As Daniel suddenly and enthusiastically opens them, the camera loses focus, becomes saturated with light for a moment, and then refocuses. In this case, perceptual realism is foregone, to an extent, for subjective and psychological realism—the camera is showing us what it is like for Daniel to be overwhelmed by light more than it is replicating a perceptual experience of looking at light. After all, at this point in the program he is only a few days out of prison, where he sat for twenty years in a windowless cell, enveloped only by cold fluorescent lights. Contextualized by the narrative of the program, therefore, this brief sequence illustrates with cinematography what it is like for Daniel to reexperience the most ordinary elements of the world—in this instance natural light. It is overwhelming, but only for a moment before he reorients himself to the world. This is reflected not just in the refocusing of the camera but also later in the scene, as Daniel moves his arm through the sunlight, feeling its warmth, reveling in that which he has been starved of, suggesting that his adjustment to the world at least in this instance has been successful.

Furthermore, it shows (along with a shot of Daniel's toes scrunching up, feeling the carpet of the bedroom) his subjective experience of these things—how his body reacts to various phenomena. Spectators can imaginatively bridge the gap between our and Daniel's embodied subjective experience—to remember the times we have been immersed in light and felt warmth on our skin. Important, though, because of the doubling of experience, we imagine these things focalized through Daniel's experience of them, drawing out the significance and meaning it has to him. As a result, we can recall the significance of our own similar phenomenal experiences of light and warmth we have had in the ordinary world and reflect on their significance and meaning to us. *Rectify*'s representation of Daniel's experience allows spectators the opportunity to contemplate what it would be like for those elements of our existence that are most familiar to instead possess an alien quality.

In "Modern Times," Daniel's sister, Amantha (Abigail Spencer), and Jon (Luke Kirby), Daniel's lawyer and Amantha's boyfriend, have been searching for Daniel across town. They eventually find him and peer at him from a car across the street from where Daniel is sitting in a park. Jon and Amantha speculate about what it's like to be Daniel—eating a candy bar and "feeling the grass." They conclude that they "can't imagine." Most spectators no doubt sympathize with this sentiment—however, central to *Rectify* is how it fixates on Daniel's subjective experience of the world as a way to artistically answer this question. In this scene, the camera responds as it did earlier—it lingers not just on the objects Daniel is experiencing but on Daniel's experiencing of them. This scene and the one mentioned earlier offer a microcosm of how the narrative form of *Rectify* functions to artistically depict Daniel's experience of readjustment. The temporally extended narrative form of the program can more gradually depict Daniel's subjective experience of readjustment and reorientation, and show more slowly what it is like to experience this process. Whereas Julie's grief in *Blue* is realized visually and aurally, Daniel's subjective experience of readjustment is necessarily a temporally extended one, so the ebb and flow of Daniel's attempts to navigate this process are reflected across the expanse of four seasons.

Daniel's subjectivity is realized through Young's performance of the character. Daniel's manner is reserved—his speech often thoughtful and contained. His face is regularly expressionless, hardened by the impossibly harsh realities of prison, emotion rarely breaking through the inscrutable and opaque exterior. This makes it difficult for spectators to connect with Daniel, but it also means that when emotion or reaction or expression do break through, they have even more impact. It also means that when the camera dwells on a phenomenon or object of experience—Daniel's experience of light, for example—the significance of such moments is amplified. The idea of the doubling of experience helps us understand how *Rectify*'s story is mediated by Daniel's subjective experience, especially in those moments when spectators are shown precisely what it is like for the ordinary to be experienced as alien or unfamiliar. Spectators can rethink anew about those ordinary elements of the world and their qualitative, subjective experience of them—to reconsider the place and meaning of the ordinary.

One way in which the narrative form of television is different from that of film is the depth through which the doubling of experience can apply to a range of characters, and that these different subjectivities can play off each other, in contrast and juxtaposition with each other (Daniel's experience of the world versus that of Amantha, for example). In *Rectify*, this is a particularly significant point. As much as spectators are presented with the challenge of connecting with Daniel's alienated experience of the world, his family—especially his mother and sister—are too. While Janet and Amantha try throughout the program to empathize with Daniel, the television program's narration affords viewers subjective access to Daniel's mental states in a way that is not possible for the other characters to have. After all, as much as the world has changed for Daniel in twenty years, so has Daniel changed for his family, and we see in a broad sense their own grief refracted through and reflected off Daniel. They grieve how things were and the possibilities in front of their son and brother; they struggle as much as Daniel does with the tension between absence and presence—Daniel is present for them, but how they remember him and how things were are lost through twenty years of incarceration.

The mismatch of experiential histories is further reflected in Daniel's flights of imagination and memories of his time in prison that revolve around his friend, Kerwin Whitman (Johnny Ray Gill), who was executed before Daniel was released. In one example, Daniel functions as a tour guide, leading Kerwin to different spots meaningful to Daniel throughout Paulie. The temporally extended form of television allows Daniel to imaginatively move back and forth between the past and present, between, paradoxically, the familiar space of created fantasy and the alien reality of the ordinary world. Throughout the television program, Daniel speaks to his dead friend, revisits their shared memories in prison, and even imaginatively places Kerwin out in the world alongside him. As *Rectify* shows us, Kerwin was essential to Daniel's survival through his time in prison, and these moments where Daniel and Kerwin share the screen are important touchstones as Daniel struggles to reorient himself in the world. By seeing the people, places, and moments that are central to Daniel—to experience his experience of them, through memory or imagination—accumulatively across episodes and seasons, spectators get a better sense of who Daniel is. We can consider how subjective experiences and their meaning can inform our understanding of who a person is—be it ourselves or someone else.

Daniel needs someone to help in this readjustment to the world. That the program uses its distinctive narrative form to return to Daniel and Kerwin's relationship throughout suggests not just the gravity and depth of their friendship built on the shared experience of prison—a shared experience that Daniel's family, and likely many spectators, cannot fathom—but also the ongoing process of readjustment with which Daniel struggles. In using editing to develop Daniel's experience in the world and his escape into memory and imagination in parallel, *Rectify* shows how Daniel attempts to draw on those things that are meaningful to him—those moments in his story that might help him now—to overcome his existential grief and readjust to the world.

Daniel's imagination is central to his attempts at readjustment—both in being imprisoned and in being released. In his transition into prison, Daniel relied on books to help stimulate his imagination, to carry him away momentarily from his cell. Reading continues as an important part of his identity outside jail too. In "Hoorah" (S03E01), Daniel is sitting on a park bench as a woman watches her children's adventures on a playset nearby. Daniel, by himself, not adjusted to his new way of being in the world and with no guide to help him navigate the change, could not seem more out of place. He attempts to kindly strike up conversation with the mother, but after a brief exchange with Daniel's clipped manner and his overly considered way of speaking, the mother and children leave with great suspicion. One of the things Daniel says to the woman is that he's "never read outside under the big blue sky; it's almost too much." It is one thing to read in the confines of a prison cell, to be taken away imaginatively by the words on the page. In a sense, one can control the imaginative experience generated by one's engagement with the work. But outside, under the big blue sky, in the wind and the sun, the qualia of this experience are completely different. Here, there is an interesting reversal of what has gone previously—sitting outside on a park bench is likely a familiar experience to many spectators of the show, but it is made unfamiliar by its association with Daniel's subjective experience of it—which acts as a concise way of summarizing the program's exploration of grief, qualia, and personal identity.

Animating Qualia

Thus far, in addressing the ways in which a film or television program can artistically represent the qualia of a character's experience, I have focused mostly on live-action works that are anchored in human experience, relying on real settings and human performers who bring to life human characters. To conclude, I will briefly examine some ways in which animation can test the limits of artistic realism, again focusing on subjective, psychological, and expressive realism.

The Pixar film *Inside Out* (2015) anthropomorphizes the emotions of a little girl named Riley (Kaitlyn Dias) such that each resembles the phenomenal features involved in experiencing them—Joy (Amy Poehler) is boundlessly optimistic, whereas as Fear (Bill Hader) is immediately timid, as we might expect. The interplay between each human-like emotion attempts to convey something of what it is like for Riley to undergo a range of experiences, including moving house, joining a new school, and running away from home. Throughout the film, we are shown, internal to Riley, the anthropomorphization of certain emotions working (or not) in concert, before switching to an external perspective to show us Riley engaged in the experience itself.

Inside Out's narrative interests preclude it from exploring fully the qualitative possibilities of this animated take on emotion. However, an earlier Pixar film deploys animation's unique characteristics to show us what it is like for a character to experience taste. Rather than just evoke a vague sense of taste, as sumptuous close-ups of a well-prepared dish might do, *Ratatouille* (2007) looks to visually represent what it is like for the central rat, Remy (Patton Oswalt), to taste food.

Early in the film, Remy is in a kitchen, savoring a piece of cheese. The background fades to black, and in voiceover he describes the tastes he is experiencing. As he does so, across the black background a symphony of abstract shapes and colors moves and morphs in time to music—in a way similar to the visual representation of sound in *Sound of Sunshine, Sound of Rain*—attempting to convey the sensorial experience of these flavors. Remy takes another bite, but this time from a strawberry, and now another, different series of shapes and colors dances alongside the satisfied rat. On a final pass, he combines the two in one mouthful, and the flash of color is at its most intense, the shapes at their most agile, and the music at its most upbeat. In this scene, the use of animation serves as a workaround to the limits of nonanimated representation—we are visually shown the qualia of Remy's experience of taste.

Later in the film, after being chaotically separated from his rat family, Remy finds himself in Paris, and in the restaurant of his gustatory idol, August Gusteau (Brad Garrett). The restaurant is but a whisper of its former glory, its namesake now deceased. Head chef, Skinner (Ian Holm), has been compelled to take on a possible relative of Gusteau himself in Alfredo Linguini (Lou Romano). On his first day, Linguini is looking to make an impression and attempts to "improve" a soup bubbling away on a stove. Looking on in frustrated horror from a hidden corner of the restaurant, his advanced sense of taste insulted by Linguini's excruciatingly hopeless adjustments, Remy delays his escape from the kitchen and cautiously makes his way to the soup. The film shows us not just Remy fixing the soup but the manner in which he does so; from a top shot, Remy's balletic leaping over the soup as he delicately and exactly drops herbs and other saving ingredients into the pot conveys the meaning and value Remy places in his experience of taste and food. Even an animated and anthropomorphized chef rat, in the terms of this chapter at least, is working in a realistic way—here in terms of expressive realism.

Gusteau's restaurant is suffering, having lost a Michelin star and being denounced to the history books by the vampiric gatekeeper of culinary greatness, food critic Anton Ego (Peter O'Toole). As the film progresses, though, and as Linguini and Remy form a partnership whereby Remy's culinary genius is channeled through Linguini via the rat's puppetry of the boy as he sits beneath his chef's hat, Ego cannot ignore the buzz surrounding the once failing restaurant. Toward the film's conclusion, Ego sits and awaits his meal, ready to pass judgment. Remy has decided to try to win Ego over in an unorthodox way by creating a variation on ratatouille, a peasant dish unlikely, at least in principle, to impress the cultured taste buds of the world's leading critic.

Rather than focusing exclusively on the qualia of the meal itself, the film shifts and represents the qualia of a different kind of experience, a memory that is conjured because of Ego's experience of the meal. Writing about the qualia of taste in film, Smith emphasizes that "the extent and depth of connectedness between the subjective experience of something as apparently simple as taste, and the network of memory, cultural association, and symbolism it can become integrated with: the way a whole life can be conjured up by a taste or smell, and the way 'thick' percepts and sensations like this—qualia laden with memory, association, beliefs, desires, values—can be created and evoked by works of art" (2017, 120). Ego skeptically skewers a small mouthful of ratatouille with his fork, and as he bites down, tastes, and swallows, he is catapulted back to his humble childhood through an instant surge of memory (fig. 4.4). A young version of Ego, having fallen over and scraped his knees, tearfully enters his small house, where his mother serves him a bowl of ratatouille. The value and meaning of these two experiences, tied together through the single subjectivity of Ego, could not be made clearer.

An individual's subjective experience of the world does not exist in a vacuum—it is informed by the multitudes of experiences that have gone before and by one's beliefs, attitudes, and histories. As Smith notes, a single moment of an experience in one sensory domain can call to mind a rush of memories or associations, so part of the significance of the qualia of that experience is precisely how it can call to mind the past. The artistic expression of qualia, therefore, is not just strictly perceptual but laden with existential meaning for that character and quite possibly for spectators, too. Animated works can open up the

Figure 4.4. The experience of memory via taste in *Ratatouille*. *Source:* Bird, Brad, dir. *Ratatouille*. 2007. Burbank, CA: Disney, 2019. 4K Disc, 2160p UHD.

ways in which these associations are forged and represented—across the senses, for example, by depicting sound or taste visually.

When we perceive a work that expressively shows us the experiences of characters—of regret, deliberation, grief, taste, memory, or any other—we are afforded an opportunity to contemplate the general features of that experience in tandem with a particular character's subjective reality. Films and television programs can do this through a systematic and interrelated use of style, form, and narrative. Beyond any single technique such as POV shots, the artistic coherence of a given work's world with the character's subjective experience of it can serve as a compelling and evocative representation of the qualia associated with that experience. Such moments can prove to be rich in meaning for us, as we compare and reflect on the similarities and differences of those value-laden and meaningful moments that make up our lives and the lives of characters.

5

Who Are Elizabeth and Philip Jennings?

Narrative and Personal Identity

In Michael Mann's *The Insider* (1999), Jeffrey Wigand (Russell Crowe) finds himself in a precarious position. He has been fired from his lucrative job at tobacco company Brown & Williamson, and, as a result, he and his family, wife Liane (Diane Venora), and two daughters, have shifted into a much more modest dwelling and lifestyle—that is, until Liane announces she is divorcing him and taking their daughters with her. Wigand's downturn in fortune stems from his decision to cooperate with Lowell Bergman (Al Pacino), a producer for CBS's *60 Minutes* program, to blow the whistle on his former employer's actions in making their cigarettes more addictive. Wigand and his family suffer death threats, his past (and especially a former marriage) is made public through various forms of the media, and he is presented as being emotionally volatile and self-serving in parts of the press. Moreover, an interview he agrees to give to Mike Wallace (Christopher Plummer) on *60 Minutes*—Wigand's chance to tell his own story—is pulled by CBS's legal department over fears of being sued by Brown & Williamson.

There are various narratives being told about Wigand—privately by his wife, for example, who is upset at their now less than luxurious lifestyle and the threats on her and their children, and by Bergman, who is tenacious in his conviction that Wigand has a duty to blow the whistle. There are public narratives being told, both by his former employer and by the media. These competing stories about Wigand largely concern not just the authenticity and veracity of his claims but his motivations for trying to bring to light what he sees to be a grave injustice. All these narratives revolve around Wigand's motivations and actions, but in doing so, also ask a question that is only partially answered by the film's end: Who is Jeffrey Wigand?

None of the competing narratives about Wigand seem to completely account for the question of his identity, though many of them do seem to contain some degree of truth—even the less than savory narratives appearing in newspapers and other media outlets. However, *The Insider* is, of course, a film, so in addition to the narratives contained within it, there is an overarching narrative that brings together the story not just of Wigand but of Bergman and the other central characters. Films and television programs have a capacity to tell stories about the ways we generate narratives about ourselves to answer questions of personal identity. Narratively constructed answers to these questions are one way in which we develop a sense of existential meaning in the actions and events that are central to our lives. *The Insider*'s examination of Wigand's story and the stories being told about him within the film captures the central concern of this chapter—how do screen narratives explore the tension between persistence and change that underpins the problem of personal identity, and in so doing, examine the difficulty in establishing a meaningful sense of continuity in response to the question, Who am I?

The metaphysical problem of personal identity comprises a cluster of questions that involve persistence, evidence, and population: How is a person the same through changes, what are the ways in which we come to know this, and how many persons are there at any one time? In this chapter, I will emphasize the question of evidence first and how this can be explored in films and television programs. Narrative identity is one way in which we can look to resolve each of these questions, and given the focus on narrative film and television, it is appropriate to consider how stories can help us reflect on the scope and limits of narrative in addressing the aforementioned metaphysical questions. Moreover, the narrative account enables us to develop a connection between metaphysical questions of personal identity and existential ones that aim to understand the meaningfulness of actions and events. The examination of narrative within films and television programs further considers the place of inauthentic narratives and the aspect of temporality, especially in terms of narrative's purported capacity to resolve changes, inconsistencies, and discordances in an individual's personal identity. Focusing on narrative, personal identity, and time also provides a way to consider the effects of television's expanded storytelling time relative to film, and the role that this feature plays in examining the scope and limits of narrative as it relates to personal identity.

Personal Identity: A Cluster of Questions

Eric T. Olson notes that "there is no single problem of personal identity, but rather a wide range of questions that are at best loosely connected" (2017, n.p.). The persistence question asks, How does a person remain one and the same despite changes through time? The evidence question asks, What kinds of evidence do we muster—which aspects of a person's personal identity do we appeal to—to answer other questions about personal identity? The population question asks, How many persons are present at any one time?

Evidence as it relates to personal identity is not just a metaphysical question in and of itself, but it is the epistemological means by which we can address the other two questions. As Olson asks, "How do we find out who is who? What evidence bears on the question of whether the person here now is the one who was here yesterday?" (2017, n.p.). The two kinds of evidence usually appealed to in identifying a person, be it oneself or someone else, is exterior appearance and personal continuity (such as memories and other cognitive or mental and psychological attributes). In the context of film, these two kinds of evidence underpin our ability to engage with characters. For Murray Smith, recognition of a character is the most fundamental aspect of the structure of sympathy—to sympathize with a character, one must recognize that character not just as distinct from others, but as the self-same character throughout the film or television program (1995, 82–83). Such recognition can be appealed to through the exterior appearance or personal continuity of characters.

Films or television programs, then, can aim to subvert or play with appearances by ambiguating likenesses between characters—twins, say, as in *The Prestige* (2006) or *Dead Ringers* (1988), as well as through mistaken identities, assumed identities, doppelgängers, and doubles. Works, too, can ambiguate personal continuity through similar means, or different ones altogether: as, for example, in *Shutter Island* (2010), which plays with the presentation of memories to ambiguate the identity and personal continuity of central character Teddy (Leonardo DiCaprio). A similar ambiguating of personal continuity is central to *American Psycho* (2000), though with different ends in mind. Works can also withhold key pieces of evidence that prevent characters from recognizing the personal identity of other characters, while imparting such knowledge to spectators, or it can withhold this knowledge from both characters and spectators.

John Campbell notes that there is a challenge posed wherein we must discern which piece of evidence should be given the most weight (2011, 339). In the context of film and television, spectators are often tasked with navigating how the external appearance and personal continuity of characters are being used to either facilitate or obstruct one's recognition of a character's personal identity. While there can be discontinuities in one kind of evidence, consistencies in others help us resolve the challenge of personal identity that a particular film or television program is posing. Moreover, in certain cases inconsistencies in evidence can enhance the depiction of a person. In *I'm Not There* (2007), Todd Haynes's inventive biopic of Bob Dylan, different performers inhabit different parts of Dylan's life. The varying appearances of the performers, each creating a "version" of Dylan from different moments of his life, do not pose an issue of recognition for spectators, nor do the different names each of these characters possess. This is due to how, despite the film's vignetted narrative form, it establishes each "episode" as relating to an aspect of Dylan's personal history, motivating the spectator's understanding that the film is a biopic (of sorts). Furthermore, in this film, the evidential disparities only enrich our sense of Dylan's enigmatic personal and artistic persona and the shifts in his personal and musical history. A sense of personal consistency is built as the vignettes are intercut across the film's progression, articulating formally that despite changes and disparities, this is a poetic film that seeks to articulate the life of an individual.

The personal continuity of characters—as understood in terms of memories and other cognitive or mental and psychological attributes—in films and television programs is arguably a more complicated feature than appearances. Artworks can show, for example, the memories of characters repeatedly, eventually arriving at (or, indeed, suspending) the extent to which these memories enable us to recognize a character as who they are—to reliably associate the memories and events being shown with some fundamental sense of that character, as is central to the film *Memento* (2000). Such a film, though, is peculiar in the way in which it uses memory to explore personal identity. More readily, spectators will look to associate events—conceivably the character's memories or experiential history, without necessarily being presented in a moment of recollection by a character—with certain characters in the process of piecing together the narrative elements of a film or television program. We might even look to glean the emotional states of characters through performance, gauging their reactions in the context of the narrative events of a film as a means of constructing some sense of stability in a character's personal identity. The internal and external, so to speak, can intersect, and thus the different kinds of evidence inform each other.

One such site where the interior and the exterior enmesh is the face. As Paul Coates suggests, the face is "widely identified as a transmitter of the essence of selfhood" (2012, 3). The face in film and television is relevant not just in terms of the performer's facial expressions but also in terms of the way this is represented. We can understand the aspect of representation in stylistic terms, such as whether or not the face is rendered in close-up, and in narrative terms as far as how the character's emotional reaction matches with their particular narrative predicament. The quality of execution—in terms of performance or the way in which the face is rendered through costume and make-up, for example—can in various ways (sometimes unintentionally) shape a film's examination of a character's personal identity. The Orson Welles film *Mr. Arkadin*, also known as *Confidential Report* (1955), follows Guy van Stratten (Robert Arden) and his attempts to uncover the true past of the mysterious Gregory Arkadin (Orson Welles). The film's concern with the mysteries of personal identity is presented symbolically, as seen in the film's use of masks and masquerade parties, Arkadin's unwillingness to be photographed, his feigning of amnesia, and the fact that it is Arkadin himself who sets van Stratten the task of composing the report and uncovering Arkadin's past. Moreover, the concern with Arkadin's identity is given an unintended metasignificance via the many different cuts of the film that exist, each shaping the exploration of personal identity and the marrying together of narrative and character development. However, as Jonathan Rosenbaum suggests, Welles's performance and aspects of costume and make-up that combine to give life to Arkadin do not so much add to the mystery—as do the perplexities of the film's labyrinthine plot or narrative design, for example—as they undercut the possibility of the character's authenticity:

> The falseness of his [Welles's] makeup and the variability of his Russian accent can't be rationalized by the elusiveness of Arkadin's character, because no norm is ever established for these traits to deviate from. One can accept the film's premise of presenting us with a gallery of grotesques, but not a title ogre whose face is little more than a Halloween mask. At separate junctures, Arkadin is linked to Neptune and Santa Claus, and at his own ball he hides behind a mask; most of the plot is devoted to uncovering his original identity as a lowlife named Akim Athabadze. (2007, 161)

Although, as Eyal Peretz suggests, we can understand Welles's output as "the development of cinema as a unique medium through which to engage, in a novel way, with the enigmatic question 'who am I?'" (2020, 247), the sophistication and richness with which such a question is explored will depend on the artfulness of the storytelling (narrative) and elements of style and performance (fig. 5.1).

In examining the intertwining of different kinds of evidence for personal identity, however, we need not limit ourselves to considering only the face. As Alan Barr notes, "Film is arguably the most wide-ranging and competent reflector of the human figure. It has the persuasive concreteness and detail of photography, plus the advantage of motion. It has the capability of literally showing us someone from every conceivable angle, even of altering the time—forward or backward—at will" (1987, 129). Therefore, the personal identity of characters is something that is explored through their entire physical presence. A character's stride or gait, their physical proportions, how they talk, and so forth are all key indicators of the identity of a given person. However, these are symptomatic—the physical continuity is informed by, and informs, the personal and internal aspects. Again, too, it is worth noting that such interplay is shaped and contextualized

Figure 5.1. Unintentional elusiveness in *Mr. Arkadin*. *Source:* Welles, Orson, dir. *Mr. Arkadin*. 1955. New York: Criterion, 2006. DVD, 480p SD.

by stylistic and narrative form (as Barr mentions). This is a central concern of René Clément's *Purple Noon* (1960), which follows Tom Ripley (Alain Delon), who is visiting his friend Philippe Greenleaf (Maurice Ronet) in Italy. Tom has a knack for imitations and subsuming the identities of others (at least the external elements). In one scene, he imitates Philippe, dressing in his clothes, adopting his mannerisms and vocal affect, checking his own performance in a mirror. After shockingly murdering Philippe, Tom adopts his identity and attempts to make himself an inextricable part of Philippe's ex-fiancée's life. The film doesn't pose the question to spectators of whether Philippe and Tom are one and the same—we know they are not. But with Tom's repeated shape-shifting in identity, it becomes difficult to establish continuous markers of who he is; we know what he does, but the motivations behind that remain somewhat ambiguous. Performatively, Delon's creation of Ripley and Ripley-as-Philippe illustrates Barr's underlying point that a character is created not by a performer in isolation but in the context of a narrative and mediated by style. In attempting to negotiate the personal identities of characters, spectators must triangulate these three features.

In the context of film and television, then, spectators are having to negotiate not just the conceptual preoccupations of certain works but the ways in which they are narratively and stylistically realized. The works themselves may look to mislead or obfuscate our attempts at recognizing certain characters, toying with a character's identity in terms of persistence, population, and evidence. Through what means can spectators aspire to resolve these challenges and apparent discontinuities? One is through the construction of a narrative that aims to achieve a sense of continuity and make coherent, stable, and complete a character's personal identity that, at times, may appear incoherent, unstable, and fractured.

Narrative Identity

When we construct a narrative of a character in tandem with the one provided by the film or television program, we adopt to varying degrees the narrative account of personal identity. While there are multiple perspectives that fall within this account, three fundamental assumptions that connect these perspectives are that "a human person is a temporal being . . . one whose identity must be a continuing identity through time"; "a person or self is, essentially, a being possessed of self-consciousness. . . . There is therefore a crucially reflexive element in the identity of a person through time"; and "a person is an agent; not just a node in a causal sequence, but a being that acts for reasons" (Rudd 2009, 61). For us to attain a stable recognition of screen characters, these underlying assumptions are also present: to recognize a character across a film is to understand them as continuing through time, distinct from others, and "acting" in various ways in the world of the film or television program. When we stitch these different features together across a work, we are able to recognize characters and resolve discontinuities or ambiguities in a character's personal identity. Such a process has a narrative shape.

Moreover, the narrative account aims not just to clarify the metaphysical questions mentioned earlier but to account for how "the lives of selves must be described in ways that make the events and actions in them *meaningful* or *significant*." (Schechtman 2011, 402). The narrative account of personal identity has an existential emphasis; it also provides a means for us to reason back from existence and experience to consider the metaphysical questions outlined in the previous section. This is due in part to the fact that narrative fosters a connection between events. In adhering to the narrative account of personal identity, one maintains that "the connectedness across time is not a mere causal connectedness (although it can also be causal); it's a connectedness of meaning—a connectedness that *makes sense* of the events" (Gallagher 2015, 405).

This intersection of narrative and meaning is central to, for example, *The Insider*. As mentioned, competing narratives in both private and public settings are trying to account not just for what has happened—what Wigand has done—but the motivations for his actions. In quiet, introspective moments of the film, not only do we see the effects of these different narratives on Wigand himself as he is gradually affected by the extreme stress of his predicament, but in hovering close-ups, we also see him silently trying to make sense of the events for himself too. In these moments, he is not so much concerned with the causal connectedness of events (after all, he knows how things have unfolded) as with trying to extract some significance and understanding, some sense of existentially meaningful connectedness between the events that have transpired in the film (fig. 5.2).

Figure 5.2. A moment's pause in *The Insider*. *Source:* Mann, Michael, dir. *The Insider*. 1999. Burbank, CA: Disney, 2013. Blu-ray Disc, 1080p HD.

Ultimately, these shots of interior sense-making—silent, obscure, and hidden beneath Wigand's densely impassive face—serve as the film's most profound examination of narrative as it relates to the existential side of personal identity. The inclusion of such shots helps to highlight why questions related to personal identity are meaningful: they emphasize one person for whom such questions apply, and in so doing, remind us of the universality of these questions, in that they apply to everyone (fictional and real individuals alike). Aside from *The Insider*'s hagiography of certain elements of the journalistic profession, its thundering storytelling with thriller-convention wrapping, and high narrative stakes, moments of reprieve that spectators share with Wigand (occasionally located in between his own substantial outbursts) provide us a chance to make sense of what has happened alongside him. The introspection encourages us, the spectators, to make sense of the events in terms of their significance to Wigand, and it is in this shared or collective context of sense-making that they add to our partial understanding of who he is. The narratives that we construct of Wigand as he tries to construct them for himself—negotiating all the other narratives from various sources contained within the film and presented as a cinematic narrative itself—somewhat reflect the process by which we look to construct narratives of ourselves and others in the ordinary world (at least according to the view of narrative identity being sketched here).

However, what is stopping us from constructing any narrative we like—leaving out or downplaying the less than savory parts that also constitute who we are? Which aspects of our own narrative get more weight than others? In *The Insider*, Wigand is at times too reluctant to acknowledge his own tendencies for emotional outbursts, for example, or to admit that he succumbs easily to his frustrations that he isn't being heard in the way he'd like, that he isn't the center of the entire narrative, or that things aren't consistently and totally falling into place for him to be able to share his story. It isn't out of the realm of possibility that we do the same in our own lives.

In considering the ways in which the narrative account functions akin to a literary narrative, Peter Lamarque argues that "to the extent that literary features are brought to bear on real-life narratives, they have a distorting and pernicious effect on the self-understanding that such narratives are supposed to yield" (2007, 117). When we can write whatever story we like about ourselves, what value could the narrative account possibly have in telling us something about who we are? What are the limits of the narrative account in terms of the meaning to be drawn—is a narrative perspective the only means by which we can aspire to develop the meaning and significance of the events and actions of our lives? These are important questions; in the context of film and television, it is in the animation of these very questions through particular works that we, the spectators, are given cause to reflect on them. A film such as *The Insider* does not derive part of its artistic value from a purported capacity or perceived attempt to "solve" philosophical questions of personal identity or resolve critiques of narrative identity. Instead, it is the artistic means by which such questions are given a life—the ways in which form, narrative, and style cohere to examine questions of evidence, population, and persistence, and the ways in which the construction of narratives can in various ways resolve these questions—that make it and other films like it compelling and provocative cinematic art.

In developing the connection between the narrative account of our lives and the narratives of artworks, literary theorist Frank Kermode notes how "men, like poets, rush 'into the middest,' *in medias res*, when they are born; they also die *in mediis rebus*, and to make sense of their span they need fictive concords with origins and ends, such as give meaning to lives and poems" (1967, 7). As is often the case, our exposure to the stories of screen characters does not begin at the start of their existence but, as Kermode notes, in their long middle. The process of recognition, a process that necessarily involves metaphysical questions to do with persistence, evidence, and population, is developed as the stories of characters continue forward as well as through whatever flashbacks into the characters' past may be presented to spectators. The process of recognition, therefore, involves both temporal directions and is a dynamic process that is subject to reformulation as spectators are exposed to the stories of characters. The recognition of screen characters, then, is influenced by the stories themselves, the way they are told, and the medium-specific features of the art form in which they are being told. As Paul Ricœur notes, "Narrative constructs the durable properties of a character," and therefore "it is first of all in the plot that one looks for mediation between permanence and change, before it can be carried over to the character" (1991b, 195). For both real-world persons and screen characters, it is the narrativization—the emplotment—of events onto or associated with the existence of an individual that allows for the navigation of permanence and change. Gallagher notes how "Ricoeur characterizes this structure in terms of *concordance* and *discordance*. Although in some way each event in the narrative is something new and different (discordance), in another way each event is part of a series (concordance), determined by what came before and constraining a sense of what is to come, allowing the story to advance" (2015, 404). The narrative account of personal identity connects metaphysical questions of persistence and population to the existential significance of actions and events, and so navigates the inextricable dynamic between permanence and change.

In Peter Weir's *The Truman Show* (1998), the narrative of Truman Burbank's (Jim Carrey) life is a worldwide sensation. Unbeknownst to Truman, the substance of his entire existence is an artificial construction that is controlled by television producer Christof (Ed Harris): Truman was born in the world of the television program and had all his significant moments from childhood to adulthood play out on television too. The world is populated by extras alongside a stable cast of recurring characters, such as Truman's wife, Meryl Burbank, who is actually an actress Hannah Gill (Laura Linney), and his childhood best friend, Marlon, an actor named Louis Coltrane (Noah Emmerich). In the opening scenes of the film, Christof notes: "While the world he [Truman] inhabits is in some respects counterfeit, there's nothing fake about Truman himself." Technically, Christof is correct; our threading the events of Truman's life together narratively helps to reveal something about the nature of narrative identity. All the things that happen to Truman during his life are real in the sense that they happen, but lack authenticity given that they are constructed and part of Christof's narrative design for Truman's life. The narrative that helps to give shape to Truman's personal identity undermines itself, given the artificiality of Truman's existence—that is, the fact that the things that come together to make up his life are orchestrated and imposed by another person.

At the film's end, by now confident in the artificiality of his existence, Truman steals a boat and intends to sail to the edge of the world—quite a feat given his carefully designed fear of water stemming from some traumatic childhood experiences at the beach. As Christof dials up the intensity of the storm to prevent Truman from confirming the nature of his unreality, Truman perseveres, eventually piercing the large canvas wall made to appear as sky at the limit of the studio set that has bound his entire life. He walks along the water, grazing his hand over fake clouds, before hearing a voice—the voice of Christof—that pierces the silence as the "sun" pierces the last remnants of the chaotic storm. As Christof speaks Truman's name, Truman turns, and asks who he is. Christof replies that he is the creator of a television show. Truman's next question is much more layered, as he stands, furrowed brow, existentially unmoored, seeking some sort of consolation in the reply of the man who has created the artificial world that has been pulled from beneath Truman over the duration of the film: "Then who am I?" he asks.

The film gives an artistic life to the process of narrativizing our personal identities—it illustrates the folly of inauthentic narratives, those accounts of ourselves that rest on unfirm ground (granted, in this case, imposed on Truman by Christof). But in the penultimate moments of the film, as Truman walks off the set to begin his own life and create his real story, we are left with a sense of unease. To return to Kermode's point, this new existence—real existence—operates in medias res. It occurs in the middle of a life that previously lacked genuine meaning, but was a life nevertheless, so Truman's new narrative, regardless of what happens, will still need to fold these experiences of his time as the star of Christof's television show into his new existence. Unlike *The Insider*'s Wigand, who is dealing with competing narratives simultaneously, *The Truman Show*'s Truman Burbank has a temporally linear task that must account for the past, the present in which he finds himself, and the future story he is hoping to create. Here, the process of recognition with which spectators regularly engage is taken to be part of the film; in the moving final moments of *The Truman Show*, we see Truman wrestling with self-recognition—something that has been shown to be lacking due to the manufactured conditions of his existence—a process that will unfold in the future as he looks to craft a meaningful story of his own life.

The film artfully illustrates the complexities of constructing narrative. As Ricœur notes, "Following a story is a very complex operation, guided by our expectations concerning the outcome of the story, expectations that we readjust as the story moves along, until it coincides with the conclusion" (1991a, 21–22). The self-reflection and self-understanding required to craft our own narratives magnify the complexities Ricœur mentions, because such understanding is constantly unfolding and being redefined as our lives and circumstances change. Nevertheless, the functional malleability of narrative is valuable as it relates to personal identity, especially the way in which personal identity is explored in films and television programs. The artistic exploration of personal identity provides spectators a kind of possible testing ground for understanding themselves via narrative. As Jane Stadler highlights: "Narrative is instrumental in our efforts to make sense of the world: it is a mode of explanation that assists interpretation by providing temporal order, describing interconnections, and rendering complex causal relationships intelligible" (2008a, 68). Moreover, "A narrative structure of understanding is necessary as a condition for the possibility of intentional action, and that narrative is the form from which such action originates" (69). *The Truman Show* illustrates a number of these observations—we might point to the relative meaninglessness of Truman's actions, given that the ends for which he is acting and the conditions in which he exists are predetermined constructions. Furthermore, narrative's interpretive function is central to both *The Truman Show* and *The Insider*.

The presuppositions of the narrative approach to personal identity afford concordance where, in relation to film and television, there may well be none. The following analysis of *3 Women* focuses, principally, on the persistence/continuity of personal identity over time, epistemological evidence of self-sameness despite change, and population. Furthermore, the analysis examines the function and limits of the narrative account of personal identity. The film motivates a breadth of interpretation: that it might operate as a dream, for example, or that the three women—Pinky Rose (Sissy Spacek), Millie Lammoreaux (Shelley Duvall), and Willie Hart (Janice Rule)—critique and parody the family structure. One relevant element of the film of interest here is its examination of the dynamics of interiority and exteriority. Robert Kolker suggests that "the interplay of interior states, exterior landscape, and the bizarre murals that punctuate the film at strategic moments is an expressionism of sorts ... created through the counterpointing of the world in its physical and ideological presence with reflections of that world off of the emotional states of the characters" (2011, 351). In attempting to address questions to do with the persistence and population of personal identity, one must weigh the evidence that usually involves physical (external) appearance and mental (personal/interior) continuity. Kolker also points toward how the film's exploration of personal identity is developed, at least partially, through the film's visual style.

In his review of *3 Women*, Roger Ebert states that "Robert Altman's 1977 masterpiece tells the story of three women whose identities blur, shift and merge until finally, in an enigmatic last scene, they have formed a family, or perhaps have become one person" (2004, n.p.). This is close to the interpretation I will offer here; however, I do not suggest that they eventually become the same woman, but rather that they are the same woman depicted at various stages of her life simultaneously. Such an interpretation will show how the film interrogates not just metaphysical questions of personal identity but also certain features of narrative identity outlined earlier.

The bare-bones plot of the film is this: Millie works at a desert spa, when one morning Pinky arrives as a new employee. Pinky eventually moves in with Millie. They work and live near a bar that is owned by the pregnant Willie. Pinky and Millie's relationship shifts and develops, until eventually, at the end of a heated argument, Pinky throws herself off the balcony of their apartment and into the complex's pool. She eventually wakes from an unconscious state in the hospital, with a more assertive, independent personality—less worshipful of Millie than when they first met.

Early in the film, when Millie and Pinky are still becoming accustomed to one another, Millie observes, talking to Pinky, that "you're a little like me, aren't ya?" Her observation contains a lot of truth—both have the birth name Mildred, both are from Texas, both hate tomatoes, and both consider as important the regular writing in their journal or notebook. Pinky says to her older friend—or, in my interpretation, her older self—that "you're the most perfect person I've met." For much of the film, Pinky's attitude to Millie is one of fawning, idealistic worship. Pinky imitates even as she latches on to Millie—it's not simply enough for Pinky to enjoy Millie's company; she needs to adopt her qualities and habits, mimicking certain attributes and interests—that is, certain superficial kinds of evidence of Millie's personal identity.

After Pinky throws herself into the pool and has returned home from the hospital, she has a harder edge. She smokes and drinks now; she has taken to writing in Millie's diary, too. In a meeting at the spa, Millie discovers that Pinky had given the spa Millie's social security and phone number, even though they had never met and did not know each other. All these similarities—both before and after the argument and what eventuates—serve to confuse personal identity both in the population of the woman's identity and in the persistence between Pinky's (younger) and Millie's (older) personal narrative. The sharing of names and the reflexive comments in dialogue, for example, also ambiguate (despite physical differences between Spacek and Duvall in the creation of their respective characters) what spectators might expect to be evidence that serves to demarcate or distinguish the characters from each other and to anchor the recognition of multiple characters rather than multiple versions of the one character.

Until this point, the questions of persistence and population remain open. How, in my interpretation of the film, can *3 Women* be seen to represent the persistence of a single, unitary person, artistically expressed as that self-same person at three different stages of her life simultaneously? A significant shift that establishes the continuity of identity between the three versions of the woman occurs when, toward the end of the film, Willie gives birth to a stillborn baby. Willie lies on the bed of her apartment, cradling the dead baby, while Millie walks out to Pinky (whom she had asked to call an ambulance, but, horrified and scared by the event, had frozen in shock). Millie's front is streaked with blood—harkening back to an earlier moment in the film when Pinky, helping Millie organize a small party, had spilled tomato ketchup down the front of her dress (fig. 5.3).

The film makes an elliptical cut to a new scene, and the three women are now running the bar. Pinky is now referred to as Millie, and Millie, who until this point had been effervescent, endlessly talkative, and upbeat, has now adopted the clipped, reserved, and impenetrable demeanor of Willie. Evidence that could have been used to distinguish the characters from one another now overlaps: whereas earlier in the film spectators may have been seeing triple, our focus is now beginning to crystallize into an image of a single woman. In the closing moments of the film, the three women—three versions of the same woman—are at a house just behind the bar. They are arranged on the front porch, at which point the camera zooms out slowly from a medium long shot of the women positioned on the porch to an extreme long shot of the house, where it pans left to the film's stunning final shot of three horizontal divisions—the lower third of tires, the middle third of dried brown shrubs, and the top third of flourishing green foliage.

Figure 5.3. Stained dresses in *3 Women*. *Source:* Altman, Robert, dir. *3 Women*. 1977. New York: Criterion, 2011. Blu-ray Disc, 1080p HD.

The movement of the cinematography in this scene is typical of the film—elaborate, slow-moving pans and zooms suffuse the story with its ruminative and somewhat unsettling qualities. That these shots are extended is a subtle way in which the film visually asserts the idea of continuity—cuts in editing, when they do occur, are sudden and shocking ends to scenes, but during the scenes themselves, the camera often moves without interruption, reinforcing the idea offered by Kolker at the start of this analysis. Extended shots do not divorce the characters from the world or from one another. The same elements of stylistic form that Kolker suggests enmesh the characters with their surroundings also show the characters' identities as being connected to one another. If the metaphysical problem of personal identity is a cluster of questions, as I suggested at the start of this chapter, it makes sense that the ambiguities in the film's exploration of persistence are reinforced and augmented via the ambiguities in its exploration of population, and vice versa.

If we take these visual considerations into account alongside the narrative and performative ones mentioned earlier, *3 Women* productively disrupts the process of recognition to pose interesting questions about the persistence, evidence, and population of personal identity. Moreover, in allowing three temporally disparate versions of the one woman to share space in the story-world of the film, *3 Women* effectively eschews the conventional temporality of Hollywood films that would influence how the narrative identity of the woman is developed. Each of the women acts as a marker on the narrative map that provides spectators with concrete sites for developing a sense of concordance. The narrative perspective's characterization of temporal identity is supported by the film's story and enables spectators to navigate the dynamics of persistence and change—the concordant and the discordant; further, the elements involved in the telling of the story (discussed earlier) support the thesis I have advanced regarding the film. The final shot offers the visual realization of this idea. It is not to suggest, of course, that tires become shrubs become foliage (or that tires are shrubs are foliage). But the counterpoising of the three women with the three elements of the final shot—and each version of the woman/element against the other two within each of these shots—offers both a visual explication of the persistence despite, or because of, change in personal identity across time, and the means by which, through evidence and narrative, we can consider fundamental questions of personal identity related to persistence, change, and evidence.

Resolving Change and Establishing Concordance through Narrative

Films such as *Purple Noon*, *The Insider*, *The Truman Show*, and *3 Women* allude to a variety of ways in which narrative can aim to unify, integrate, and resolve changes, inconsistencies, and developments across an individual's existence. Moreover, narrative can help us not just reflect on and resolve the metaphysical questions of persistence and population but understand the existential significance of these questions in the first place. As Stadler notes, "Narrative is crucial to theorizing personal identity because it is uniquely able to articulate the complex interrelatedness of our identities with others and accommodate the changes that a person experiences over the span of her or his life, retaining a sense that these differences are integrated aspects of the same self" (2008a, 70). Underpinning these insightful remarks is a keen attention not just to the interplay of concordance and discordance, of the dynamic between continuity and change, and of questions of population, evidence, and persistence, but to how a narrative approach seeks to cohere and integrate the realities of existence into a unitary understanding of a single self. Furthermore, narrative helps us understand individuals (screen characters or real-life individuals, including ourselves) partly in terms of how it navigates population—how it distinguishes us from others and others from us. The ways in which narrative folds together an individual's changes and discontinuities can take into account those changes and discontinuities as they play off others, thereby giving us a clearer view of a particular individual by exploring the interrelatedness of personal identity.

To return to the example of *Purple Noon*: as mentioned earlier, Tom Ripley's penchant for assuming identities—especially that of Philippe, the former friend he murders—makes it difficult to develop a coherent, rich sense of who Tom is. Writing on a more recent adaptation of the same story, Anthony Minghella's *The Talented Mr. Ripley* (1999), Murray Pomerance identifies as key to the character of Ripley his "talent for spontaneous invention—*authorship*—and . . . his desperate conviction for maintaining the fantasy architecture he builds" (2018, 81). Pomerance's further comments on the 1999 film are equally applicable to *Purple Noon*, where he sees *The Talented Mr. Ripley* as "a fascinating exploration of the limits of sincerity and truth": a film that is "a construction about construction" (82). In *Purple Noon*, this is seen most clearly in Ripley's performative mimicry and his construction of himself as Philippe, but it is also notable via the absence of a clear and concrete sense of who Tom is. To try to develop a deeper sense of Tom's personal identity (something, I would argue, that is not possible—and by design—in *Purple Noon*) we can turn to narrative to track what happens to Tom and what he does, plot point by plot point. This account of what happens would ideally lead us back to who Tom is; narrative identity and a focus on experience and existence ordinarily work as the lens through which to examine the metaphysical questions of personal identity. However, the film's unwillingness to make clear his motivations at a fundamental level for acting as he does—to reach back into the temporally prior motivations for where he is in the film and how things unfold—ensures that such a thread is lost.

As fictional constructions, all screen characters are to a certain extent unknowable. The process of recognition that is central to spectatorial engagement with characters, however—especially recognition that seeks to "write" narratives as a means of understanding the characters we see in films and television programs—operates, at least according to the view developed throughout this chapter, in a way that is instructive to our thinking about personal identity outside the context of film and television. Moreover, that this recognition is occurring in the context of art means that there are scenarios, characters, and ways in which personal identity can be explored as distinct from the ordinary world of experience. And even if certain works deal ostensibly with a realistically plausible cast of characters and collection of stories, the fact that these are stylistically, narratively, and formally realized establishes them as a unique means of thinking through questions and issues related to personal identity.

In the Preston Sturges film *Sullivan's Travels* (1941), we follow movie director John L. Sullivan (Joel McCrea)—a man renowned for his comedic work—as he attempts to change artistic pace and create a socially moving, realistic drama. To ensure that his understanding and knowledge of the people who will populate the film—the poor, lower classes far removed from his glamorous lifestyle—is an authentic one, Sullivan assumes the identity of a tramp to accumulate firsthand the experiences of those the film will be exploring. Certain questions regarding Sullivan's identity are easily answered—spectators never lose a sense of which character is Sullivan (though other characters do, such as the actress [Veronica Lake] who accompanies him on much of his journey), and we are always aware of Sullivan's identity (though he, late in the film, loses his own sense of personal continuity after he is knocked unconscious). The ways in which Sullivan inhabits a stratum of society not his—willingly in the beginning as a tramp, unwillingly later in the film after his accident, when he hazily stumbles onto a railyard, is arrested for trespassing, and eventually sent to a labor camp—involve both inauthentic and authentic narratives, respectively. That is, the first is an artificial construction and the second scenario is not, so the significance and meaning generated by each is different. However, the very way in which we understand whether these experiences are meaningful or not is by connecting them to Sullivan and unifying them into the overarching narrative of his life.

The film doesn't test the limits of narrative identity—after all, for the reasons stated earlier, Sullivan's experiences are easily unified by the narrative and integrated into his existence in the film. Instead, the film provides a provocative means of considering the connection between narrative unity and meaning. When Sullivan is playing the part of a tramp, we can understand him as knowingly writing a narrative that does not account for his own identity but that of a hypothetical other whose life he then subjectively inhabits as a means of gaining experiences that would be meaningful to that person, as well as experiences that he would otherwise not have access to. This is a deliberately inauthentic narrative; Sullivan isn't kidding himself in the sense that he thinks he is a tramp. After all, his willingness to live as one implies his awareness that he is from a different part of society. It is noteworthy, though, that this inauthentic narrative does not help him achieve his aims—he does not gain any great insight into the human condition or the art he is aspiring to create by playing a tramp.

Sullivan's insight comes later in the film when the narrative of his life authentically and legitimately involves his becoming a disenfranchised member of society (even though by accident). Initially, this change occurs because of his lack of personal continuity resulting from amnesia caused by the accident. He eventually regains his memory, but cannot convince anyone at the labor camp that he really is who he says. His sense of personal continuity and self-identity is undercut then, first internally and then externally when he is made to live at least for a while the life of an inmate. However, because these are real experiences to Sullivan—not manufactured constructs designed to generate insight into the human condition—he attains a genuine revelation. He can see and experience firsthand the value of comedic art, precisely because he is inhabiting a kind of narrative that, while unintended, is in fact authentic.

One way in which we can understand the meaningfulness of events in *Sullivan's Travels* is in terms of how they relate to Sullivan—that they are things that happen to him and events that he experiences, and as such are anchored in his overarching life narrative. The first scenario involving his "performance" of a tramp—a kind of narrative in its own right—lacks meaning given its artificiality, and it is this scenario that provides much of the comedic basis of the film. While the second part of the film provides us with Sullivan's revelations about the value of comedy, it is noteworthy that the more comedy-heavy first part of the film, which does not provide Sullivan with insight, does do so for spectators. Here we can see the folly of inauthentic narratives, that Sullivan's aims (while admirable in one respect) are doomed to fail and shown to be absurd through the comedic trappings of this part of the film. Moreover, spectators can draw such conclusions because of the events' relevance to Sullivan—that they are unified in his narrative and in relevant aspects of who he is. The earlier part of the film subsequently provides a depth to the revelations that occur in the second part of the film, which mirrors authentically what unfolded inauthentically in the first part; Sullivan experiences a genuine revelation because the experiences he has are authentic elements of his story. Narrative identity enables spectators to meet the straightforward challenge of recognizing Sullivan: despite changes in appearance and temporary gaps in personal continuity, Sullivan remains to spectators identifiably himself throughout the film.

However, ambiguating for whom experiences and events are happening—by obscuring the undercurrent of personal identity in various ways and, through an emphasis on persistence or population rather than evidence as discussed earlier, making difficult the process of recognizing who a character is—allows for a more nuanced examination of narrative identity and its capacity to unify changes and discordances. In David Cronenberg's *A History of Violence* (2005), we follow apparent small-town family man Tom Stall (Viggo Mortensen), who is also Joey Cusack, a violent criminal from Philadelphia who has attempted to leave his former life behind him. The film tracks Tom's reluctant confrontation with the ghosts of the past that pervade and threaten the quiet family life he has forged in Millbrook, Indiana. With the arrival of gangster Carl Fogerty (Ed Harris) and his henchman, Stall's existence is unraveled. Carl's purpose is to convince Joey to return to Philadelphia and face his crime lord brother, Richie (William Hurt), so there is a clash between past and present that brings to the forefront Tom/Joey's discordance in identity, as well as the dissonance in meaning that results. The key event through which this takes place is Tom's expertly violent and precise stopping of a robbery at the diner he owns. Receiving widespread media coverage for his acts brings Richie's attention, the appearance of Carl, and the slow return of Joey to Millbrook.

The discordance in identity of Tom and Joey is anchored in Mortensen's performance of different characters who make up one and the same man. Tom is mild-mannered, kind, devoted, and meek: he and his family—wife, Edie (Maria Bello), and children, Jack (Ashton Holmes) and Sarah (Heidi Hayes)—are presented to the point of caricaturing the idyll of the small-town American household. The relations between Tom/Joey and Edie help track the effects of his discordant identity, and particularly how narrative can attempt to unify contradictory features of an individual's existence via their interrelatedness with others.

In one key scene, the Stall family home has been visited by Carl and some henchman, who have taken Jack hostage. They're willing to return Jack to his family provided Joey returns with them to Philadelphia. However, the deal, unfolding in the Stall's front yard, goes completely awry—we see Mortensen morph Tom into Joey through subtle but discernible changes in performance. His face hardens, his voice levels out, and he conducts himself with an edge and a snarl (fig. 5.4). Joey manages to kill the henchmen while taking a bullet himself, and as Carl leans over Tom/Joey as the latter lies on the ground, a shot rings out that signals Carl's death rather than Tom/Joey's—Jack has picked up a discarded weapon and saved his father. Due to the injuries he sustained, Tom/Joey finds himself in a hospital, and Edie, who watched the earlier confrontation unfold in the relative safety from within the Stall home, and who to this point has stood by her husband and maintained that his being taken for Jocy is simply a case of mistaken identity, is disheveled and betrayed as she approaches Tom/Joey while he lies in a hospital bed.

As the confrontation between the two (or three) continues, Tom/Joey offers a reflective insight into his self-identity. He notes that the people he killed were killed by Joey, not Tom, and mentions the difficulties of shedding one identity—one sense of self, or one version of the narrative—and developing another. Ultimately, though, the challenge is really in how both stories are to be assimilated or unified into a single, coherent one that envelops both Joey's and Tom's life. That is to say, the perspective of narrative identity crystallizes the meaningful, existential effects of a person's life (Tom/Joey), but it is not enough to say that he once was Joey and then became Tom, only to become

Figure 5.4. The difference in demeanor between Tom and Joey in *A History of Violence*. Source: Cronenberg, David, dir. *A History of Violence*. 2005. Burbank, CA: Warner Bros. Pictures, 2009. Blu-ray Disc, 1080p HD.

Joey again temporarily. As the narrative approach to personal identity relates to the metaphysical questions of evidence, population, and especially persistence, it needs to account for the person who exists as an undercurrent beneath the personae of Joey and Tom—it must navigate the discordant and contradictory evidential characteristics seen in the two personae, as well as the performative differences that Mortensen creates. In this film, we are given artistic ways of thinking through both the scope and limits of narrative and the connection between metaphysical and existential questions of personal identity. Moreover, we can further understand these aspects of narrative and personal identity through the interrelatedness of personal identity, considering how the shifts in one individual's self-understanding can influence other individuals' self-understanding. This is illustrated in the film's closing moments.

Having returned from Philadelphia, his brother and the remainder of his gang violently dispatched, Tom/Joey walks into the front door of his home as his family has just sat down to dinner. A wreck, Tom/Joey gradually makes his way over to the table and takes his place. After a lengthy and uncomfortable silence, his daughter, Sarah, gets up, collects a plate from the kitchen bench, and sets it down in front of her father. The narrative of his life has reset again—the narrative of his family's life, because of this shift in identity, resets again too. But the shift in identity is an ambiguous one—we can't be sure who it is that has walked through the front door. Joey's/Tom's comments in the hospital room regarding the difficulty of shedding one identity are once again relevant, but so is a question Richie posed to his brother only moments earlier in the film: "When you dream, are you still Joey?" Despite any external changes and consistencies, the evidence of personal continuity cannot be resolved, masked, or unified quite so easily.

Two further scenes between Tom/Joey and Edie illustrate this point further. Early in the film, before the appearance of Joey, Tom and Edie are sharing an intimate moment. Edie tells Tom playfully that they never got to be teenagers together. Dressed in a cheerleader's outfit, Edie is looking to provide a kind of stereotypical fantasy for her husband, who is initially a little taken aback and awkward. As with the early scenes of the family home, this moment is a hyperreflexive construction of identity: here Edie is providing a performance for Tom. In hindsight, we also realize that Tom is providing a performance for his wife every moment of his existence. As husband and wife make love, it is as though the character's themselves—Edie and Tom—are performing to a prescribed script. This contrasts with a later scene after Tom/Joey returns home from hospital. Edie and Joey get into a fight that escalates, and they trade some blows as the intense disagreement proceeds up the stairs. They fall, and as Joey moves to get up, she pulls him in and they make love once again—here, in contrast to how they behaved in the somewhat empty performance of the earlier scene, husband and wife act completely differently, with messiness and aggression toward each other. We can certainly gather something about Edie's personal identity across both scenes as much as about Tom/Joey's—we can stitch together a narrative that accounts for the differences in her behavior and consider what this tells us about her. But in both instances, such a narrative construction is motivated by the external change in identity of Tom/Joey, and thus the interrelatedness of personal identity is made central once more.

Both McRea's performance of Sullivan and Mortensen's performance of Tom/Joey bring to life characters who are themselves reflexively performing identities in various ways. It is in this kind of performance of performance that the scope and limits of narrative identity's capacity to unify discordance and change within an individual's existence is offered as a source of reflection to spectators. Questions of personal identity are more easily resolved in *Sullivan's Travels*—we know who Sullivan is throughout the film, and it is the story of his experiences motivated by the artificial narrative construction he provides at the film's beginning that emphasizes not so much narrative's limits as its scope. By formulating a narrative understanding of Sullivan, we can see that his revelations about the importance of comedic art and its value to life are born from firsthand experience and a juxtaposition of his playing the role of the tramp (an inauthentic narrative) against his authentic experience as a disenfranchised member of society (an authentic narrative of the character's actual experience). It is the latter that provides Sullivan his epiphany, rather than the former.

A History of Violence instead offers a more open-ended view of narrative. It poses a challenging problem to narrative's purported capacity to unify discordances, inconsistencies, and changes to an individual's personal identity. Nevertheless, the film's balance of narrative identity and the metaphysics of personal identity is shown through the links between the personae of Joey and Tom, and the interwoven and interrelated quality of personal identity.

Long-Form Storytelling and Narrative Identity

Both *Sullivan's Travels* and *A History of Violence* are on some level concerned with a multilayered understanding of performance as it relates to personal identity, and especially the interrelatedness of personal identity—how who one is shapes others' sense of self as much as one's own. *The Americans* shares these concerns and also examines how the narrative account of personal identity uses its existential and experiential emphasis on meaning and significance of events and actions to lead back to the metaphysical questions associated with personal identity. It explores the limitations of narrative identity and develops these issues through the medium-specific features of television, most notably television's expansive storytelling time. While a film such as *3 Women* inventively exploits the medium-specific temporal constraints in its artistic consideration of personal identity, *The Americans* makes full use of the elongated temporal form of television.

As Robert Blanchet and Margrethe Bruun Vaage note, "Television series can enhance familiarity with a particular story world and characters to a greater extent than can feature films" (2012, 24). This has distinctive effects on the narratives of television series and on the richness of our recognition of characters. As Elliott Logan suggests, "Serial television drama is produced in an unfolding series of discrete but nevertheless interrelated parts, namely episodes and seasons. What follows from this fact is that the textual composition of such works is characterised by ... a peculiar tension between the unified and the fragmentary, between the discrete part and the greater whole, which are at once separate and connected" (2016, 2). The medium-specific features of television—temporal interruption and elongation—as compared to that of film dictate how such stories can be told and the sorts of stories that can be told. Television programs that explore personal identity—as *The Americans* does—have a fundamentally challenging task. Roberta Pearson suggests that "the lack of an immediate denouement requires that the core psychological traits and behaviors of television characters remain stable" (2007, 50) and that the "repetitive nature of the television series dictates a relative state of stability for its characters, whose failure to perform key narrative functions and to interact with other characters in pre-established fashion could seriously undermine a series' premise" (55–56). However, in our experience of television programs that explore personal identity, we should not expect the characters' traits to be outlined and stable for the entire program.

A distinction can be made here between a television program that is a series and one that is a serial. The former would require the stability of which Pearson writes, whereas a serial need not. As Logan suggests, "Serial television drama is especially, perhaps even uniquely, well suited to depicting how the build-up of personal history places pressure upon the always-shifting constitution of a person's present identity as a foundation for the future" (2016, 90). Therefore, for television serials, recognition of characters is an ongoing process that is subject to a complex dynamic of persistence and change. More specifically, for television serials such as *The Americans*, narrative is key in navigating the personal identity of characters—a process that accumulates across episodes and seasons, rather than being concretely outlined in the earlier moments of a program (as in the case of a series)—and informing the expectations of spectators. Fundamentally a spy narrative, *The Americans* follows two KGB agents—Philip (Matthew Rhys) and Elizabeth Jennings (Keri Russell)—who, as part of the USSR's efforts in the Cold War, live and work undercover in the United States posing as American travel agents. As Alberto N. García and Pablo Castrillo note, the program is preoccupied with a trio of dichotomous themes that suit an artistic exploration of personal identity and narrative: "secrecy and revelation, identity and disguise, authenticity and performance" (2020, 783).

In "The Clock" (S01E02), Philip and Elizabeth are in Viola Johnson's (Tonye Patano) home. Her son, Grayson (Grantham Coleman), lies on his bed in a barely conscious state, having been covertly poisoned by Elizabeth earlier in the episode. Viola, a maid at the home of Secretary of Defense Caspar Weinberger, had been tasked by Elizabeth to steal a clock from Weinberger's office so that it could be bugged and then returned for surveillance purposes. Although Viola had complied with the request to steal the clock, she had not returned it, and her son lay dying on the bed, refused the antidote promised by Elizabeth because Viola had failed to complete the task set for her. Due to complications to the mission, Philip has become involved—in a previous scene, he beat Viola's brother in a fistfight, and at this point in the episode he is smothering Grayson with a pillow, hastening the poison's course and conveying to Viola exactly what is at stake for her and her family if she does not comply. Viola, emotionally ruined and weeping, repetitiously screaming "no," finally and hysterically poses two questions: "What kind of people are you?! Who are you?!"

The Americans shows characters wrestling with these questions throughout the program. For a character such as Viola, her understanding of Philip and Elizabeth can be shattered in a moment when she becomes aware that her sense of Philip and Elizabeth—and of the kind of people she would expect them to be, based on her perception of them—is false. That is to say, the evidence Viola has at hand to infer the personal identity of (primarily) Elizabeth turns out to be misleading, and therefore the narrative constructed to establish persistence and coherence to Elizabeth's identity requires reformulation.

Throughout the program, Philip and Elizabeth deploy a range of disguises relying on intricate uses of makeup, dress, wigs, and so on to shield their true appearance from those they are involved with—that is to say, to falsify the evidence used for others to identify them (fig. 5.5). Philip becomes Clark Westerfeld, a member of the Office of Personal Responsibility (responsible for overseeing and auditing all US federal intelligence agencies), who seduces and uses Martha Hanson (Alison Wright), secretary to the director of counterintelligence. Their relationship (to which I will return in a moment) lasts across several seasons of the program. Philip also becomes James to Kimberley Breland (Julia Garner), the high school–age daughter of Isaac Breland (Frank Deal), the head of the CIA's Afghan War Division. Philip-as-James uses Kimberley, as Philip-as-Clark does Martha.

Figure 5.5. Philip and Elizabeth disguised in *The Americans. Source:* Weisberg, Joe, creator. *The Americans.* 2017. Los Angeles: 20th Century Fox, 2019. DVD, 480p SD.

One of Elizabeth's most notable personae is Stephanie, a home nurse caring for the terminally ill wife of Glenn Haskard (Scott Cohen), a key part of the US State Department negotiation team. Elizabeth also plays Patty, a Mary Kay door-to-door saleswoman, whose role is to get close to fellow saleswoman Young-Hee Seong (Ruthie Ann Miles) so as to seduce her husband, who possesses security codes for a scientific research facility.

Elizabeth and Philip also collaborate, as in the scene with Viola and Grayson mentioned earlier. In other parts of the program, Elizabeth plays Clark's sister, Jennifer, and throughout season 5, Philip and Elizabeth play Brad and Dee Eckert, a pilot and hostess couple who have an adopted son, Tuan (Ivan Mok), who spy on and live in the same neighborhood as a Soviet defector. In addition to these named characters are the nameless personae that populate various isolated missions across the program.

These external aspects destabilize the evidence normally used to ground personal identity, and the resultant mutability is supported by elegant and nuanced performances by the central stars, as well as through the temporal aspects of the medium-specific features of television's narrative form. Philip Drake highlights the importance of the interplay between the extended narrative form of television and the performance-driven aspects of *The Americans*. He notes that "accumulated performances—the building up of detail and the use of familiar facial expressions, gestures, movements, and vocal signs—are just as important to an understanding of character development for nonstar and supporting actors. Across a thirteen-episode US television series, for example, a viewer will spend approximately ten hours accumulating knowledge of a character through the details of performance, the repeated gestures, glances, eye movements, expressive use of body and face, inflection of voice, and so on" (2016, 9). Drake also highlights how the quality of the performances and the long-form nature of the medium mutually benefit each other (13). In our experience with television programs, therefore, we accumulate evidence that feeds our recognition of the personal identity of characters in the world of the work. For serials such as *The Americans*, furthermore, it is the development of character—the dynamic between concordant and discordant features of characters—that plays out across seasons, and continually and repeatedly draws into question our recognition of characters. Drake highlights how "the face, eyes, and voice of the performer are potent signs in the performance idiolect in that they are often read as the site of presence, anchored through the body" (2016, 9). In posing as a variety of personae to other characters in the world of *The Americans*, Philip and Elizabeth disrupt the usual sites of evidence to obscure their true identities—who they actually are. Spectators, however, are always aware that Clark, for example, is Philip-as-Clark and Stephanie is Elizabeth-as-Stephanie. Whereas *3 Women*, for example, sustains an ambiguity as to the recognition of the woman that I suggest is resolved in taking each of the women as different versions of the same woman, the population question as it relates to Philip and Elizabeth is not ambiguous for spectators. As Drake notes, "*The Americans* uses wigs and other devices as ostensive tools to rekey the actors' performances, indicating to the viewer that the character onscreen is a performance of a performance" (11). The narrative suspense throughout *The Americans* instead becomes a question of when or whether certain characters will eventually possess the same knowledge—the same recognition—as spectators.

One key example is the aforementioned arc involving Philip-as-Clark and Martha, which continues across four seasons. Clark's persona and behavior relative to that of Philip change in line with his disguise—what starts as a romantic fling of sorts builds across seasons to an eventual marriage. The narrative climax of the fourth season centers around the revelation to Martha of Philip's identity in what Emily Nussbaum describes as "the end of a powerful arc about intimacy and betrayal" (2019, 276). The relationship's demise had been simmering for a number of episodes, with Martha beginning to question Clark's long absences due to work, the tasks Clark was asking Martha to complete that were making her feel increasingly uneasy, and, despite Clark's honeyed declarations of love and attempts at comfort, Martha's curiosity regarding his unwillingness to have children (attributed to work). At the conclusion of "I Am Abassin Zadran" (S03E12), Philip, sitting with a distraught and pensive Martha in their living room, removes his glasses and wig, showing to her his true appearance. The question of population along with the question of who Clark really is has, for Martha, supposedly been resolved due to the clarification of evidence.

In one of the final conversations between Martha and Philip, it is unclear, though, just how much clarity has been achieved. Clearly still in the shock of the revelations of Philip's/Clark's betrayal and deceit, now in a USSR safe house and talking face-to-face, Martha is unsure whether there was ever any love, feelings, or care that anchored their relationship. After all, the narrative perspective of personal identity doesn't just seek to reconcile questions of persistence, evidence, and population. It aims to provide not just metaphysical clarity but existential meaning. For Martha, the revelation of Philip-as-Clark might resolve some of these questions at a metaphysical level, but the question of meaning lingers for her as it does for spectators in regard to Tom/Joey in *A History of Violence* (and for Edie in that film, too). The narrative constructed between her and Clark has been broken and needs to be rewritten, and there is an ambiguity as to what of that relationship—what of their shared narrative—can be retained. This aspect of *The Americans*, through performance and the medium-specific temporal form of television, illustrates the limits of the narrative account of personal identity.

Not all of the relationships that Philip and Elizabeth have with other central characters require such elaborate disguises—some are more subtle. Philip and Elizabeth's relationship to their children, Henry (Keidrich Sellati) and the ever-inquisitive Paige (Holly Taylor), brought the tension inherent to the performance of their identities into the intimacy and, as would normally be expected, privacy and security of the domestic household. In "Stingers" (S03E10), Paige confronts her parents about the abnormality of their family life—that Philip and Elizabeth are frequently up in the middle of the night or leave in the middle of the night, and how she doesn't know whether her parents will be home when she arrives there from school. Philip and Elizabeth tell Paige who they are—that they are KGB agents working for the USSR, trying to improve the state of things (as they see it). Such a revelation is not readily accepted by Paige.

As mentioned earlier, the narrative account of personal identity attempts to generate meaning, to make sense of the story that connects the concordance and discordance of an individual's existence. In the example mentioned earlier of Philip-as-Clark and Martha, we can see that when the evidence of Clark's personal identity is shown to be false, the narrative falls to pieces—the story told to that point faces fatal plot holes, so to speak, and, in a Ricœurian mode, Martha is faced with the prospect of accounting for a mammoth discordance—of editing the narrative—that obliterates her understanding of who Clark is.

Paige must endure something similar. Her parents' revelation not only shatters her understanding of who they are but also has a run-on effect, calling into question her own narrative formed about her own identity. As noted earlier, the narrative perspective of personal identity is reflexive and deals with the interrelations of different individuals—the narrative Paige had of herself to this point is challenged because of the revelations of her parents. These different narratives intertwine because the lives of the people to whom the stories refer intertwine. To what extent does Paige's understanding—the meaningful narrative she constructs—of herself change because of the revelations of her parents? This question extends throughout the rest of program, as Paige's arc faces twists that mirror her own attempts to formulate a new narrative about her and her family's personal identity. *The Americans*' development of Paige's story, therefore, offers an opportunity to consider the extent to which the narratives of our own personal identities rest not just on our own personal continuity but on how that continuity is informed by those who are a close part of our lives.

Emily Nussbaum highlights two relevant features to this discussion of *The Americans* that possess a tragic quality: "the fate of Philip and Elizabeth's marriage—a deep bond between two well-trained fakes—and the one about the fate of the Soviet Union itself, which is due to collapse soon, not long after the show's eighties setting" (2019, 276). The latter, oriented in history, is a foregone conclusion—given the program's setting in real events that have already taken place and despite the program's setting in medias res, our foreknowledge of what eventuates helps reassert the tragic tenor that characterizes *The Americans*, extending into the very relationship in which the program is anchored.

The relationship between Philip and Elizabeth is one that was orchestrated by the USSR—they knew nothing of each other prior to meeting and being sent to the United States, and they had children so as to better fit in with their surroundings and not arouse undue suspicion. Having dropped spectators into the story of the Jenningses in medias res, the program dots flashbacks throughout as needed to enrich the histories of the two central characters and to develop some context for their behaviors and motivations (their agency). This begins, appropriately enough, in "Pilot" (S01E01), in which Philip is watching Nikolai Timoshev (David Vadim), a KGB defector to the United States. Timoshev is captured and taken back to the Jennings' house and left in the trunk of their car. Through a flashback, we see a young Elizabeth, back in the USSR, training in hand-to-hand combat with her instructor. A young Timoshev enters the scene, taking the place of the instructor, and the training session escalates, violently culminating in Timoshev raping Elizabeth. In the program's present again, Elizabeth, Philip, and Timoshev are in the Jennings' garage. Elizabeth beats Timoshev almost until the point of death, and the defector apologizes for what he did to Elizabeth. Philip, bewildered, asks what it is he is apologizing for. Receiving no response, he breaks Timoshev's neck and kills him, failing the mission in the process.

This example illustrates how a significant aspect of the narrative form of *The Americans* is to key spectators into moments that inform who the characters are and why they behave in the way that they do. And, as mentioned earlier, the program does not always provide the same information to that of the characters in *The Americans*. Therefore, one of the effects of the program's artistic exploration of personal identity is its generation of anticipation in spectators regarding other characters' recognition of Philip and Elizabeth. The flashback in the scene just mentioned—as with other flashbacks, another of which I will discuss in a moment—provides a depth of understanding to Elizabeth and why she reacts to Timoshev in the way that she does. The narrative we formulate about her identity, about her attributes as a person that persist through time, are developed in such moments. However, as with the example of Paige mentioned earlier, given the domestic and intimate nature of the family, the narrative we formulate about Elizabeth also informs the narrative we formulate about Philip. That he reacts in the way that he does—without the knowledge of Elizabeth's past that spectators possess—further serves to enrich our understanding of him, too.

In seasons 5 and 6 of *The Americans*, the relationship between Philip and Elizabeth becomes strained. The different effects of their decisions during missions and in their personal lives have affected their marriage and called into question their understandings of each other and themselves in a way not completely dissimilar to the predicament experienced by Martha. As much as they are being tested as a couple, the narratives they have constructed of their own identities, their own sense of who they are, are equally tested. Season 5 of *The Americans* frequently draws on flashbacks to Philip's childhood in the USSR—desperately poor, and characterized by violence. Traveling into the city center from his rural hometown of Tobolsk to retrieve milk and bread for his family, a school-age Philip would have to outrun gangs who would often violently rob him for money and food. One flashback shows Philip as a boy eventually standing up for himself and beating one of the members of the gang—a slightly older boy—to death with a rock. Philip also has an experience similar to that of Paige, though he experiences his revelation as an adult. For most of his life, Philip understood his father to be a logger working at the nearby forest. Through one of the regular KGB contacts disclosing missions to Philip and Elizabeth in the United States, Philip learns that his father was actually a guard at a prison camp that required the prisoners to work as loggers to the point of exhaustion and death.

These moments come at a critical point in Philip's narrative—ever more disillusioned with the missions to which he is tasked and the cause they are supposed to be advancing, and nearly lifeless in his relationship with Elizabeth. It is no coincidence that these interruptions of his personal history come at a time of crisis in personal identity—a crisis of meaning that the narrative perspective of personal identity looks to resolve. Philip draws on the earlier moments of his narrative to search for something constant—a thread that connects his existence then to now, one that looks to eradicate the disillusionment he feels at the current state of his life. He is searching for something that persists, something that gives his story meaning. He looks to the evidence of personal continuity, taking a deep dive into the past that might give him some clarification, some sense of resolution, though the program, in my estimation, remains agnostic as to whether he achieves this.

Nussbaum eloquently summarizes one of the themes that runs through *The Americans* as follows: "When you're known, you're in danger" (2019, 278). The shock and ambiguity experienced by Martha—in attempting to resolve the discordance in the narrative that encompasses Philip-as-Clark and Philip—are similar to what Philip experiences himself in terms of his own narrative. In order to be successful in his missions, Philip must deceive; he must become the character—the identity—he is playing. There is thus a sense in which he must deceive himself too. The different performative identities that he must maintain—often simultaneously—have taken their toll and bled back into the narrative that is meant to act as a straight path beneath those constructed and deceitful identities of Philip's missions. Performances such as Clark testify to the dangers of being known—but in the latter seasons of *The Americans*, Philip's existential exhaustion, his crisis of narrative, testify equally to the dangers of being unknown, especially to oneself.

As mentioned, that the thematic concerns in *The Americans* make their way into the domestic space of the family home means that the narrative identities of characters are not easily teased apart, with each mutually informing the others. This is clearly seen in the relationship between Philip and Elizabeth and Paige, and the marriage between Philip and Elizabeth. In "Dead Hand" (S06E01), Philip remarks to Elizabeth that "your whole way of being seems off." Because of the medium-specific temporal form of television, and the way in which it is used by *The Americans*, spectators can understand where Philip is coming from. The complete observation by Emily Nussbaum, only part of which I included earlier, is that "when you're known, you're in danger. To be loved, you have to be known" (2019, 278). The deceptions I described earlier that feed into Philip's ambiguous sense of self further inform his relationship with Elizabeth. The dynamics of the relationship that see it increase in strength as often as it seems ready to give way make use of the temporally elongated narrative form of television. It is never completely clear how much Philip and Elizabeth know of each other—and the ambiguity of one's recognition of the other is mirrored in the ambiguity of the recognition spectators have of each. Certainly, we recognize Elizabeth and Philip when they are onscreen, but we are never completely sure *who* they are in the meaningful sense that the philosophical perspective of narrative identity aims to clarify.

These existential questions are not divorced from the metaphysical questions; rather, they lead back to them. The depiction of Philip and Elizabeth's relationship in *The Americans* enables spectators to contemplate the extent to which the narrative perspective can track the existential and experiential quality of personal identity, the limits of the narrative account in drawing out the meaning and significance of events and actions. In experiencing *The Americans*, spectators can consider the narratives they construct of themselves and others in light of those narratives they have witnessed onscreen. And again, it is worth pointing out that these aspects of the program are inextricably tied to the temporally elongated narrative form of television. As Blanchet and Bruun Vaage note, "Television series are better equipped to allow spectators to develop a bond with fictional characters than feature films. This is because television series more effectively invoke the impression that we share a history with their characters: first, because of the series' longer screen duration and, second, because our own lives progress as the series goes on" (2012, 28). The medium-specific features of television also allow for spectators to develop a shared history with multiple characters—*The Americans* often makes use of crosscutting to ensure that spectators are kept abreast of missions that are occurring simultaneously. But these features are also used to great effect to develop the personal identity of characters on their own terms—to allow the space for the narratives of characters to fully encompass the concordance and discordance of their individual stories. Whereas *3 Women* exploited, or worked around, the medium-specific temporal restraints of film, *The Americans* makes full use of the prolonged temporal capacities of television to deeply develop the existences of a core group of characters, enabling their stories to be rich on their own terms as well as in terms of how they intersect with others.

In "Jennings, Elizabeth" (S06E09), the penultimate episode of *The Americans*, the program cuts to a flashback of Elizabeth's final briefing in the USSR before she leaves for America. It is a brief flashback, and the agent simply tells her that "you must make the right choices over there. But most importantly, we don't want you to lose who you are." At this point we might recall the two questions that Viola posed to Philip and Elizabeth in an earlier season of the program: "Who are you? What kind of people are you?" While *The Americans* does, at times, resolve these questions for certain characters, it leaves them open for spectators upon the program's conclusion. Making full use of the temporally elongated narrative form of the serial, *The Americans* demonstrates through the inextricability of form and content how the narrative perspective of personal identity can be deployed to account for the concordance and discordance of an identity and make explicit the sensitive interrelationships among multiple individuals through an emphasis on the existential questions surrounding personal identity, thereby leading back to certain metaphysical aspects of who a person is. At the same time, it can nevertheless be limited in not totally and meaningfully providing answers, both for characters and spectators.

The emphasis *The Americans* places on performance, personal identity, narrative, and time represents a sophisticated examination of many of the ideas central to this chapter. That the cluster of metaphysical questions regarding personal identity—questions addressing evidence, population, and persistence—can be explored through films and television programs with a narrative shape naturally invites us, the spectators, to reflect on the nature of narrative and its scope and limits. Narrative can act as a tether between the aforementioned metaphysical questions and existential ones, the latter providing us a means of identifying the significance of events and actions that are central to our lives. In telling stories about stories and stories about storytelling, films and television programs also provide novel means of rethinking what narrative is capable of and in what it consists: the extent to which it can in fact render our lives meaningful, the way in which it can unify and cohere together inconsistencies, discordances, and changes in an individual across time, the artistic and medium-specific ways in which these issues are brought to light in different artistic works.

6

What Can Film and Television Do?

Narrative, Mimesis, and Wonder

CHARLIE KAUFMAN's *Synecdoche, New York* (2008) finishes with the death of protagonist Caden Cotard (Philip Seymour Hoffman). The film depicts—*in media res*—Caden's life after his wife and daughter leave him. Caden wins a MacArthur Fellowship and moves to New York City, where he develops a play that looks to examine the ordinary, the tedious, the mundane, and the quotidian in all their depth, detail, and richness. The play is developed in a warehouse where Caden attempts to reconstruct places and events of significance to his life, and his cast of characters plays versions of the people in Caden's existence, including himself. He essentially aims to create a play that is a complete replication of an ordinary life—his ordinary life. The film's narrative gradually and continually eradicates the boundaries between the reality of the world of the film (Caden's world) and the constructed world of the play (the world Caden creates). Whereas the latter began as an attempt to reconstruct the reality of Caden's existence, it instead starts to overwhelm and shape it. The artwork begins to influence reality as much as reality gives birth to the artwork.

The idea of mimesis is unquestionably central to the film. The dual role of Cotard's play—reconstructive as much as it is generative—resembles the mimetic qualities of art that are central to the metaphysical screen. As Paul Ricœur reminds us, "*mimesis* is not a copy, but a creative imitation.... a concept which distinguishes human crafts and arts from nature. In this sense, it separates more than it connects" (1983, 8). The mimetic aspects of art—artworks of the metaphysical screen, and artworks such as Caden's play—create a gap that is not a deficient feature of the work but a laudable one. It is because of this creative remaking of a preexisting world that we can examine reality in the light of our experience with art and come to better understand how our experiences with art can enrich our capacity to wonder about the world and our place in it.

The Worth of Wonder

What characterizes our willingness to wonder through our engagement with art? Why might we be so open to seizing art and to investing our selves into the worlds we experience—worlds like those of the metaphysical screen—and the lives of those who populate those worlds? What of the fact that art acts on and seizes us, too, in ways unexpected and sometimes unsought? Rita Felski notes:

> We need to do justice to what the artwork does. The poem intervenes; the painting arrests a nonchalant viewer; the movie makes something happen. Someone is drawn to a haunting refrain, a quirky narrator, a burst of pigment: features that beg to be described, detailed, captured. For the fan, the enthusiast, the aficionado, such qualities matter. This mattering is built into the meaning of attachment: that we are drawn to one thing and emphatically not to another; that its specialness is nonnegotiable; that we are riled when we see it being treated as a stand-in for something else. (2020, 6)

That we form attachments to certain artworks is a given. That we cannot always understand why or how or which artworks those attachments cling to is seemingly a given as well. But one reason we are drawn to art—that we continue to intrude on it and allow it to or have it intrude on us—is the wonder that it evokes. Wonder about the work itself and how it uses the capacities of its medium and form to create worlds and tell stories through those worlds, as well as wonder that is manifest in whatever contemplation an artwork may evoke about the ordinary world we experience. One way to better understand this wonder is by attempting to better understand the experience that generates it: to articulate in language the wondrous, wonder-filled moment with an artwork as well as the work's artistic qualities and the effect those qualities had on us; to articulate, for example, the wonder of the metaphysical screen (as I have done throughout this book).

Attachment and wonder are not alienated from each other. Martha C. Nussbaum writes that wonder "responds to the pull of the object, and one might say that in it the subject is maximally aware of the value of the object, and only minimally aware, if at all, of its relationship to her own plans. That is why it is likely to issue in contemplation rather than in any other sort of action toward the object" (2001, 54–55). In Nussbaum's view, wonder's value is not realized through a preordained instrumentalization of some end we have in mind. However, we at times know that we are seized by an artwork (or a moment or detail that is part of it) without knowing why. The contemplation that can result can be a response to this uncertainty as much as it is to marvel in the "pull" (the attachment) of the object of experience that has motivated such contemplation. We don't doubt the value, but it isn't always clear how the value will act on us and motivate us to action. (Here, Nussbaum is writing of wonder as an emotion, and thus her concern with action.) And even after the experience has concluded, the fruits of it can continue to act on us. After all, we take our experiences with us.

The wondrous and wonder-filled moments of our experience with art need not be experiences with, for example, unfamiliar films or television programs. The familiar and unfamiliar alike can invoke a sense of wonder. Joerg Fingerhut and Jesse J. Prinz write that "wonder arises when we experience things that transcend common categories, things that are unusual, special, larger than life, or pull us away from our mundane activities. These may be things that are unexpected, but wonder also arises for familiar and expected things, such as a sunset, a waterfall, or a baby's hands. Even if we have seen these before, each encounter can remove us from the workday flow of life" (2018, 116–17). To adapt these comments to the domain of art: the activity of the work upon us can be from familiar works or unfamiliar ones, familiar details and moments in works or unfamiliar ones. It might be that a scene we have experienced countless times before resonates differently with us. It might inspire something not inspired before (despite its familiarity), and not because the art has changed but because we have and because of who we now are and what has occurred to us in our time away from the artwork. The changes in us can enable us to be receptive to a detail, moment, or work in a new way.

Fingerhut and Prinz draw attention to an important aspect involved in wonderment: that we are dealing with an object of experience some aspect or quality or detail of which is difficult to describe or understand through preexisting categories and modes of experiencing the world around us. We may recognize something that is familiar—an object or situation, for example, or, in the context of art, a depiction of a familiar object or situation. However, as familiar as that object or situation might be, the manner of its representation and the way it is situated in a narrative could strike us and draw us in in a way that we are unused to. Because of the way that such a moment transcends our ordinary understanding of the familiar, we have cause to wonder at the object or situation itself, as well as its artistic realization. These sorts of experiences motivate wonder and foster our attachments to works of art, so it is reasonable that such experiences and moments are ones we are motivated to understand. Sophia Vasalou writes,

> For if wonder is the gasp torn from us as children when we are confronted with something hitherto unseen, there is also another kind of gasp that is torn from us as adults when we study more closely—as scientists, as philosophers, as students of spiritual techniques—what has already been a thousand times seen and see it again. If wonder sends us looking, there is also a kind of wonder for which we may later seek—seeking out starlit skies and mountain tops, bending closer to lines of poetry, leaning closer to drops of water or snowflakes or the wings of flies to look. (2015, 3)

There is a delight in wonder that is absent from something like the sublime. There is a quality of gratitude that is not diminished once the initial surprise of the moment—of the experience—has passed and the reflection and contemplation set in, nor that is necessarily diminished as we seek out that moment over and over to understand it. The attempt to understand the source and nature of wonder with art through analysis and articulating the content of our contemplation both establishes wonder's significance and helps to delineate it from other sorts of emotional (or emotion-laden) experiences. Vasalou continues:

> If wonder is the exclamation of delight faced with the *aurora borealis* or the wide-eyed look of the scientist as she watches the dance of fabulous animals or the dance of objects in the sky, this pleasured response often shades dangerously into others—to a look of pained confusion, or frozen anxiety, or awed terror, before a spectacle that disturbs our expectations or overwhelms our ordinary frames of thought, pulling us too far away from the zone in which the extraordinary can be contemplated without disturbance; to something darker, bearing the texture of fear, as we confront the grandeur and enormity of the world that surrounds us. (2015, 3)

Wonder motivates other sorts of emotional experiences—it can lead to awe or terror or anxiety when we are confronted with certain complex questions. The experience of wonder itself, though, is valuable, as it tears us from our ordinary mode of experience, opens us to thinking about familiar things in new ways or new things altogether, and causes us to reckon with ourselves and our place in the world. It expands the horizons of our experience.

What can be gained by experiencing films with an openness to wonder, or indeed, by bringing such perception to films that explore the presence of wonder itself? In Henry Koster's *Harvey* (1950), Elwood P. Dowd (James Stewart) has a best friend—a six-and-a-half-foot rabbit who is invisible to nearly everyone except Elwood. In the opening scene, Elwood and Harvey have opened the front door to a beautiful morning. They walk happily to the front gate and open it, too—Elwood, ever the gentleman, lets Harvey through first. The postman arrives with a special letter, remarking happily and politely, "Beautiful day." As he signs for his letter, Elwood replies in Stewart's familiar cadence: "Oh, uh, every day's a beautiful day."

Elwood's amiability is limitless—he is personable, interested in others, and only too willing to make friends. He has an aloof air, but only in the sense that he is somewhat detached from the ordinary, everyday troubles of those he comes across—most notably his older sister, Veta (Josephine Hull), and his niece, Myrtle Mae (Victoria Horne). His detachment and pleasant, faraway quality, paired with his enthusiasm to introduce Harvey to everyone he comes across, concerns his family, as it undercuts the social standing they are trying to establish in the community (the ends of which are marrying Myrtle Mae off to the "right man"). Veta and Myrtle Mae's solution to the problem of Elwood and Harvey is to have him committed. Elwood, though, continues to win over those at the sanatorium who would approve such a decision, including Dr. William Chumley (Cecil Kellaway), who sees and befriends Harvey toward the film's conclusion.

In the penultimate moments of the film, Elwood is in the foyer of the sanatorium, finally convinced by his exasperated sister (who has gotten the attending psychiatrist on her side) to now willingly take a serum guaranteed to ensure that Elwood won't see Harvey anymore. In wanders a cab driver who has been impatiently waiting outside for his fare after having brought Veta and some of her entourage in tow to the sanatorium. Unable to find her coin purse, Elwood moseys over to pay the driver before going into the room for his so-called cure. The cab driver is familiar with the sanatorium, having taken many people to visit inpatients and undergo various treatments, and is familiar even with the serum Elwood is to receive. He remarks that the serum will work, and Elwood will become "normal," adding, "and we know what stinkers they [normal people] are."

Fortunately, Veta eventually intervenes, and as Elwood leaves the sanatorium by himself—he is under the impression that Harvey has decided to stay behind with Dr. Chumley—there is an air of melancholy before man and rabbit are reunited once more. The film's identification with wonder is made clearer in the context of the cab driver's comments, which are insightful especially when taken with some other moments in the film. In another scene, a disheveled Chumley emerges from his office to greet Elwood and some employees of the sanatorium who have been looking for the missing doctor. The doctor ushers Elwood into his office for a conversation; it appears Chumley has seen and befriended Harvey. After talking for a while, Chumley informs Elwood of his sister's plan (Elwood simply replies that Veta is a "whirlwind"). The doctor then asks Elwood whether he has any righteous indignation. Elwood replies, "Well, doctor, years ago my mother used to say to me, 'in this world, Elwood, you must be'—she always called me Elwood—'in this world, Elwood, you must be oh so smart or oh so pleasant.' Well, for years I was smart. I recommend pleasant. You may quote me." Elwood has a commitment to his friend, Harvey, who helps him navigate the world and make sense of things. In a way, Harvey simplifies Elwood's life—the latter bounces ideas off the former, he asks questions of him, and they enjoy conversations together of which we only hear the human's side. The possibility that Elwood's wonder could slide into anxiety, worry, and other less pleasant things is ameliorated by the presence of the rabbit. He provides Elwood with a kind of safety and stability. With Harvey, Elwood is free to revel in and wonder about the ordinary and everyday things of life, to maintain his sense of gratitude for every beautiful day, to regularly see the familiar anew and to wonder in ways that he tragically wouldn't otherwise. Is it smart to rely on a gigantic invisible white rabbit? Perhaps not, but his presence provides Elwood the means of "safely" (and pleasantly) wondering about the world.

The one moment in the film that most strongly attests to this occurs toward its conclusion, as Elwood says goodbye (or what he thinks is goodbye) to Harvey at the front door of the sanatorium. Instead of leaving with Elwood, Harvey has decided to spend some time with Chumley instead. Ever gracious, Elwood amiably enough agrees. But in medium close-up we see Elwood's face shattered, as his eyes dart and bounce chaotically all around. Suddenly without his friend, things instantly seem more difficult, more chaotic, more terrifying. Life itself has lost its ability to evoke wonder, and life itself seems much less pleasant.

What is it that Elwood is losing with the absence of his friend? Earlier moments in the film help us understand what is being lost in the separation. With the disappearance of Chumley that occurs partway through the film, Elwood is being escorted by Dr. Sanderson (Charles Drake) and Nurse Kelly (Peggy Dow)—employees of the sanatorium—through town to search for the missing doctor. Elwood had enjoyed Chumley's company earlier for a drink and is the last to have seen him. Together, they return to the bar in question—one of Elwood and Harvey's favorite haunts—and as nurse and doctor enjoy a long-awaited heartfelt dance together (orchestrated by Elwood), he wanders out a side door and into an alley, closely followed by a panicked Sanderson and Kelly. After Elwood mentions that he used to dance quite often himself, but doesn't seem to have the time, as he has "so many things to do," the nurse asks a plausible question, one that may have even crossed spectators' minds as well: "What is it you do, Mr. Dowd?"

Elwood is only too happy to oblige—he sits in the bars with Harvey; they enjoy a drink together and listen to the jukebox: "And soon the faces of all the other people turn toward mine, and they smile. And they're saying, 'We don't know your name mister, but you're a very nice fellah.' Harvey and I warm ourselves in all these golden moments. We've entered as strangers and soon we have friends." Lives are transformed in the repetitious and familiar—lives are transformed by the wonder found and evoked by these moments. Elwood tells us that nobody brings anything small into a bar—no one has any small problems, well-moderated hopes and dreams. And he notes with a tinge of sadness and regret that when he introduces his friend Harvey to his new friends—as Elwood remarks, a rabbit grander than anything anyone else brings into the bar—these people seldom return to them.

Earlier in the scene, as Kelly and Sanderson had entered the bar looking for Elwood, doctor and nurse see him apparently by himself in a booth. Elwood stands to greet them, and after some conversation, Sanderson implores Elwood to face reality. Coyly, Elwood replies: "Well, I wrestled with reality for thirty-five years, doctor, and I'm happy to state I finally won out over it." This selection of moments from and attributes of the film I have sketched—including the quest for a cure for Elwood's way of seeing the world through and with Harvey, Elwood's capacity to wonder, and his sadness and regret over others without that capacity—is a gesture to the ways in which the film artistically explores the process and value of wondering. These examples are significant illustrations of the ways in which *Harvey* works to transcend our ordinary understanding of seeing the world by dwelling on and celebrating Elwood's wonder-filled appreciation of the ordinary. He wins out over reality not by ignoring it but by appreciating it, reveling in it, and being grateful for it.

On the other hand, we might ask: Is Harvey an invention of Elwood's imagination? Is the rabbit a somewhat sad way for him to justify an entrenched drinking habit in a world he finds too difficult to face soberly? There may be some truth to this, but Chumley sees Harvey as well. And Veta, even in a state of distress, admits to seeing the rabbit on occasion. I prefer to see in Harvey—as real as any other character that populates the film—an embodiment of wonder. This is clear in the scene where Harvey and Elwood say goodbye, only to be reconnected minutes later. The look of sudden and intense unease on Elwood's face at the thought of being without his friend is matched by the sparkle, joy, sense of gratitude, and indeed sense of wonder at the sight (invisible to us) of that big rabbit's return (fig. 6.1).

Nothing is more ordinary or familiar to Elwood than the presence of his best friend, yet he wonders anew at the sight of him, beholding him with an upward glance in a posture we associate with wondering. Through the moments described earlier we can piece together important aspects of Elwood's character, a character that is expertly and richly created through Stewart's performance. Elwood devalues the ordinary troubles of reality and opts for kindness, being pleasant, and taking an interest in others (even though he knows how things often will go once strangers meet his most cherished friend). For Elwood, Harvey is the friend whom he wonders at and who also enables him to wonder about the world, to be safely befuddled by the things that unfold around him—never with a hardness or sense of interrogation, but instead with a gentility and curiosity that afford him the joy of finding every day to be a beautiful one. As Harvey meets Elwood at the front gates of the sanatorium in the closing moments of the film, Elwood's face couldn't be more opposite to the one that registered his sadness of living without his friend. Wondering what happened with Chumley, we can, through Elwood's reply, intimate Harvey's answer without hearing it: "Well thank you, Harvey. I prefer you, too." Who could blame him?

The imagination as it relates to wonder runs beneath the surface of *Harvey*, which opts more to focus on the concrete effects and experience of wondering. But the imagination, wonder, and mimesis—the capability of wonder and the imagination to creatively remake the world and see it anew—are central to another film, Norman Z. McLeod's *The Secret Life of Walter Mitty* (1942). Walter Mitty (Danny Kaye) is an editor at a publishing company, and he is ground down, harassed, and bothered by the characters that populate his life, including his mother, boss, and fiancée. Too timid to stand up for himself, he instead frequently resides in his imagination, especially as the often courageous, swashbuckling, adventurous lead of scenarios inspired by the pulp magazines he proofreads in his job. Mitty's imagination, though, can be spurred on by anything. For example, passing a billboard for Sea Drift soap chips, he transforms into a brave sea captain (fig. 6.2).

Figure 6.1. Elwood says farewell (top), and Elwood is reunited (bottom) in *Harvey*. *Source:* Koster, Henry, dir. *Harvey*. 1950. Los Angeles: Universal Studios, 2014. Blu-ray Disc, 1080p HD.

Figure 6.2. A billboard creates a brave sea captain in *The Secret Life of Walter Mitty*. *Source:* McLeod, Norman Z., dir. *The Secret Life of Walter Mitty*. 1947. Burbank, CA: Warner Bros. Pictures, 2013. DVD, 480p HD.

Ordinary tasks, too, allow Mitty to wander (and wonder) freely in his mind. The fantasies, though, occasionally break through the surface of reality: imagining himself as a courageous RAF pilot while he stokes a fire with a hot poker, he places the poker under his arm and salutes when his mother calls him to dinner.

Mitty's real problem with the overlap of fantasy and reality arises when he becomes the protagonist of a real-life thrilling adventure involving Dutch jewels hidden from the Nazis, and a range of interested but shady parties engaged in their retrieval. The fantasy has become reality, yet Mitty finds himself needing time to adapt to his role as hero and develop the courage to overcome those seeking him harm (the real-life players in the apparent fantasy). He must also stand up to those who have been overwhelming him (the real-life players in Mitty's everyday life).

Mitty is constantly making and remaking the world around him into fantasy worlds for him to imaginatively inhabit. There is a kernel of the ordinary reality he endures day-to-day, but for the most part this is a starting point for him to mimetically construct the world around him as something else, and as such it affords him the opportunity to mimetically construct himself anew as well. Wonder is not wishful thinking or fantasy, but in all of Mitty's fantasies, we see the fruits of his wondering as expressed through the mimetic worlds he creates. He imaginatively tests the waters, moves to the edge of his reality, and wonders about how things could be—his fantasies are born from a recognition of the ordinary categories and modes of experience that shape his life, and his wondering enables him to move beyond them.

Walter's existential change occurs when the sorts of things he imagines and wonders about flow back into his ordinary sense of reality. Here we see the call to action that wonder-as-emotion demands—he must respond to meet the challenges of the seemingly new world in which he finds himself. The example he looks to regarding how he needs to act is the one embodied in the courageous and confident fantastical personae that have populated his imaginative wondering to this point. Once he realizes that he must act as he has always imagined he would like to—once he allows the wonder to shape his existence—he sees his ordinary reality in a new way, in light of what has happened. He sees the world around him in light of wonder and in light of mimesis.

Internal Reflections

As mentioned earlier, one of the central concerns of *Synecdoche, New York*, and something that is shared with *The Secret Life of Walter Mitty*, is the ways in which the mimetic worlds we create flow back into and influence our experience of the ordinary world, the ways in which we understand ourselves and the world we inhabit. One of the many ideas explored in *Synecdoche* is the attempt to achieve some sort of self-understanding through the creation of art. Caden's re-creation of his existence in a play can be seen as the externalization of his experiences into a mimetic world so as to gain a degree of self-knowledge that can only be attained, not in his everyday experience, but as such experience is refracted through the re-creation and performance of the everyday. He is authoring the story that is continually unfolding, so the play can only be complete once he dies.

Caden is left in a horrible existential predicament, so his play is an attempt to achieve some manner of understanding of the world and himself, to see the performance of his life laid before him. But in this creative remaking of the world—the mimetic transformation of his life—something is lost. The very force or momentum behind and driving self-discovery is dampened somewhat. The more Caden attempts to know of himself through the past, through the locked-in memories of the play and through the orchestration of each new day performed by others but not experienced by him, the more the mimetic world Caden creates becomes increasingly removed from his experience. The thread connecting it to the world becomes ever weaker, ever more frayed.

How do works that expressly illustrate the mimetic creation of worlds reflect the process of experiencing artistic worlds? In Jim Jarmusch's *Paterson* (2016), Paterson (Adam Driver) is a poetry-writing bus driver in the city of Paterson, New Jersey. We follow Paterson over a week of his life. In *Synecdoche, New York*, Caden doesn't so much engage in wonder (perhaps, as Nussbaum would point out, he is too instrumental in his approach to art), but we often see Paterson doing so: he is struck by the wonder evoked by the ordinary, mundane, familiar, and repetitious. The strangeness of the ordinary is expressed through the motif of twins, and Paterson's attention is occupied by the recurrent presence of twins throughout the film. For example, on the first Monday, Paterson's wife, Laura (Golshifteh Farahani), dreams that they had twins ("one for each of us"); on Tuesday while driving his bus, he notices two passengers who are mirror images of each other in terms of behavior, both making excuses for their failed romantic pursuits; Wednesday, Paterson looks quizzically at twin girls crossing the road; and on Thursday he sees twin girls on the bus, before meeting his own twin—a young girl who is also a poet waiting for her sister and mother.

Paterson looks to transform the ordinary experiences of the world through poetic form and into mimetic worlds. For example, he writes about matchboxes as a means of expressing the personal history of a loving relationship. He also writes of the experience of writing and creating poetry, and of time, too. Time is one of the most central themes of the film and so of Paterson's poetry. Often, we see the words of the poem onscreen as Paterson recites the poem in voiceover. Paterson's ruminations on time occur during a montage sequence of sorts, representing a standard slice of his workday driving a bus. We are treated to the experience that has likely given rise to and is expressed in the poetic form of his poem "Another One"—the world and his experience of it is remade cinematically as Paterson remakes it poetically.

The scene in question employs several techniques to convey Paterson's experience of time. The use of superimposition doesn't demarcate or delineate moments, but rather—in layering two, three, even four shots on top of each other—visually represents the amorphous nature of Paterson's temporal experience of working through the rhythm generated by his bus route. Some of these shots are shots of passengers, the streets of Paterson, or Paterson himself. Others align with certain parts of the poem; a beer glass, for example, makes an appearance at the appropriate time as it is buried in the densely layered images just mentioned. There is a sense, then, in which memories or ideas impose themselves on Paterson's experience too, and thus there is a lack of a clear delineation between the world he experiences and the poetic world of "Another One." The layering of images in the scene reflects a layering of worlds. Paterson's world is remade in the world of the poem, and these worlds are remade in the world of the film, itself a remaking of the world of ordinary experience.

The metaphysical screen has a myriad of ways to examine the mimetic world's influence on the ordinary world. Early in Oliver

Assayas's film *Irma Vep* (1996), we see a chaotic film production office: hurried conversations about finances and promotional aspects of a film, assistants rushing to correct misunderstandings and address complications—the office personnel all attempting to balance director René Vidal's (Jean-Pierre Léaud) thought process and creative vision with the practical realities of filmmaking. The film he is making is a remake of a silent film masterpiece, *Les Vampires*, which follows a group of thieves. The leader of the group is named Irma Vep, played in *Irma Vep* by Maggie Cheung (Maggie Cheung). Even here we can see a layering of mimetic worlds—a director making a film, an adaptation of an older film, which is part of the film *Irma Vep*, a key character of which is a fictionalized version of a real-life actress. This density of worlds is made more of than the moment in *Paterson* described earlier, and it structures the entirety of *Irma Vep*. It is one of several films that show us the cinematic process of remaking—familiar in works as varied as *Singin' in the Rain* (1952), *8½* (1963), *Day for Night* (1973), *The Player* (1992), *Get Shorty* (1995), *Mulholland Drive* (2001), and *Tropic Thunder* (2008).

The details of the mimetic world matter. In one scene, with some assistants and employees from the costume department, Maggie is trying out different possibilities for Irma's costume, a skintight latex catsuit. The costuming possibilities are interrogated and compared with other possibilities down to the finest detail—how each one sits and looks on Maggie, how it feels, how it allows her to move. In another scene—this time a scene of a scene being shot in the film *Les Vampires* (part of the film *Irma Vep*)—Irma Vep is kidnapped by another criminal and replaced with another character who has been hypnotized, and we watch this second woman jump the railing of the small apartment in which the switch takes place, wearing the same catsuit as Irma. In a later scene, after René has had a violent breakdown after being animatedly distraught with the final product of the film, *Irma Vep*'s Maggie Cheung is at his apartment after he had left messages with her hotel asking her to meet him. Hearing the chaos of sirens and checking that René is all right, she leaves, jumping a small fence to take a shortcut back to her room. This gesture recalls the earlier one, foregrounding the remaking and inviting our attention to the layering of mimetic worlds. The film unmistakably signals the mutual influence of the densely populated and layered mimetic realities operating within *Irma Vep*, of which the film itself is the metaworld containing all the others. As in *Paterson*, there is a persistent refraction in *Irma Vep* and a sense of internal reflection. It works as a hall of mirrors that highlights the variable mimetic worlds and the ever-knotted threads connecting them.

Loving Perception

Irma Vep is hardly an ode to filmmaking. It isn't a love letter to cinema, despite its preoccupation with the creation of worlds that film affords. The attention to detail given to filmmaking throughout the film—the exploration of filmmaking via the making of a film—invites a reflection not just on what cinema is capable of but on the appreciation and love for cinema that attracts so many to try to explain the wonder it invokes. That is, in its peculiar depiction of mimesis and wonder, it is also at once an example of cinematically depicted cinephilia.

Cinephilia has many manifestations. Thomas Elsaesser notes that "cinephilia . . . wherever it is practiced around the globe, is not simply a love of the cinema. It is always already caught in several kinds of deferral: a detour in place and space, a shift in register and a delay in time" (2005, 30). The means of cinephiliac practice are stronger than ever despite the downturn in theatergoing. Contemporary cinephilia relies on and affords deferrals and detours of space and time through home media, streaming, and film societies. In these different forms and manifestations, cinephilia may not merely represent a love of cinema. All its forms and manifestations are surely motivated by, at the very least, an appreciation of the art form, a kind of wondering about cinema that is prompted by cinema itself.

The concept and practice of cinephilia have a complex scholarly history. The idea of it I have in mind here, which has informed the preceding chapters, is something along the lines of a consciously appreciative means of navigating the objective artistic qualities of a work and one's subjective interest in and experience of that work. This idea is implied in some reflective comments made by François Truffaut. Describing the process of falling in love with the cinema, he writes:

> I am often asked at what point in my love affair with films I began to want to be a director or a critic. Truthfully, I

don't know. All I know is that I wanted to get closer and closer to films.

The first step involved seeing lots of movies; secondly, I began to note the name of the director as I left the theatre. In the third stage I saw the same films over and over and began making choices as to what I would have done, if I had been the director. (1978, 4)

A willing exposure to a volume of films develops into a keen interest for details of the players involved, which then extends into repetitive viewing and a critical reflection of the details and choices within the films themselves. How does this attraction to art—a motivated attempt to grow closer to films—manifest itself in the critical attempt to understand the moments, details, and works that encourage and invoke wonder? For Truffaut, the cinephiliac tendency I suggest he is describing is one that is characterized by gratitude. He continues: "Those who do the judging . . . are cognizant of the enormous privilege of the act of creation, of the risks incurred by the one who exposes himself thus, and in turn feel a *secret* admiration and respect which would at least partially restore the artist's peace of mind if he could know it" (13). Truffaut's somewhat unique position as both filmmaker and critic—as someone who, to return to the idea of threefold mimesis briefly, navigates the move from prefiguration to configuration in the creation of films, and articulates the configurative nature and refigurative value of works in his role as critic—enables a distinctively "wonder-filled" appreciation of film.

The sort of cinephilia at play here—the sort I hold Truffaut to be advocating—is at odds with other ways in which it is often treated. Christian Keathley builds on the work of Paul Willemen to develop a somewhat different view of cinephilia. Willemen prioritized the "cinephiliac moment" whereby the spectator engages with "fleeting, evanescent moments" in their experience with a film, which is wrapped up in what he calls a "discourse of revelation" (1994, 232). On the back of this view, Keathley held maximal value in "the gesture of a hand, the odd rhythm of a horse's gait, or the sudden change in expression on a face" as moments celebrated by the cinephile "who beholds them as nothing less than an epiphany" (2006, 7). Keathley emphasizes as the source and focus of cinephilia the accidental, the unintended, and the peripheral moments that make their way into films. Although these moments can be shared with others, Keathley observes that "such details remain one's own, no doubt in large part because the initial encounter was a private one" (31). There is some overlap between my understanding of cinephilia and Keathley's, and that is that each spectator, each cinephile, gradually builds a repertoire of cinematic moments that is particular to them, celebrated by them, important to them, and not necessarily shared by any other spectator. Keathley provides a concise definition: "the cinephiliac moment may be understood as a kind of *mise-en-abyme* wherein each cinephile's obsessive relationship to the cinema is embodied in its most dense, concentrated form" (32).

But why so much talk about obsession and fetishizing? Or why use the language of desire, or of film as a dose and a drug as another writer has it (Keller 2020, 27)? The original formulation of *philia* is a form of love with dimensions of friendship and companionship, affection, and familiarity developed across time. Aristotle's understanding of philia prevents it from encompassing nonhuman relationships, given the importance of reciprocity and activity, but because the term *cinephilia* has already entered critical discourse and enjoyed (as Hodsdon [2017] ably demonstrates) a long and changing history, why not at least try to respect the root idea it looks to evoke in the context of our experience with films? Is there not more gained rather than lost by an understanding of cinephilia that is developed more gently across multiple, accumulating experiences—no doubt peppered with the epiphanic, the revelatory, and at times even the marginal without this prescriptively being the case?

After all, as Barrett Hodsdon highlights, to privilege the marginal, the accidental, and the incidental is to therefore denigrate a "premeditative director like Hitchcock or Fritz Lang" who "rarely catered for the occurrence of chance factors" (2017, 172). Here, Hodsdon echoes another of Truffaut's implied observations: that the filmmakers—the creators, including all the cast and crew who give life to a work—are designing their artistic world with something in mind, some end point. Is this intention less valuable merely because it is not always accidental? Is the hyperconcentrated design of a Hitchcock film less artistically impressive than the aesthetic freedom of a Cassavetes movie? Or is it the task of cinephilia to search for the unique value that these different forms of filmmaking create in their own respective worlds?

Hodsdon goes to some length to develop an understanding of cinephilia that beautifully articulates the idea I have in mind here. It involves a sort of perspective or attitude that balances the objective and subjective, that moves between the two, that is sensitive to wonder and the mimetic and imaginative process of remaking the world:

> Rather than restricting the epiphanous moment to the unseen seen, it is more fruitful to locate it on a more expansive canvas of numerous possibilities for the concise and rhythmic execution of mise-en-scéne, with a space for the inclusion of the accidental and incidental, and their potential fusion with authorial makership. These moments can emanate from the director's ability to translate his mode of perception into an aesthetic ordering of performance, gesture, and detail alongside the overall framing and organization of scenic and narrative dynamics. This can amount to rich and subtle inflections of the image that almost imperceptibly shift from the prosaic mode of expression to a poetic register. Such a shift can imbue the image with an indelible quality reverberating back through the narrative, condensing or redoubling thematic concerns or motifs (2017, 172).

Hodsdon sees cinephilia as a kind of perception, a kind of attention—a mode of wonder-filled experience that revels in any detail, any texture, any surface, any moment, or any work. Cinephilia seeks to understand the way in which cinematic wonder fulfills its capacity in transcending the ordinary modes of understanding, perceiving, and experiencing. Cinephilia, then, is not limited to the experience of the spectator but is also represented in the work of the filmmakers themselves, prompting these questions: Can films re-create or remake the very way in which we attend to things, through the very fact they have been ordered according to a preexisting perception? And what can films tell us about the process of looking and perceiving via their own cinematic looks and the way in which they explore the very idea of experiential perception itself?

Lynne Ramsay's *Morvern Callar* (2002) follows Morvern (Samantha Morton), who discovers on Christmas morning that her boyfriend has committed suicide. He has left, among other things, a note, a mixtape, and the unsubmitted but complete manuscript of his book. Morvern sends the book off to a publisher, after replacing his name with hers. She uses the money he left behind to arrange his funeral to instead go with her friend Lanna (Kathleen McDermott) on a holiday to Spain. After a few days and before heading off, Morvern cuts up her boyfriend's corpse and buries it in an isolated field. The film ostensibly tracks Morvern's grief, which manifests itself in erratic and often unexplained behavior, compounded by Morvern's impassive countenance and emotional restraint. We have no frame of reference for what Morvern is like prior to her boyfriend's suicide. This lack of knowledge of her personal history, augmented by how emotionally withdrawn and obscure she is, makes it difficult at times to understand what she does. And yet we spend the entirety of the film with her.

Through an intimate series of close-ups, we watch Morvern discover her boyfriend's body on Christmas morning. The image is suffused by the blinking lights decorating the house and tree. This motif is repeated throughout the film: at a party sequence before Lanna and Morvern leave for Spain, at various nightclubs they frequent while on holiday, and in the closing scene of the film as well. While the blinking lights in these moments are appropriate given the setting, the film's attachment to Morvern suggests a significance beyond this. They serve as a reminder of that morning, of her boyfriend, of the means by which she has paid for the holiday, of the entire history she shared with him that exists not for spectators but for her. She carries parts of this history with her throughout the film—a jacket, a lighter, the mixtape, and, in a way, the trip itself. We are invited to search for the details that give us a hint as to what she is experiencing, but the film's paradox is that despite spending its entire duration alongside Morvern, we gain little in the way of understanding her motivations and who she is.

The film's cinematography reveals a preoccupation with and sensitivity to surfaces, details, and texture. It is a sensorial and tactile film that relies repeatedly on close-ups of faces and hands, caresses between humans, and touches and contact with objects. That the film emphasizes this felt experience of the world is again a compelling paradox given that the person whose experience it is we are following is so hidden from us. The film does not just present itself as an object of experience but is an object of experience that represents an experiencing character. In the burial scene, Morvern takes her time to experience her surroundings, the area where she has just laid her boyfriend to rest: she strokes a branch and holds her hand in a puddle (fig. 6.3). She cannot hold him or be near him anymore—there is no material, embodied proximity that is possible—but she takes her time to spend her last moments with him being as close as possible, the natural world now intervening and severing their capacity for a felt connection.

This lack of intimacy, of relational proximity, is a feature of the film. *Morvern Callar* is a sophisticated analysis of a life untethered from the world and a character trying to make sense of the world from which she feels removed. The superficial markers of experience are present throughout, but these are intercut with Morvern's existential isolation and reservation. She tries to envelop herself with the world, to establish contact with objects and people, but on the level of meaning or significance there is no connection, no substance to the surface of proximity and intimacy she is trying to create. The final scenes of the film show Morvern in a sweaty nightclub somewhere, completely removed from what is happening, her cassette player plugged in and her headphones wrapped around her ears. It suggests that she is still listening to her boyfriend's mixtape, with the blinking lights that opened the film pulsating through the scene. The details

Figure 6.3. Morvern touches the earth in *Morvern Callar*. *Source:* Ramsay, Lynne, dir. *Morvern Callar*. 2002. New York: Fun City Editions, 2022. Blu-ray Disc, 1080p HD.

Morvern is attending to reside in her past, the little snapshots are frozen memories of what once was, the present world around her fading in importance. *Morvern Callar* uses the artistic attributes of cinema to represent a character's experiential perception of her world. It artfully attunes spectators to fine details and to the embodied and tactile modes of experiencing a world. The film thereby invites us, via its treatment of experiential perception, to reflect on the means by which we experience our world day-to-day.

In Jim Jarmusch's *The Limits of Control* (2009), Lone Man (Isaach de Bankolé) is an assassin for hire carrying out jobs in Spain. The plot is bare-bones, and each extended sequence works as a kind of variation on a single idea—Lone Man meets other characters at a café in the same way, he has multiple meetings on trains, phrases are repeated, and locations are revisited. The familiar is made more familiar in returning to it, the differences and remaking that occur via experience offering a case of wonder and cinephiliac perception untethered from a clear and conventional narrative.

The initial encounter that has Lone Man sent to Spain is abstruse; little is explained. His employers state that "everything is subjective" and that "the universe has no center and no edges; reality is arbitrary." The film's lack of character history and motivation and lack of clear narrative direction open up an interpretive and experiential space for spectators to fill in the gaps with their own subjectivity. The narrative's openness and inexplicable qualities motivate a shift in emphasis away from what happens toward how the world and characters are represented. Therefore, *The Limits of Control* amplifies and fixates and on shapes, lines, and surfaces of characters, objects, and settings.

Reflections off surfaces, windows of buildings, and mirrors are rife throughout the film. The angles of buildings are brought into highly composed relief. So too are the sharp lines of the performers' faces: de Bankolé's prominent cheekbones (fig. 6.4); Tilda Swinton's unnamed contact; and Paz de La Huerta's mysterious, thwarted femme fatale are all reveled in by the camera. The positioning of the camera varies to stridently compose the faces, buildings, and images we see. Occasionally perching high and sometimes sitting low as is necessary to accentuate these bodily features and the features of the modernist architecture surrounding the characters, it cherishes the curves of the Torres Biancas apartment tower Lone Man stays in in Madrid, and the straight edges of the Museo Nacional Centro de Arte Reina Sofía

Figure 6.4. Facial and architectural angles in *The Limits of Control*. Source: Jarmusch, Jim, dir. *The Limits of Control*. 2009. Hertfordshire, England: Arrow Films, 2019. Blu-ray Disc, 1080p HD.

where he often goes to gaze at art. Lone Man conducts himself in silence for much of the film, so we are left to adhere to his weighty, analytic looks and glances—the camera fixates on these moments of looking in long static shots or slow tracks in, magnifying the intensity.

As the film progresses, Lone Man moves to increasingly wilder and more alienated territory, eventually landing in a desert town. On the way, he encounters a new character, Mexican (Gael García

Bernal), who passes on some local knowledge: "The old men in my village used to say, 'Everything changes by the color of the glass you see it through.' Nothing is true. Everything is imagined. Do you know these reflections? For me sometimes the reflection is far more present than the thing being reflected." What is being reflected in *The Limits of Control* is a certain way of examining the world. The film is a celebration of looking, the camera's orchestrated capacity to select and cherish what falls before it, to show us characters looking (especially Lone Man), to give spectators a cinematic means of reflecting on what it is to reflect and perceiving what it is to perceive. Whereas *Morvern Callar* strongly emphasizes a single character's story that is paradoxically obscured, *The Limits of Control* offers little to no character whatsoever and places the camera as the protagonist. They are both examples of cinematic works that can potentially intervene and motivate us to wonder about how we wonder; they invite us to think about how we think about ourselves and the world in which we find ourselves, and about the priority we give to details, to the past, or to art itself.

Ricœur suggests that "the sense or the significance of a narrative stems from the *intersection of the world of the text and the world of the reader*" (1991a, 26). In an aesthetic experience with a work, we are attentive to the objective features of that work, but the meaning and significance we draw from such an aesthetic experience can, in principle, be as varied and numerous as there are spectators. In an aesthetic experience—an experience of and through an attitude of cinephilia—the subjective significance is drawn out through attention to the work's objective qualities. As philosopher Alva Noë notes, "Art provides us an opportunity to catch ourselves in the act of achieving our conscious lives, of bringing the world into focus for perceptual (and other forms of) consciousness. And so art is a field in which we can take seriously the . . . question . . . why do we see so little?" (2015, xii). The sort of experience motivating the chapters of this book rests on a kind of loving consciousness—that our attention and experience are at times exhausted by the works before us, and that because of this we can understand how rich such an experience can be. It is not just that our attention to the work is sensitive to its objective features but that we interpret them in terms of our own unique existence. As Caden notes in *Synecdoche, New York*, nobody "is an extra. They're all the leads of their own stories. They have to be given their due."

The wonder about the world that emerges from such an experience enlarges and expands the richness of our own lives. The narrative of our existence only becomes deeper and livelier through the aesthetic experiences we have with art.

We take these experiences with us, and they shape how we perceive things, how we experience and understand ourselves and the world. Others may only see the effects; as Harvey is to Elwood, our aesthetic experiences may only truly be present to us. Our aesthetic experiences may only provide us the very means by which we are able to continue through the world. Wonder derived from our experiences with art can give us a renewed existential momentum, sending us out seeking with active, contemplative vigor the things that are of deepest importance and most profound significance to us. Our openness to understanding and contemplating the richly meaningful attachments we form to certain artworks and the moments they contain, motivated by the gratitude-laden perception of cinephilia, affords a sensitivity to and awareness of the thread connecting remade worlds with the one we inhabit day-to-day. Such inhabitation can be increasingly expanded with the presence of wonder.

Afterword

What Does Jerry Do? The Riddle of Selection and the Metaphysics of Performance

Run Lola Run, *The Shootist*, *The Americans*, and *Dekalog*. Free will and causality, goodness, qualia, and cinephilia and wonder. Harpo through to Danny Kaye, John Barrymore and Carole Lombard, Cyd Charisse, and Jerry Lewis.

While there are a range of ways to treat the aforementioned collection of films and television programs, concepts, and individuals (as well those others treated throughout this book but not again listed here), here I would like to consider two that are particularly instructive as they relate to selection. The first is the primary point and purpose of the book—that all of these works, ideas, and human beings inhabit and help to create, in various ways, the metaphysical screen. They all participate in what I have attempted to show across the chapters I have written: that films and television programs can give an artistic life to metaphysical concepts that, in the artistic bearing they possess onscreen, give us cause to wonder in different ways about the world, about ourselves and our place in it. The metaphysical screen invites us to contemplate the ways in which films and television programs can be tethered to this world, and so to ourselves.

The other perspective—not contradictory, but merely a different register—is that they have been selected and put into conversation with one another by me. I could have selected other films, other concepts, and other performers and individuals to make the case that

I do throughout this book. Indeed, this afterword, focusing as it will on specific performances (Danny Kaye in *The Court Jester* [1955], John Barrymore and Carole Lombard in *20th Century* [1934], Cyd Charisse and Fred Astaire in *The Band Wagon* [1953], and Jerry Lewis in *Cracking Up!* aka *Smorgasbord* [1983]), could easily have emphasized others. In fact, it almost did: Billy Bob Thornton in *Bad Santa* (2003), Nicole Kidman in *The Others* (2001), Rosanna Arquette in *After Hours* (1985), and George C. Scott in *Hardcore* (1979). Why one group of films and performers over others? That is, why this collection of selections, and not the alternatives listed? Why does selection matter, what does it achieve, and why might we be given cause to think about the central place of selection in our experience with films and television programs?

Selection shapes. Much as the abstract reality of metaphysics shapes existence, much as the concepts treated throughout this book shape the works in which they are explored (and the works, too, shape the expression of the concepts), the fact of selection shapes the process of writing about film and television, the way in which works of the screen (metaphysical or otherwise) are experienced, and the way in which films and television programs are created.

Any person attempting to write meaningfully about film and television will be aware of the process of selection—selecting concepts, selecting the films and television programs themselves, selecting the scholars to include alongside one's own interpretations, arguments, and analyses. Selection is involved, too, in the words used to describe a scene, a moment of performance, the texture or quality of a shot, the movement of the camera, the lighting, sound, music, and so on. Selection, and an awareness of the process of selection, underpin criticism and interpretation. They shape the act of translation that is the displacing of the experiential process of reveling and participating in a work of art into language. The critical and interpretative dimension to this act of translation involves an attempt to select the appropriate order and rhythm of the language used to bring back to life the texture or substance of a moment from a work, the formal shape of the work itself, or anything in between (or, indeed, outside).

The experience of spectatorship itself involves selection too. There is a choice to take the film or television program seriously as a work of art and to undistractedly (as much as one can) actively immerse oneself in a story, a flow of narrative events, the aesthetic qualities of the image, and all other elements of the work one is experiencing. A selection is made in affording oneself the time and space to contemplate the substance and source of the experience, to wonder about the work's connection to the world, to consider why certain elements have stuck long after the final credits have rolled.

To cultivate aesthetically motivated wonder—wonder that grows out of the experience with art—is a selection, a choice made by the spectator. To be willing to treat the work with a kind of artistic respect, or to at least give the work a chance of having such an effect, is a selection, a choice too. There are no guarantees that a work will deliver, or deliver in the way we might expect. As mentioned in the previous chapter, wonder does not tend to work in an instrumental way. In not giving an artwork a chance, though, we are all but guaranteed that it cannot work on us at all.

Selection is threaded throughout this book: in the decision to consider the metaphysical screen itself, in the particular examples used to bring this idea to life, and in the way those selections intersect with the observations and work of scholars of varying stripes. Selection is not infrequently invoked in our evaluation and attempt to better understand the works we experience. We might contemplate a particular directorial "choice" (perceived or actual), or the decisions involved in how the story is told, or the selections made regarding performance (in terms of both casting and how a performer has crafted a particular character). This final consideration is the lens I have selected to examine selection's role in a number of films: to use performances where the very idea of selection and its significance is made explicit, as an invitation to spectators to reflect on the very idea, the very process, the very importance, of selection itself.

Danny

In *The Court Jester*, Hubert Hawkins (Danny Kaye) is the minstrel member of a band of rebels lead by the Black Fox (Edward Ashley); the rebels are trying to restore to the throne of England the rightful king (an infant child) by usurping the faux king Roderick (Cecil Parker). Hawkins and fellow rebel Jean (Glynis Johns) have infiltrated Roderick's well-fortified castle, having kidnapped a court jester named Giacomo (John Carradine). Hawkins has taken Giacomo's place, though unbeknownst to him, Giacomo is in fact an assassin, hired by Lord Ravenhurst (Basil Rathbone)—a member of Roderick's court—who is trying to make a power play of his own.

The narrative backdrop is a vehicle for Kaye's most proficient and joyous hallmarks as a performer, and the film's reflexive take on selection has it operate as a no less joyous ode to performance itself. *The Court Jester* has Kaye at his most facially expressive, vocally dexterous, and musically gestural. The opening credits key spectators in to the reflexive, self-aware nature of the film. They feature Kaye as Hawkins in the traditional jester attire (an outfit not worn during the film itself) of cap 'n' bells and marotte, interacting with the names of the cast as they appear. Singing the song "Life Could Not Better Be," Kaye prances across the screen contained within the medieval-esque design of the border, alluding to the film to follow in various ways. For example, the lyric "villains full of villainy" has Hawkins dispatching the third appearance of Rathbone's name. Late in the film, Kaye's Hawkins does in fact dispatch his formidable opponent.

As might be expected given the aforementioned synopsis of the film, and the way it trades (with levity) in deceit, subterfuge, and revenge, performances of performance take a central role. Hawkins's embodiment of Giacomo is a performance that contains, nested within it, Kaye's performance of Hawkins. The creation of Giacomo is a performative Russian doll. Hawkins, having never met the actual Giacomo, has to improvise his way through conversations with Roderick and Ravenhurst, as well as fulfill his role as a court jester. In order for Hawkins's performance of Giacomo to be authentic and successful—in order for him to assimilate with and meet the expectations of those who have brought Giacomo to the castle—Hawkins needs to be funny, witty, musical, and willing to be made fun of. That is to say, the Russian doll of performance requires the performative attributes that are characteristic of Kaye's screen persona. The film that *The Court Jester* is relies on the selection of Kaye to fulfill the central role. The way he imbues the role with his own suite of performative attributes shapes not just the character but the aesthetic distinctiveness of *The Court Jester*. The selection of Kaye, then, possesses a type of metaphysical function—it shapes and conditions the unique artistic life that *The Court Jester* possesses.

At one point in the film, Hawkins has been fast-tracked through the trials of knighthood, having been found out as an imposter and so set up to be eliminated by the visiting knight Griswold (Robert Middleton) in a duel. However, Griselda (Mildred Natwick), the resident witch and advisor to Roderick's daughter, Gwendolyn (Angela Lansbury), has other plans. Griselda informs Hawkins that one of the two goblets used in the pre-duel toast has been poisoned, but he needs some assistance in remembering which one.

The wordplay in the scene requires Kaye's particular brand of linguistic dexterity. We see him both retain the labyrinthine phrases offered by Griselda while effortlessly confusing them as the scene unfolds. The combination of Kaye's persona as out of place, innocent, even easily bewildered is selectively combined with his adeptness for delivering complex dialogue at a rapid and rhythmic pace. Intricate lines such as "Where the pellet with the poison's in the vessel with the pestle, the chalice from the palace has the brew that is true" are with staccato relentlessness repeatedly turned over by Hawkins and increasingly muddled as he makes his way alongside Griswold to the table where the vessels themselves rest (fig. A.1):

> The pestle with t ... the pellet with the poison's in the vessel with the pestle, the palace from the chalice has the brew that is blue. Eh, no ... The pellet with the poison's

Figure A.1. A selection by Hubert Hawkins in *The Court Jester*. *Source:* Frank, Melvin, and Norman Panama, dirs. *The Court Jester*. 1955. Hollywood, CA: Paramount Pictures, 2001. Blu-ray Disc, 1080p HD.

in the vessel with the pestle. The cha- eh, the pellet with the plip ... the pellet with the poisle's in the vessel with the plazzle. Eh, the plazzle with the vlessle. Eh, the the bless ... The vessel with the plozle is the plazzle with the ...

The selection of the dialogue is tied to the selection of Kaye for the film, and the fact of selection is foregrounded in the necessary choice between the two goblets (as well as in the choice that follows, where Griswold and Hawkins must select their weapons for combat). *The Court Jester* relies on Kaye's inclusion in order for the other selections to be successful. The film's overall tone, its use of dialogue, its comedic sensibility, and the lighthearted adventure that runs through it all depend on Kaye's casting and his delivering on the recognizable attributes of his performative persona.

Toward the end of *The Court Jester*, with the Black Fox and his band of renegades storming the castle, Hawkins and Ravenhurst face each other in an apparent fight to the death. Selection is at play in this scene, too. Hawkins is, predictably enough, not a swordsman, and he is barely hanging on in the fight. His "skill" is recognizably desperate as he slaps and waves the sword wildly in front of him. The selection of Rathbone to play Ravenhurst is an important one to the comedic intentions of the scene. Rathbone's well-deserved reputation for his proficiency at fencing and swordplay is on full display—he is mannered, artful, elegant, and composed in the face of Kaye's chaos. Although in many of Rathbone's onscreen battles he does not emerge the victor, this particular duel seems to suggest that he will. However, with the help of a spell from Griselda, at the snap of her (or anybody else's) fingers, Kaye's Hawkins instantly transforms into a scoffing, poised, immeasurably confident swordsman. Where before he flailed wildly, getting caught in the stone of the castle's upper walls, he now stands with an endearing arrogant smile across his face, his blade cutting the air and immediately putting Ravenhurst on the back foot.

But *The Court Jester* is a vehicle for Danny Kaye, so Hawkins cannot stop being imbued with Kaye's performative and comedic tendencies. His very arrogance is comedic because we know that Kaye's screen personae are imbued with the haplessness displayed in Hawkins throughout *The Court Jester*. The selection of Kaye dictates how the action will play out—he will win, of course (the opening credits have told us as much), but not yet. Hawkins has parried Ravenhurst onto the precipice of the castle's high walls, overlooking an unforgiving cliff face that recedes down to the bottomless depths of the ocean. The newly gloating master swordsman takes this opportunity to mock his opponent: "At this moment, my dear Ravenhurst, your life isn't worth that." Hawkins punctuates the final syllable of his playful jeer with a snap of his fingers, thereby undoing Griselda's spell, and the fight continues back and forth in this fashion until the film's inevitable close.

A snap of the fingers is a small gesture that has a significant outcome. It is a necessary selection for the scene to unfold in a way that makes sense with what we know of Danny Kaye's notable performative qualities. It is also another way in which selection is brought to the surface of *The Court Jester*, a film that is littered with explicit selections—choosing the right goblet, picking the right weapon, inadvisably selecting to snap one's fingers at an inopportune time. But this last example, of course, is not inopportune at all—none of them are. It is perfectly timed, because this moment, as with all the others mentioned, is demanded by the inclusion of Kaye in the film; it is demanded by not just the selection of him but the selections by him, too.

John and Carole

In Howard Hawks's *20th Century*, Carole Lombard plays model Mildred Plotka turned aspiring actress Lily Garland. Mildred has been selected by Broadway theater director Oscar Jaffe (John Barrymore) to become the breakout star of his next breakout play. Jaffe has selected Plotka not for her acting ability or reputation (after all, she has none in the realm of the theater) but for the ineffable star quality that her beauty is perceived to exude. Earlier in the film, an extended moment does much to set up the challenges of employing a performer on the basis of anything other than acting ability. In a key rehearsal sequence, Mildred is tasked with producing a guttural scream of anguish. Take after take, she can but offer only the meekest imitation (if anything at all).

In writing about Barrymore's portrayal of Oscar Jaffe, George Toles observes:

> One reason Oscar Jaffe is widely regarded as Barrymore's lodestar film role is because it places no limit on his transforming impulses. Jaffe is free to improvise his attitudes, needs, values and behavioral language with reckless abandon and no fealty to coherence. His temperament contains multitudes of evanescent personages, and he can get by with no ground beneath his feet other than the license to pretend in all directions. Only the chalk-marked space of a rehearsal stage makes sense to Jaffe as a realm where things have a dependable order and intelligibility. (2021, 142)

Barrymore's realization of Oscar Jaffe is extraordinarily compelling, but here I am interested more in drawing out some of Toles's remarks in relation to selection, especially as they involve the interplay between Jaffe and Plotka/Garland. The transformation of Mildred into Lily is shown to be inextricably tethered to Jaffe's capacity as a director. The moment of transformation itself occurs during the scene in question, in which Jaffe pricks Mildred with a pin to create the necessary scream (fig. A.2). It is in this very moment that Mildred is left to the past, and Lily—future star and intermittent lover and muse of Jaffe—is created.

William Rothman offers a close analysis of the rehearsal scene that does much to contextualize the dynamics of Oscar and Lily that unfold throughout the film (2019, 102–13). The subtitle of this section of Rothman's chapter, "How to Scream," articulates the insightful and pertinent implication that there are many different ways one might scream, but that, in this moment in *20th Century*, there is but one correct, acceptable way. That is, there are any number of possibilities to choose from—to select—but only one of those will do. How to draw out the correct scream? What does it look and sound like? The film, as much as Jaffe's planned production, depends on the right scream being produced. The film and show cannot go on until the scream—signifier of Mildred's becoming Lily—rattles the rehearsal space, a kind of performative proof of concept for Jaffe's casting decision.

Toles alludes to the fact that for Jaffe there is no selection that is off the table so long as it achieves what he needs it to. He transforms and shape-shifts himself in whatever way is necessary to fit the need—romantically and artistically with Lily, professionally with producers and backers. When it comes to Jaffe's artistic creations—

Figure A.2. Oscar Jaffe forcibly selects the right scream in *20th Century*. *Source:* Hawks, Howard, dir. *20th Century*. 1934. London: Powerhouse Films, 2021. Blu-Ray Disc, 1080p HD.

the play and, in a sense, Lily herself—there is a rigidity of order, an uncompromising reality to the artistic vision that nobody else is privy to except in the way it is made public and available to his cocreators (though Jaffe would scoff at the very idea of cocreation). Every single element of the play must resonate with his intentions; otherwise the rehearsal cannot progress to the next scene or progress to a public production, and the film itself cannot continue. *20th Century*, then, is dependent on the right scream being delivered in order for it to exist. It requires Mildred to become Lily, which requires Jaffe's involvement (intrusive though it is), and Jaffe's involvement is necessitated by the interior artistic vision he has for the production. Everyone else participates, guided by their own intuitions and skill that are deployed in the direction Jaffe needs. They are guided by the selections that Jaffe demands, but that they must make.

The specific facts of Jaffe's authorial intentions are incidental, unimportant, and arbitrary when treated in the context of selection. If rather than a scream Jaffe needed a whimper, a sharp gasp of shock, a nonreaction of indifference, or a maniacal laugh, the importance of the rehearsal to his play and the importance of the scene to the film would remain unchanged. The importance lies not in the specificity of facts but in the fact of specifics: not that Jaffe requires a scream, but that there is only one scream that is required.

20th Century's achievement as a high point of screwball comedy demands the erratic, melodramatic, and combustible interplay between Oscar and Lily. The central relationship of the film requires Mildred's transformation into Lily. This transformation is made possible by Jaffe's aggressive direction with the pin. It produces not just the scream but Lily herself. With one violent gesture, Jaffe creates a star, a hit show, and, in a sense, *20th Century* too. The artistic justification of Jaffe's selection of Mildred is delivered by a scream that is plucked from an imaginary and limitless pool of possible screams. This moment of transformation occurs in the context of a rehearsal space that is loaded with the hidden intelligibility (the metaphysical force) of Jaffe's artistic vision.

Cyd and Fred

Selection, rehearsal, and production are also central to *The Band Wagon*. Fred Astaire plays Tony Hunter, an aging star of movie musicals. Fearing his career is beyond revitalization, he agrees to perform as the lead role in a Broadway play, pitched to him by his friends and writers of the play, Lester (Oscar Levant) and Lily Marton (Nanette Fabray). With Hunter's involvement, the Martons acquire the services of theater director Jeffrey Cordova (Jack Buchanan). Cordova casts ballerina and Broadway amateur Gaby Gerard (Cyd Charisse), despite the reservations of her boyfriend-manager-choreographer Paul Byrd (James Mitchell). The Martons' original pitch for the show has it as a fizzy, light, comedic musical production. Cordova, though, perceives within it something else: a contemporaneous and adventurous reworking of Faust. The Martons rework the play into a darker musical production, while Gerard and Hunter spend many of the early rehearsals treating each other with hostility. Hunter eventually walks out on the production before Gerard brings him back into the fold. Of course, they also fall in love.

I will consider in a moment the "Dancing in the Dark" number—an astonishing moment from the film. First, though, a brief detour. Rothman assimilates his own interpretation of an earlier number featuring only Astaire ("By Myself") with an analysis by Stanley Cavell. Rothman highlights how, in Cavell's view, "the routine's philosophical bearing resides in its achievement of 'emblematizing' the ordinary; making uneventfulness manifest is the remarkable event it makes manifest" (2021, 234). For Cavell, what is compelling about this routine is how its philosophical substance is derived from the ways in which the ordinary is made emblematic; what is commonly ignored or goes unnoticed is instead designated by the film as exemplary. Preceding the number, Hunter is mobbed by reporters as he gets off a train. He is greeted by Ava Gardner (playing herself), who turns out to be the actual subject of interest for the reporters. They implore her to walk off the train one more time, as the photographers missed the original opportunity. The ordinary, then, is emblematized—made momentous and worthy of record—before Astaire's number even takes place.

Rothman's observations on "By Myself" extend Cavell's original concerns to draw out the nuances of authorship (performative and directorial) as key to the staging and presentation of the routine. Performative and directorial authorship, the use of staging, and the spatial design of the number all coalesce in emblematizing the ordinary. This formal or intentional unification is key to the aesthetic interest and achievement of the scene:

> But if we pay close attention to the fact that Astaire delivers his song and "proto-dance" on film, rather than on stage, we can see that this paradigmatically uneventful "photographed song" is, *cinematically*, remarkably eventful. Discovering its eminently missable way of being eventful requires attending to what the camera is doing—what the director is doing with the camera—at each moment, seeing Astaire's delivery of the song as also Vincente Minnelli's "delivery" of this sequence of shots, the passionate utterance by which he presents to us the star's passionate utterance (2021, 234).

The number follows Astaire's Hunter along the train platform; he is singing as much to himself as to us, the spectators. It is a moment of introspection that is afforded by the conditional privacy of the setting and circumstances. Any possible attention is reserved for other people, other things—bigger movie stars, for example. The setting is public—it is not Hunter's private train station, after all—but it is now largely deserted, populated sparsely by nobody other than the workers taking care of the trolleys of luggage. Despite this, and as Rothman notes, the scene is nevertheless filmed, and filmed for an audience. In this sense it could hardly be more public. The interplay of privacy and publicity is interwoven with the exemplarity of the ordinary that Rothman, following Cavell, sees as important to the scene. For Rothman, these concerns are brought out through attention to the camera—that is, to the way space and staging have been selectively designated by the director. Once the visual and spatial bounds of the scene are set, Astaire then selectively delivers his lines and expressively moves in parallel to the platform. He is by himself, but he has been selectively placed there, selectively represented as such; and selectively this conditionally private moment is at the same time public to spectators of the film.

The selection of space and setting, the dual presence of privacy and publicity, and the performative and expressive selections on the part of the performer reach beautifully realized heights in the "Dancing in the Dark" number. Gerard has followed Hunter after he has walked out on their production, and in a bid to give their working (and blossoming personal) relationship one last chance, they take a carriage ride to Central Park. The driver asks Hunter, "Where to?" Hunter hesitates and replies, "Leave it to the horse." (A number of selections are at play in so concise a line.)

Walking through the park, they happen upon a collection of couples dancing. The camera tracks back as Hunter and Gerard part the crowd without breaking stride, silently pondering their troubles and finding a more secluded spot for a dance of their own. Spontaneously, Gerard makes the first move, and Hunter rapidly follows. They dance—often mimicking each other, especially in footwork and the lines of their arms, but complementing each other too, as Hunter works as the catalyst for Gerard's artful pirouettes, or the support for her bends and leans (fig. A.3). For much of the scene, the movement is predominantly lateral across the frame, the performers responding to the selection of choreography, setting, and space designated by the camera. They have brief sojourns to a park bench that is placed marginally in the background, but only move through the depth of

Figure A.3. Selections of staging, setting, and performance in *The Band Wagon*. *Source:* Minnelli, Vincente, dir. *The Band Wagon*. 1953. Burbank, CA: Warner Bros. Pictures, 2015. Blu-Ray Disc, 1080p HD.

the scene toward the camera as it recedes backward through the ever-expanding foreground. Gerard and Hunter dance toward and then across the screen before fluidly returning to their seats in the waiting carriage.

The cluster of selections informing the scene underpins the dual presence of the private and the public. This is an unquestionably intimate moment between the two characters. It is set late in the evening in a secluded part of the park. However, their having made their way through a crowd, and the dance having been set in a park establish the publicity that plays alongside the privacy and intimacy of the dance itself. Moreover, it is a scene in a film, which—like all films—is made for spectators. As with the earlier number, there are multiple layers of the interplay between private and public. The performance—with each other, for the other, and for spectators—is conditioned by the selections of setting, staging, and camera movement. Selection is made explicit, and it is interwoven with the dual concern of the public and private.

A *Saturday Night Live* sketch from 1978 serves as an homage to the "Dancing in the Dark" number from *Band Wagon*, nevertheless reinforcing its preoccupation with selection, publicity, and privacy. At points it is of course played for laughs, where the elegance and intimacy of the dancers—here, Steve Martin as Astaire and Gilda Radner as Charisse—is interrupted by chaotic twirls or Martin's happy feet. Underscoring the performance, though, is an awareness of selection as it relates to the number's attunement to the dissolution of publicity and privacy. Martin and Radner's version begins in the setting of a bar. Martin sits at the bar itself smoking a cigarette, Radner at a circular table across the room with two other men. Suddenly, they lock eyes, the camera zooming slowly into alternating close-ups of each as the music starts to play, removing the upbeat disco soundtrack that was playing in the bar. The pair magnetically meet in the space in the center of the set and begin to dance together. The background characters freeze, the background noise grows into silence, and all other lighting fades to darkness except for the spotlight that isolates the two dancers.

Before too long, though, Martin and Radner's version of the routine crosses the boundary of the set and into the audience's domain, with no regard for the viewers' presence (except for the implied awareness embodied in the number's comedic moments). We see various crew members, cameras, video assists, and other spectators as Martin and Radner make their way to a raised stage, before Martin with great effort carries Radner back to the barroom setting, where they reclaim their places and separate. The music in the bar resumes, the extras start moving and talking again, and the camera cranes outward to raucous applause from the audience. The selection of artistic construction is made more explicit in the homage than in the original: we, as spectators, are made more aware of the fact that the selection to construct *for* an audience implies the construction for an audience *by* an author.

Jerry

Warren Nefron (Jerry Lewis) cannot seem to do anything right. This includes delivering on the most absolute of all selections, the decision to end his own life. In the earliest scenes of *Cracking Up*, Nefron attempts to hang himself, but instead accidentally demolishes an entire building. He tries to shoot himself with an elaborate rig involving a rifle. It is designed to fire once the room service he has called for opens the door. A Western is playing on the hotel room's television as this attempt at suicide unfolds. Room service arrives, but it seems Nefron has locked the door. He disentangles himself from the rig, unlocking and opening the door. The rifle fires and shoots the television set, as the cowboy on that screen is shot as though from Nefron's rifle. Another cowboy shoots from within the television to without, killing the room service attendant. Nefron lives.

Nefron visits a psychiatrist to seek help, to turn things around. He is a misfit who does nothing right and fits in nowhere, so he needs professional help. What follows in *Cracking Up* is a series of loosely connected vignettes that unfold moments from Nefron's past (including that of his ancestors). Via hypnosis, the psychiatrist succeeds only in transferring Nefron's loosely defined condition onto himself. The vignetted structure of the film matches closely with Lewis's approach to comedy: "I use the term 'joke' to mean something funny, either verbal or visual, but there is a great difference between a joke, as such, and a visual-comedy sequence. I distinguish a joke or gag as being rather short or quick-cut. A visual comedy sequence can be quite long" (2021, 150). *Cracking Up* embeds jokes and gags within the sequences (the structuring vignettes themselves). Narrative continuity and coherence are selected to take a backseat to Lewis's densely populated comedy—dense in its mise-en-scéne as much as its volume of jokes. The intricacy of the comedy is matched in the intricacy of the visual design that supports and represents the jokes and sequences. As Lewis himself confirms: "There is a refinement of jokes on the soundstage and infrequently the lucky flash... but most of it is written in detail and prepared well in advance of filming. Once I write a joke I give it to a sketch artist for rendering. I explain how I plan to shoot it, name the characters involved, and estimate the camera moves through to the cut or dissolve. It is almost frame-by-frame planning" (150). In choosing to prioritize humor over narrative richness, Lewis's film opens up the possibilities of what can be included creatively, comedically, and cinematically. As Chris Fujiwara observes, this is a common thread that ties together Lewis's form of cinematic comedy: "His films make an equally strong demand to be read as the most vivid and emotionally wrenching American show-business hallucinations ever put on film: representations and creations of a modern world in part naturalistic and plausible, in part fantastic and implausible, partly real, partly staged. In describing them like this, I don't mean to say that they are films in which, simply 'anything goes' (though *Cracking Up* comes close to such a condition)" (2009, 98–99). The film is an exclamation point at the end of Lewis's comedic career in cinema, especially those works where he operates both as director and actor. The film offers multiple conscious nods to Lewis's dual role as selector and selection—director and performer (of more characters than just Nefron)—of which I will consider just one.

A bank heist is unfolding. The underlings of the suited gang of thieves enthusiastically enter the expansive space of the bank's lobby, asserting their control over security guards and patrons. One of them waves toward the bank's front door, and Lewis as head robber walks through the parting queue of terrified customers. He strides confidently past them all before stopping, noticing a security camera. Lewis's character starts playing to the camera—which now, through cutting, means he plays directly to us. He makes faces, showing the crooked fake teeth populating his mouth, showing us his profile before rapidly turning back to the camera straight on. Lewis's character is making choices in front of the security camera and in front of Lewis's movie camera. He selects the faces and selects the timing and rhythm of their expression. The shot cuts from close-up to medium shot and then to long shot, showing Lewis's character take his bag to a desk. He takes out a boater-style hat and music player and begins performing a dance number to the tune of "New York, New York" that involves the robbers and eventually the security guards. Lewis—director and performer—is making selections in these moments too.

The dance number is intercut with some shots of the security camera, reminding us of the device that acts as catalyst for Lewis's character's performance, as well as the tool that unites Lewis the director's comedic intentions with the art form of cinema. We are reminded that he selects the movement of the camera, its positioning across cuts, and the performative gestures that play for laughs. Everyone else except Lewis is a bit player—an arbitrary selection. Fujiwara observes that *Cracking Up* is one of Lewis's films "in which he directly confronts the possibility of his own character's death" and that the film tries "to define and preserve selfhood even as [the film] ... play[s] with its disappearance, only to end up acknowledging the fictional and optional nature of selfhood" (2009, 29).

We are returned, then, as much to Harpo as to Lewis. That is, we are returned to the selection that inaugurated this book and all the selections that followed—the metaphysical Harpo, the Harpo that encourages us to ask whether he is free in any number of ways. I selected those too.

References

Augustine. 2012. *The Confessions*. Translated by Maria Boulding. San Francisco: Ignatius Press.
Bandy, Mary Lea, and Kevin Stoehr. 2012. "Eastwood and the American Western: *High Plains Drifter*, *The Outlaw Josey Wales*, and *Unforgiven*." In *Ride Boldly Ride: The Evolution of the American Western*, 238–68. Berkeley: University of California Press.
Baracco, Alberto. 2017. *Hermeneutics of the Film World: A Ricœurian Method for Film Interpretation*. Basingstoke, UK: Palgrave MacMillan.
Barfield, Owen. 1988. *Saving the Appearances: A Study in Idolatry*. Middletown, CT: Wesleyan University Press.
Barr, Alan. 1987. "The Unraveling of Character in Bergman's *Persona*." *Literature/Film Quarterly* 15 (2): 123–36.
Barzun, Jacques. 1989. *The Culture We Deserve*. Hanover, NH: Wesleyan University Press.
Bateman, John A. 2019. "Multimodality and Materiality: The Interplay of Textuality and Texturality in the Aesthetics of Film." *Poetics Today* 40 (2): 235–68. https://doi.org/10.1215/03335372-7298536.
Baumberger, Christoph. 2013. "Art and Understanding: In Defence of Aesthetic Cognitivism." In *Bilder Sehen. Perspektiven der Bildwissenschaft*, edited by Christoph Wagner, Marc Greenlee, Rainer Hammwöhner, Bernd Körber, and Christian Wolff, 1–23. Regensburg: Schnell + Steiner. Available at: https://www.academia.edu/2284624/Art_and_Understanding_In_Defence_of_Aesthetic_Cognitivism._In_Marc_Greenlee_et_al._Bilder_sehen._Perspektiven_der_Bildwissenschaft._Reg ensburg_Schnell_Steiner_2013_41–67.
Bazin, André. 1998. "The Evolution of the Western." In *The Western Reader*, edited by Jim Kitses and Gregg Rickman, 49–56. New York: Limelight Editions.

Bazin, André. 2010. "The Evolution of the Language of Cinema." In *The Film Theory Reader: Debates and Arguments*, edited by Marc Furstenau, 95–103. London: Routledge.

Berg, Charles Ramírez. 2006. "A Taxonomy of Alternative Plots in Recent Films: Classifying the 'Tarantino Effect.'" *Film Criticism* 31 (1/2): 5–61.

Blanchet, Robert, and Margrethe Bruun Vaage. 2012. "Don, Peggy, and Other Fictional Friends? Engaging with Characters in Television Series." *Projections: The Journal for Movies and Mind* 6 (2): 18–41.

Bordwell, David. 1985. *Narration in the Fiction Film*. New York: Routledge.

Bordwell, David. 1989. *Making Meaning: Inference and Rhetoric in the Interpretation of Cinema*. Cambridge, MA: Harvard University Press.

Bordwell, David. 2002. "Film Futures." *SubStance* 31 (1): 88–104.

Bordwell, David. 2005. *Figures Traced in Light: On Cinematic Staging*. Berkeley: University of California Press.

Bordwell, David. 2006. "Subjective Stories and Network Narratives." In *The Way Hollywood Tells It*, 72–103. Berkeley: University of California Press.

Bordwell, David. 2008. "Cognition and Comprehension: Viewing and Forgetting in *Mildred Pierce*." In *Poetics of Cinema*, 135–50. London: Routledge.

Branigan, Edward. 1984. *Point of View in the Cinema: A Theory of Narration and Subjectivity in Classical Film*. New York: Mouton.

Branigan, Edward. 1992. *Narrative Comprehension and Film*. New York: Routledge.

Branigan, Edward. 2002. "Nearly True: Forking Plots, Forking Interpretations: A Response to David Bordwell's 'Film Futures.'" *SubStance* 31 (1): 105–14.

Buckland, Warren. 2009. "Introduction: Puzzle Plots." In *Puzzle Films: Complex Storytelling in Contemporary Cinema*, edited by Warren Buckland, 1–12. Oxford: Wiley-Blackwell.

Buckland, Warren. 2014. "Introduction: Ambiguity, Ontological Pluralism, and Cognitive Dissonance in the Hollywood Puzzle Film." In *Hollywood Puzzle Films*, edited by Warren Buckland, 1–14. London: Routledge.

Cameron, Allan. 2008. *Modular Narratives in Contemporary Cinema*. Basingstoke, UK: Palgrave Macmillan.

Campbell, John. 2011. "Personal Identity." In *The Oxford Handbook of the Self*, edited by Shaun Gallagher, 339–51. New York: Oxford University Press.

Campora, Matthew. 2014. *Subjective Realist Cinema: From Expressionism to Inception*. New York: Berghahn Books.

Carroll, Noël. 2002. "The Wheel of Virtue: Art, Literature, and Moral Knowledge." *Journal of Aesthetics and Art Criticism* 60 (1): 3–26.

Carroll, Noël. 2012. "Recent Approaches to Aesthetic Experience." *Journal of Aesthetics and Art Criticism* 70 (2): 165–177.

Cavell, Stanley. 2005. "The Thought of Movies." In *Cavell on Film*, edited by William Rothman, 87–106. Albany: State University of New York Press.
Choi, Jinhee. 2005. "Leaving It Up to the Imagination: POV Shots and Imagining from the Inside." *Journal of Aesthetics & Art Criticism* 63 (1): 17–25. https://www.jstor.org/stable/1559136.
Choi, Jinhee, and Mattias Frey, eds. 2013. *Cine-ethics: Ethical Dimensions of Film Theory, Practice, and Spectatorship*. London: Routledge.
Coates, Paul. 2012. *Screening the Face*. Basingstoke, UK: Palgrave Macmillan.
Critchley, Simon. 2005. "Calm: On Terrence Malick's *The Thin Red Line*." In *Film as Philosophy: Essays on Cinema after Wittgenstein and Cavell*, edited by Rupert Read and Jerry Goodenough, 133–48. Basingstoke, UK: Palgrave Macmillan.
Currie, Gregory. 1995. *Image and Mind: Film, Philosophy, and Cognitive Science*. Cambridge: Cambridge University Press.
Currie, Gregory. 2011. "The Representation of Experience in Cinema." In *Subjectivity: Filmic Representation and the Spectators' Experience*, edited by Dominique Chateau, 41–51. Amsterdam: Amsterdam University Press.
Danto, Arthur C. 2014. *Remarks on Art and Philosophy*. New York: A.S.A.P.
Day, Kirsten. 2016. *Cowboy Classics: The Roots of the American Western in the Epic Tradition*. Edinburgh: Edinburgh University Press.
Donaldson, Lucy Fife. 2014. *Texture in Film*. Basingstoke, UK: Palgrave Macmillan.
Drake, Philip. 2016. "Reframing Television Performance." *Journal of Film and Video* 68 (3–4): 6–17.
Ebert, Roger. 2004. "Great Movie: *3 Women*." Rogerebert.com. https://www.rogerebert.com/reviews/great-movie-3-women-1977.
Eliot, T. S. 1993. *The Varieties of Metaphysical Poetry: The Clark Lectures at Trinity College, Cambridge, 1926, and the Turnbull Lectures at the Johns Hopkins University, 1933*. London: Faber and Faber.
Elsaesser, Thomas. 2005. "Cinephilia or the Uses of Disenchantment." In *Cinephilia: Movies, Love and Memory*, edited by Mrijke de Valck and Malte Hagener, 27–43. Amsterdam: Amsterdam University Press.
Elsaesser, Thomas. 2009. "The Mind-Game Film." In *Puzzle Films: Complex Storytelling in Contemporary Cinema*, edited by Warren Buckland, 13–41. Oxford: Wiley-Blackwell.
Elsaesser, Thomas. 2014. "Philip K. Dick, the Mind-Game Film, and Retroactive Causality." In *Hollywood Puzzle Films*, edited by Warren Buckland, 143–64. London: Routledge.
Fabe, Marilyn. 2004. "Expressive Realism: Orson Welles's *Citizen Kane*." In *Closely Watched Films: An Introduction to the Art of Narrative Film Technique*, 78–98. Berkeley: University of California Press.

Felski, Rita. 2020. *Hooked: Art and Attachment*. Chicago: University of Chicago Press.

Fingerhut, Joerg, and Jesse J. Prinz. 2018. "Wonder, Appreciation, and the Value of Art." *Progress in Brain Research* 237:107–28. https://doi.org/10.1016/bs.pbr.2018.03.004.

Flaherty, Matthew. 2019. "Expressive Realism and the Phenomenological Turn: A Canon for Postcritical Literary Studies." *Poetics Today* 40 (1): 135–58. https://doi.org/10.1215/03335372-7259929.

Fuchs, Thomas. 2018. "Presence in Absence. The Ambiguous Phenomenology of Grief." *Phenomenology and the Cognitive Sciences* 17 (1): 43–63. https://doi.org/10.1007/s11097-017-9506-2.

Fudge, Erica. 2000. *Perceiving Animals: Humans and Beasts in Early Modern English Culture*. New York: St. Martin's Press.

Fujiwara, Chris. 2009. *Jerry Lewis*. Chicago: University of Illinois Press.

Gallagher, Shaun. 2015. "Self and Narrative." In *The Routledge Companion to Hermeneutics*, edited by Jeff Malpas and Hans-Heimuth Gander, 403–14. London: Routledge.

Gallagher, Shaun, and Dan Zahavi. 2012. *The Phenomenological Mind*. 2nd ed. New York: Routledge.

García, Alberto N., and Pablo Castrillo. 2020. "'Just Being Us'—Secrecy, Authenticity and Identity in *The Americans*." *Quarterly Review of Film and Video* 37 (8): 782–803. https://doi.org/10.1080/10509208.2020.1747354.

Garwood, Ian. 2013. *The Sense of Film Narration*. Edinburgh: Edinburgh University Press.

Gibson, John. 2008. "Cognitivism and the Arts." *Philosophy Compass* 3 (4): 573–89.

Gorfinkel, Elena. 2015. "Exhausted Drift: Austerity, Dispossession and the Politics of Slow in Kelly Reichardt's *Meek's Cutoff*." In *Slow Cinema*, edited by Tiago Luca and Nuno Barradas, 123–36. Edinburgh: Edinburgh University Press.

Grodal, Torben. 1997. *Moving Pictures: A New Theory of Film Genres, Feelings, and Cognition*. Oxford: Clarendon Press.

Hanich, Julian. 2011. "Experiencing Extended Point-of-View Shots: A Film-Phenomenological Perspective on Extreme Character Subjectivity." In *Subjectivity across Media: Interdisciplinary and Transmedial Perspectives*, 127–44. New York: Routledge.

Hark, Ina Rae. 2012. "Language, Decent and Otherwise." In *Deadwood*, 31–40. Detroit: Wayne State University Press.

Herman, David. 2018. *Narratology beyond the Human: Storytelling and Animal Life*. New York: Oxford University Press.

Hodsdon, Barrett. 2017. *The Elusive Auteur: The Question of Film Authorship throughout the Age of Cinema*. Jefferson, NC: McFarland.

Hutson, Richard. 2007. "One Hang, We All Hang: *High Plains Drifter*." In *Clint Eastwood, Actor and Director: New Perspectives*, edited by Leonard Engel, 99–118. Salt Lake City: University of Utah Press.
Jacobs, Jason. 2012. *Deadwood*. London: Palgrave MacMillan.
Kearney, Richard. 2002. "Narrative Matters." In *On Stories*, 125–56. London: Routledge.
Keathley, Christian. 2006. *Cinephilia and History, or The Wind in the Trees*. Bloomington: Indiana University Press.
Keller, Sarah. 2020. *Anxious Cinephilia: Pleasure and Peril at the Movies*. New York: Columbia University Press.
Kermode, Frank. 1967. *The Sense of an Ending: Studies in the Theory of Fiction*. New York: Oxford University Press.
Kickasola, Joseph G. 2004. *The Films of Krzysztof Kieslowski: The Liminal Image*. New York: Continuum.
Kind, Amy. 2008. "Qualia." *Internet Encyclopedia of Philosophy*. https://www.iep.utm.edu/qualia/.
Kitses, Jim. 1998. "Authorship and Genre: Notes on the Western." In *The Western Reader*, edited by Jim Kitses and Gregg Rickman, 57–68. New York: Limelight Editions.
Kolker, Robert. 2011. "Radical Surfaces and Independent Means: Robert Altman." In *A Cinema of Loneliness*, 349–430. New York: Oxford University Press.
Lamarque, Peter. 2007. "On the Distance between Literary Narratives and Real-Life Narratives." In *Narrative and Understanding Persons*, edited by Daniel Hutto, 117–32. Cambridge: Cambridge University Press.
Lewis, C. S. 2002. "A Grief Observed." In *The Complete C. S. Lewis Signature Classics*, 647–88. London: HarperOne.
Lewis, Jerry. 2021. *The Total Film-Maker*. Studio City, CA: Michael Wiese Productions.
Lis, Marek. 2016. "*Dekalog*: 'Someone Should Make a Film about the Ten Commandments.'" In *Krzysztof Kieślowski: Dekalog and Other Television Works*, edited by Michael Brooke, 19–25. Manchester, UK: Arrow Academy.
Logan, Elliott. 2016. *Breaking Bad and Dignity: Utility and Fragmentation in the Serial Television Drama*. Basingstoke, UK: Palgrave Macmillan.
Loht, Shawn. 2015. "Phenomenological Preconditions of the Concept of Film-as-Philosophy." *Journal of Aesthetics and Phenomenology* 2 (2): 171–85.
Loht, Shawn. 2017. *Phenomenology of Film: A Heideggerian Account of the Film Experience*. New York: Lexington Books.
MacIntyre, Alasdair. 1999. *Dependent Rational Animals: Why Human Beings Need the Virtues*. Chicago: Open Court.
MacIntyre, Alasdair. 2007. *After Virtue: A Study in Moral Theory*. Notre Dame, IN: University of Notre Dame Press.

Matheson, Sue. 2013. "Introduction." In *Love in Western Film and Television: Lonely Hearts and Happy Trails*, edited by Sue Matheson, 1–6. Basingstoke, UK: Palgrave Macmillan, 2013.
Merten, Jennilyn. 2013. "Right or Wrong, You Side with Your Feelings." In *Dirty Words in Deadwood: Literature and the Postwestern*, edited by Melody Graulich and Nicolas Witschi, 141–64. Lincoln: University of Nebraska Press.
Mitchell, Lee Clark. 1996. *Westerns: Making the Man in Fiction and Film*. Chicago: University of Chicago Press.
Mittell, Jason. 2006. "Narrative Complexity in Contemporary American Television." *Velvet Light Trap* 58 (1): 29–40.
Mumford, Stephen. 2012. *Metaphysics: A Very Short Introduction*. Oxford: Oxford University Press.
Murdoch, Iris. 1993. *Metaphysics as a Guide to Morals*. Sydney: Penguin.
Murdoch, Iris. 1997. "The Sovereignty of Good over Other Concepts." In *Existentialists and Mystics: Writings on Philosophy and Literature*, edited by Peter Conradi, 363–85. Sydney: Penguin.
Nagel, Thomas. 1980. "What Is It Like to Be a Bat?" In *Readings in Philosophy of Psychology*, edited by Ned Block, 1:159–68. Cambridge, MA: Harvard University Press.
Nannicelli, Ted. 2016. "The Medium." In *Appreciating the Art of Television: A Philosophical Perspective*, 51–87. London: Routledge.
Noë, Alva. 2015. *Strange Tools: Art and Human Nature*. New York: Hill and Wang.
Nussbaum, Emily. 2019. "*The Americans* Is Too Bleak and That's Why It's Great." In *I Like to Watch: Arguing My Way Through the TV Revolution*, 275–78. New York: Random House.
Nussbuam, Martha C. 2001. *Upheavals of Thought*. Cambridge: Cambridge University Press.
Olson, Eric T. 2017. "Personal Identity." *Stanford Encyclopedia of Philosophy*. https://plato.stanford.edu/archives/sum2017/entries/identity-personal/.
Parshall, Peter F. 2002. *Altman and After: Multiple Narratives in Film*. London: Scarecrow Press.
Paulus, Irena, and Graham McMaster. 1999. "Music in Krzysztof Kieślowski's Film *Three Colours: Blue*. A Rhapsody in Shades of Blue: The Reflections of a Musician." *International Review of the Aesthetics and Sociology of Music* 30 (1): 65–91.
Pearlman, Karen. 2009. *Cutting Rhythms: Shaping the Film Edit*. Sydney: Focal Press.
Pearson, Roberta. 2007. "Anatomising Gilbert Grissom: The Structure and Function of the Televisual Character." In *Reading CSI: Crime TV under the Microscope*, edited by Michael Allen, 39–56. London: I. B. Tauris.

Peretz, Eyal. 2020. "From the Mark of Kane to the Artistic Signature: Orson Welles as Self-Portraitist." *Res: Anthropology and Aesthetics* 73–74 (Spring-Autumn): 247–55. https://doi.org/10.1086/711585.
Perkins, V. F. 1990. "Must We Say What They Mean? Film Criticism and Interpretation." *Movie* 34/35: 1–7.
Perkins, V. F. 1993. *Film as Film: Understanding and Judging Movies.* New York: Da Capo Press.
Perkins, V. F. 2020. "Where Is the World? The Horizon of Events in Movie Fiction." In *V. F. Perkins on Movies: Collected Shorter Film Criticism*, edited by Douglas Pye, 270–300. Detroit: Wayne State University Press.
Pippin, Robert B. 2010. *Hollywood Westerns and American Myth: The Importance of Howard Hawks and John Ford for Political Philosophy.* New Haven, CT: Yale University Press.
Pippin, Robert B. 2013. "Vernacular Metaphysics: On Terrence Malick's *The Thin Red Line.*" *Critical Inquiry* 39 (2): 247–75.
Plantinga, Carl. 2009. *Moving Viewers: American Film and the Spectator's Experience.* Berkeley: University of California Press.
Pomerance, Murray. 2018. "Tom Ripley's Talent." In *Patricia Highsmith on Screen*, edited by Wieland Schwanebeck and Douglas McFarland, 81–97. Cham, Switzerland: Palgrave Macmillan.
Poulaki, Maria. 2014. "Puzzled Hollywood and the Return of Complex Films." In *Hollywood Puzzle Films*, edited by Warren Buckland, 35–53. London: Routledge.
Prince, Stephen. 2006. "Beholding Blood Sacrifice in *The Passion of the Christ*: How Real Is Movie Violence?" *Film Quarterly* 59 (4): 11–22.
Pye, Douglas. 2014. "The Western (Genre and Movies)." *Film Genre Reader IV*, edited by Barry Keith Grant, 239–54. Austin: University of Texas Press.
Ratcliffe, Matthew. 2017. "Grief and the Unity of Emotion." *Midwest Studies in Philosophy* 41 (1): 154–74. https://doi.org/10.1111/misp.12071.
Reinerth, Maike Sarah, and Jan-Noël Thon. 2017. "Introduction: Subjectivity across Media." In *Subjectivity across Media: Interdisciplinary and Transmedial Perspectives*, edited by Maike Sarah Reinerth and Jan-Noël Thon, 1–25. New York: Routledge.
Ricœur, Paul. 1983. "Can Fictional Narratives Be True?" In *Analecta Husserliana*, edited by Anna-Teresa Tymieniecka, 14:3–19. London: Springer.
Ricœur, Paul. 1984. "Time and Narrative: Threefold *Mimesis.*" In *Time and Narrative*, 1:52–87. Chicago: University of Chicago Press.
Ricœur, Paul. 1991a. "Life in Quest of Narrative." In *On Paul Ricoeur: Narrative and Interpretation*, edited by David Wood, 20–33. London: Routledge.
Ricœur, Paul. 1991b. "Narrative Identity." In *On Paul Ricoeur: Narrative and Interpretation*, edited by David Wood, 188–99. London: Routledge.

Rosenbaum, Jonathan. 2007. "15. The Seven Arkadins." In *Discovering Orson Welles*, 146–62. Berkeley: University of California Press.

Rothman, William. 2019. "'I Never Thought I Should Sink So Low as to Become an Actor': John Barrymore in *Twentieth Century*." In *Tuitions and Intuitions: Essays at the Intersection of Film Criticism and Philosophy*, 99–114. Albany: State University of New York Press.

Rothman, William. 2021. "On Stanley Cavell's *Band Wagon*." In *The Holiday in His Eye: Stanley Cavell's Vision of Film and Philosophy*, 217–40. Albany: State University of New York Press.

Rudd, Anthony. 2009. "In Defence of Narrative." *European Journal of Philosophy* 17 (1): 60–75. https://doi.org/10.1111/j.1468-0378.2007.00272.x.

Ruokonen, Floora. 2008. "Iris Murdoch and the Extraordinary Ambiguity of Art." *Journal of Value Inquiry* 42 (1): 77–90.

Santilli, Paul C. 2006. "Cinema and Subjectivity in Krzysztof Kieślowski." *Journal of Aesthetics and Art Criticism* 64 (1): 147–56.

Schechtman, Marya. 2011. "The Narrative Self." In *The Oxford Handbook of the Self*, edited by Shaun Gallagher, 394–416. New York: Oxford University Press.

Sinnerbrink, Robert. 2006. "A Heideggerian Cinema? On Terrence Malick's *The Thin Red Line*." *Film-Philosophy* 10 (3): 26–37.

Sinnerbrink, Robert. 2011. "Questioning Style." In *The Language and Style of Film Criticism*, edited by Alex Clayton and Andrew Klevan, 38–53. London: Routledge.

Sinnerbrink, Robert. 2014. "Cavellian Meditations: How to Do Things with Film and Philosophy." *Film-Philosophy* 18: 50–69.

Sinnerbrink, Robert. 2015. *Cinematic Ethics: Exploring Ethical Experience through Film*. London: Routledge.

Smith, Murray. 1995. *Engaging Characters: Fiction, Emotion, and the Cinema*. New York: Oxford University Press.

Smith, Murray. 1997. "Imagining from the Inside." In *Film Theory and Philosophy*, edited by Richard Allen and Murray Smith, 412–30. New York: Oxford University Press.

Smith, Murray. 2016. "Film, Philosophy, and the Varieties of Artistic Value." In *Current Controversies in Philosophy of Film*, edited by Katherine Thomson-Jones, 182–201. London: Routledge.

Smith, Murray. 2017. "Papaya, Pomegranates, and Green Tea." In *Film, Art, and the Third Culture: Toward a Naturalized Aesthetics of Film*, 106–26. New York: Oxford University Press.

Sobchack, Vivian. 2004. "The Expanded Gaze in Contracted Space: Happenstance, Hazard, and the Flesh of the World." In *Carnal Thoughts: Embodiment and Moving Image Culture*, 85–108. Berkeley: University of California Press.

Sobchack, Vivian. 2011. "The Man Who Wasn't There: The Production of Subjectivity in Delmer Daves' *Dark Passage*." In *Subjectivity: Filmic Representation and the Spectators' Experience*, edited by Dominique Chateau, 69–83. Amsterdam: Amsterdam University Press.

Stadler, Jane. 2008a. "Losing the Plot: Narrative Structure and Ethical Identity." In *Pulling Focus: Intersubjective Experience, Narrative Film, and Ethics*, 66–95. London: Continuum.

Stadler, Jane. 2008b. *Pulling Focus: Intersubjective Experience, Narrative Film, and Ethics*. London: Continuum.

Stadler, Jane. 2013. "Cinema's Compassionate Gaze: Empathy, Affect, and Aesthetics in *The Diving Bell and the Butterfly*." In *Cine-Ethics: Ethical Dimensions of Film Theory, Practice, and Spectatorship*, edited by Jinhee Choi and Mattias Frey, 27–42. New York: Routledge.

Stevens, Kyle. 2015. *Mike Nichols: Sex, Language, and the Reinvention of Psychological Realism*. New York: Oxford University Press.

Taylor, Charles. 2014. "Iris Murdoch and Moral Philosophy." In *Dilemma and Connections: Selected Essays*, 3–23. Cambridge, MA: Belknap Press.

Thanouli, Eleftheria. 2009. *Post-Classical Cinema: An International Poetics of Film Narration*. New York: Columbia University Press.

Thompson, Kristin. 1981. *Eisenstein's Ivan the Terrible: A Neoformalist Analysis*. Princeton, NJ: Princeton University Press.

Thompson, Kristin. 1988. *Breaking the Glass Armor: Neoformalist Film Analysis*. Princeton, NJ: Princeton University Press.

Thomson-Jones, Katherine. 2005. "Inseparable Insight: Reconciling Cognitivism and Formalism in Aesthetics." *Journal of Aesthetics and Art Criticism* 63 (4): 375–84.

Toles, George. 2021. *Curtains of Light: Theatrical Space in Film*. Albany: State University of New York Press.

Truffaut, François. 1978. "What Do Critics Dream About?" In *The Films in My Life*, 3–20. New York: Touchstone.

Tye, Michael. 2018. "Qualia." *Stanford Encyclopedia of Philosophy*. plato.stanford.edu/archives/sum2018/entries/qualia/.

Van Inwagen, Peter. 2014. *Metaphysics*. 4th ed. New York: Westview Press.

Vasalou, Sophia. 2015. *Wonder: A Grammar*. Albany: State University of New York Press.

Willemen, Paul. 1994. "Through the Glass Darkly: Cinephilia Reconsidered." In *Looks and Frictions*, 223–57. Bloomington: Indiana University Press.

Wilson, George. 1988. *Narration in Light: Studies in Cinematic Point of View*. Baltimore: Johns Hopkins University Press.

Winkler, Martin M. 1985. "Classical Mythology and the Western Film." *Comparative Literature Studies* 22 (4): 516–40.

Wright, Edmond, ed. 2008. *The Case for Qualia*. Cambridge, MA: MIT Press.

Wright, Will. 1977. *Sixguns and Society: A Structural Study of the Western*. Berkeley: University of California Press.

Yacavone, Daniel. 2015. *Film Worlds: A Philosophical Aesthetics of Cinema*. New York: Columbia University Press.

Index

12 Monkeys (Terry Gilliam, 1995), 55–56
20th Century (Howard Hawks, 1934), 215–218
3 Women (Robert Altman, 1977), 158–162
3:10 to Yuma (Delmer Daves, 1957), 81–83, 94

aesthetic cognitivism, 20
Americans, The (2013–2018), 171–182
Animal Crackers (Victor Heerman, 1930), xxiii
Assassination of Jesse James by the Coward Robert Ford, The (Andrew Dominik, 2007), 88–91
Augustine, 127–128

Babel (Alejandro González Iñárritu, 2006), 47–49
Band Wagon, The (Vincente Minnelli, 1953), 218–222: and *Saturday Night Live* sketch (1978), 222
Bandy, Lea, 97
Baracco, Alberto, 27
Barr, Alan, 150
Barzun, Jacques, 28–29
Baumberger, Christoph, 21

Bazin, André, 6, 72
Blanchet, Robert, 171, 180–181
Blind Chance (Krzysztof Kieślowski, 1987), 41–42, 43
Bordwell, David, 32, 34–35, 38, 44, 58–59, 62
Branigan, Edward, 39, 118–119
Buckland, Warren, 36, 37

Campora, Matthew, 32, 35, 120
Carroll, Noël, 6, 73, 77
Castrillo, Pablo, 172
Cavell, Stanley, 18
cinephilia, 198–201
Citizen Kane (Orson Welles, 1941), 125–126
Coates, Paul, 149
Code Unknown (Michael Haneke, 2000), 44–45
complex narratives, 35–39
Contagion (Steven Soderbergh, 2011), 117–118
Court Jester, The (Norman Panama and Melvin Frank, 1955), 211–215
Cover Girl (Charles Vidor, 1944), 122–123
Cracking Up aka *Smorgasbord* (Jerry Lewis, 1983), 223–225

Critchley, Simon, 22
Currie, Gregory, 116–117, 120

Dark (2017–2020), 56–58
Day at the Races, A, (Sam Wood, 1937), xxv
Danto, Arthur C., 4
Dark Passage (Delmer Daves, 1947), 116
Deadwood (2004–2006), 97–102
defamiliarization, 17
Dekalog (Krzysztof Kieślowski, 1989–1990), 7–12
Diving Bell and the Butterfly, The (Julian Schnabel, 2007), 118
Donaldson, Lucy Fife, 15
Drake, Philip, 174–175
Duck Soup (Leo McCarey, 1933), xxii–xxiii

Ebert, Roger, 159
Edge of Tomorrow (Doug Liman, 2014), 40–41
Eliot, T.S., 4
Elsaesser, Thomas, 198

Fabe, Marilyn, 125–126
Fargo universe, 49–53
Felski, Rita, 184
film-philosophy, 19–20
film and ethics, 3
Fingerhut, Joerg 185
Flaherty, Matthew, 125
forking-path narratives, 33–34, 39–43
form and content, 4–7, 19
Fuchs, Thomas, 129
Fujiwara, Chris, 223–225

Gallagher, Shaun, 109, 156
García, Alberto N., 172
Garwood, Ian, 15

Gibson, John, 20–21
Good, the, 74–75, 77–78, 85–86, 93
Gorfinkel, Elena, 91
Grand Canyon (Lawrence Kasdan, 1991), 45–47
grief, 126–130
Groundhog Day (Harold Ramis, 1993), 40–41

Hark, Ina Rae, 99
Harvey (Henry Koster, 1950), 187–191
Herman, David, 114
High Noon (Fred Zinnemann, 1952), 78–79
High Plains Drifter (Clint Eastwood, 1973), 96–97
History of Violence, A (David Cronenberg, 2005), 166–170
Hodsdon, Barrett, 200–201
Hutson, Rich, 96–97

I'm Not There (Todd Haynes, 2007), 148
Iñárritu, Alejandro González, 47
Inside Out (Pete Docter, 2015), 141–142
Insider, The (Michael Mann, 1999), 145–146, 153–154, 155
Irma Vep (Olivier Assayas, 1996), 196–198

Jacobs, Jason, 97, 100
Jonathan Livingston Seagull (Hall Bartlett, 1973), 113–114, 115–116

Kaye, Danny, 212–215
Kearney, Richard, 13, 14, 25
Keathley, Christian, 199–200
Kermode, Frank, 155
Kind, Amy, 108
Kitses, Jim, 72

Kolker, Robert, 158–159

L'Argent (Robert Bresson, 1983), 59–61
Lamarque, Peter, 154
Lewis, C.S., 127
Lewis, Jerry, 223–224
Limits of Control, The (Jim Jarmusch, 2009), 204–206
Lis, Marek, 7
Logan, Elliott, 171–172
Loht, Shawn, 18, 20, 26–27
Looper (Rian Johnson, 2012), 54–55

MacIntyre, Alasdair, 73, 74, 75, 77, 85, 93, 100
Magnolia (Paul Thomas Anderson, 1999), 47
Malick, Terrence, 25–6
Man Who Shot Liberty Valance, The (John Ford, 1962), 75–76, 77–78
Man Who Wasn't There, The (Coen Brothers, 2001), 110–111
Marx, Harpo, xv–xxvi
Matheson, Sue, 103
McMaster, Graham, 132
Meek's Cutoff (Kelly Reichardt, 2010), 91–92
Merten, Jennilyn, 101
metaphysics, 2–3
mimesis, 12 14, 25, 27, 184
Mitchell, Lee Clark, 94
Mittell, Jason, 36–37
Morvern Callar (Lynne Ramsay, 2002), 201–204
Mr. Arkadin aka *Confidential Report* (Orson Welles, 1955), 149–150
Mr Nobody (Jaco van Dormael, 2009), 31–32
multimodal narratives, 34, 49–53
multiple draft narratives, 39–41
Mumford, Stephen, 2, 3

Murdoch, Iris, 28, 73, 85, 86

Nagel, Thomas, 107, 114
Nannicelli, Ted, 6
Nashville (Robert Altman, 1975), 44
Night at the Opera, A (Sam Wood, 1935), xvi–xix
Nussbaum, Emily, 175, 177, 179
Nussbaum, Martha C., 185

Olson, Eric T., 147

parametric form and narration, 34–35, 58–68
Paterson (Jim Jarmusch, 2016), 195–196
Paulus, Irena, 132
Pearlman, Karen, 33
Pearson, Roberta, 171
Peretz, Eyal, 150
Perkins, V.F., 14, 16, 19, 24–25
personal identity, 146: and narrative, 153–156, 162–163; and population 147; evidence of, 147–152; persistence of, 147
Phantom of Liberty, The (Luis Buñuel, 1974), 62–68
Pippin, Robert, 21, 22
Plantinga, Carl, 121
Pomerance, Murray, 163
Poulaki, Maria, 35
POV shots, 116–119
Prince, Stephen, 93, 94
Prinz, Jesse J., 185
Purple Noon (René Clément, 1960), 151, 163–164
Pye, Douglas, 82

qualia, 106, 107

Ratatouille (Brad Bird, 2007), 142–144

Ratcliffe, Matthew, 128, 129
realism, 119–120: expressive, 125–126; perceptual, 120; psychological, 121–122; subjective, 120–121
Rectify (2013–2016), 134–141
Reinerth, Maike Sarah, 124
Ricœur, Paul, 13, 27, 155–156, 157–158, 184, 206
Rosenbaum, Jonathan, 150
Rothman, William, 216, 219
Run, Lola, Run (Tom Tykwer, 1998), 41–42, 43
Ruokonen, Floora, 73, 85

Santilli, Paul C., 9
Scarlet Street (Fritz Lang, 1945), 122
Secret Life of Walter Mitty, The (Norman Z. McLeod, 1942), 191, 194
selection, 209–211
Shane (George Stevens, 1953), 79–81
Shootist, The (Don Siegel, 1976), 86–88
Sinnerbrink, Robert, 20, 22, 23–24
Smith, Murray, 4, 110, 112–113, 143, 147
Sobchack, Vivian, 8–9
Sound of Sunshine, Sound of Rain (Caroline Hayward, 1983), 126
spatial convergence narratives, 34, 43–49
spectatorship, 25–28, 38–39, 108–109, 115, 210–211
Stadler, Jane, 118, 158, 163
Stoehr, Kevin, 97
Sullivan's Travels (Preston Sturges, 1941), 164–166, 170
Synecdoche, New York (Charlie Kaufman, 2008), 183–184, 195, 206

Taylor, Charles, 72
television, 6–8, 36–37, 171–172

telos, 75, 83–84
Ten Commandments, 7–8, 10
The Circus, At (Edward Buzzell, 1939), xix–xxii
Thin Red Line, The (Terrence Malick, 1998), 1, 21–24
Thompson, Kristin, 17, 59, 61–62
Thomson-Jones, Katherine, 5, 25
Thon, Jan-Noël, 124
Three Colours: Blue (Krzysztof Kieślowski, 1994), 108, 109, 121, 126, 130–134
time-travel narratives, 34, 53–58
Toles, George, 215–216
Truffaut, François, 198–199
Truman Show, The (Peter Weir, 1998), 156–157
Turin Horse, The (Belá Tarr, 2011), 15–16
Tye, Michael, 107, 109

Unforgiven (Clint Eastwood, 1992), 95–96

Vaage, Margrethe Bruun, 171, 180–181
van Inwagen, Peter, 2–3
Vasalou, Sophia, 186, 187
violence, 92–93
virtue, 74–78, 93

Wayne, John, 86
We Need to Talk about Kevin (Lynne Ramsay, 2011), 105–107, 110, 111–112, 113
Wild Bunch, The (Sam Peckinpah, 1969), 71–72
Willemen, Paul, 199
wonder, 184–187, 206–207
worldbuilding, 14–19

Yacavone, Daniel, 14, 18

Zahavi, Dan, 109

www.ingramcontent.com/pod-product-compliance
Lightning Source LLC
Chambersburg PA
CBHW020328240426
43665CB00044B/889